THE COMPLETE GUIDE TO COACHING GIRLS' BASKETBALL

Date Due

The Complete Guide to
COACHING GIRLS' BASKETBALL

Building a Great Team the Carolina Way

SYLVIA HATCHELL, Head Coach, University of North Carolina

WITH JEFF THOMAS

McGraw-Hill

Camden, Maine • New York • Chicago • San Francisco • Lisbon • London • Madrid
Mexico City • Milan • New Delhi • San Juan • Seoul • Singapore • Sydney • Toronto

Dedication

To my loving parents, Veda Shepard Rhyne (died 12/22/04) and Carroll Costner Rhyne, from whom I learned countless valuable lessons, and built my life and success on their faith, hope, and love.

To my husband, Carl (Sammy) Hatchell, and my son, Van Davis Hatchell, the loves of my life.

To my loyal staff, Andrew Calder, Tracey Williams-Johnson, Charlotte Smith-Taylor, and Greg Law.

And to all the wonderful players I've had the good fortune and privilege to coach at Francis Marion University and the University of North Carolina.

Sylvia Hatchell

To Burke and Catherine. I can't believe how lucky I am to be your Pop.

Jeff Thomas

The McGraw·Hill Companies

1 2 3 4 5 6 7 8 9 DOC DOC 0 9 8 7 6

Library of Congress Cataloging-in-Publication Data
Hatchell, Sylvia.
    The complete guide to coaching girls' basketball : building a great team the Carolina way / by Sylvia Hatchell with Jeff Thomas.
        p.   cm.
    Includes index.
    ISBN 0-07-147394-7 (pbk. : alk. paper)
    1. Basketball for girls—Coaching.   I. Thomas, Jeff, 1949–   II. Title.
    GV885.3.H39 2006
    796.323'8—dc22   2006006586

Questions regarding the content of this book should be addressed to
McGraw-Hill/Ragged Mountain Press
P.O. Box 220
Camden, ME 04843
www.raggedmountainpress.com

Questions regarding the ordering of this book should be addressed to
The McGraw-Hill Companies
Customer Service Department
P.O. Box 547
Blacklick, OH 43004
Retail customers: 1-800-262-4729
Bookstores: 1-800-722-4726

Photographs by Jeffery Camarati
Illustrations by International Typesetting Composition

CONTENTS

ACKNOWLEDGMENTS

My heartfelt thanks go to the women who demonstrated the basketball skills in this book's photographs. I am proud to have coached them:

La'Tangela Atkinson, Meghan Austin, Heather Claytor, Christina Dewitt, Erlana Larkins, Ivory Latta, Camille Little, Rashanda McCants, Iman McFarland, Alex Miller, Jennifer Nelms, Latoya Pringle, Jessica Sell, Martina Wood.

So many people have influenced my coaching career—far too many to list—but I'd like to acknowledge three people who have helped me more than I can ever repay them for: Jerry Green, Head Coach at various universities; Hubie Brown, former NBA Head Coach; and Howard West, Head Varsity Coach at Ronald Reagan High School (Pfafftown, North Carolina).

Sylvia Hatchell

INTRODUCTION

This book is based on the knowledge and insight I've gained over many years of coaching. My focus is on how to coach girls who are 11 to 18 years old; that is, girls who play middle school, AAU, and high school basketball. I address everything you need to know to be a successful coach, whether you're a first-timer or you've coached for twenty years. My goal is that this book will be the only reference you need, the one source for information on how to be successful at whatever level you coach. My goal is for this book to be a complete guide to coaching girls' basketball.

I begin with how to teach the fundamentals—footwork, dribbling, passing, shooting, and all the individual skills that are critical to becoming a good player. In many games, the proper execution of the individual skills is the difference between winning and losing. Talent, strategy, psychology, and luck affect the outcome of a game, but often when a team loses it's due to a lapse in fundamentals—a missed layup or bad pass at a critical moment, the dribbler not protecting the ball, the rebounder not blocking out, a defender losing sight of the ball, or poor footwork that results in an untimely travel. The basis for coaching basketball successfully at every level is fundamentals. At North Carolina, though my teams have highly talented players who have played basketball for years, we spend the first several days of every season on nothing but fundamentals.

Next, I go beyond the fundamentals into how to teach advanced individual skills. Then, I cover team skills, from elementary offensive and defensive principles to more complicated principles and alignments. I also cover many other essential topics, including how to choose your team, how to motivate players, how to decide what offenses and defenses are best for your team, and how to pick the best strategies and tactics for various situations. I explain a variety of offenses and defenses so you can choose what best fits your players and coaching philosophy. Throughout, I use diagrams to make the explanations easy to understand.

Lastly, I include seventy-five drills, ranging in difficulty from beginner level to advanced level, that will allow you to match drills to the experience and abilities of your players.

I'm proud to bring this book to you. I hope you find coaching as fulfilling, enjoyable, and exciting as I do.

The Head Coach's Role

When you have the first team meeting of the new season and see a dozen eager faces, you become aware of how much the players are counting on you. Their expectations are huge. They may be nervous about how they'll fit in with the rest of the team and how much they'll be asked to do, but you're the all-knowing, omnipotent coach, the person who will ease their fears and make everything good. Middle school players will put you on a pedestal, as will most ninth graders. While older players will likely have the more skeptical outlook of a teenager, both younger and older players will initially trust that you'll have their best interests at heart. With young players, what you do and teach is the gospel. They don't question what you say. Even with older kids who have played for years and who have had a number of different coaches, you're their role model, at least at first.

The power you have as a coach is both a great opportunity and a great responsibility. You wield tremendous influence over your players, so it's incumbent that you use this influence wisely. Your players will watch and note everything you do and say. To some

Above all else, coaching girls should be fun!

extent, they'll behave as they see you behave, because your actions tell them that it's the right way to behave. How you handle pressure, how you handle referees, how you treat each player, how you treat the team as a whole—the girls will see you in roles they don't see their parents in, and they'll pattern their behavior after yours. More than your words, more than the number of wins and losses, your actions and behavior will determine how successful the season is for them.

If you're an experienced coach, you know how multifaceted coaching is. If you're a rookie, you'll be amazed at how much is involved. To lead a successful team, you must master many aptitudes, you must learn many skills, and you must be many things.

Possessor of All Knowledge

You must know your subject. You don't have to be John Wooden or Dean Smith, but at a minimum, you have to acquire a working knowledge of the game. This takes time, but if you're interested (I assume that's why you're reading this book), the sources of information are many. Talk to other coaches. They're an excellent source of information. Attend clinics (a great place to meet and trade ideas with other coaches).

Search the Internet. Subscribe to coaching magazines. Read books and study tapes. There's a ton of information out there, and most of it is easy to find.

Another way to add to your knowledge is through your assistant coaches. Surrounding yourself with one or two capable assistants will make you a better coach. Ideally, they'll have experience with the game (coaching experience or playing experience). Even if you're a rookie coach, having one or two assistants who know what they're doing will quickly make you a knowledgeable head coach (at least, your girls will think so).

Teacher

It's one thing to know how to run a pick-and-roll. It's another thing to know how to teach it. The first requirement of good teaching is that you know your subject. I covered this in the prior section.

The second requirement is that you know how to communicate what you know. Some coaches are natural communicators and some are not. If you're in the latter category, the good news is this is a skill anyone can learn. Brevity is important. When addressing your players, keep it short and sweet. The attention span of girls is limited. If you drone on for 10 minutes, you'll lose their attention and waste time that could be used to develop skills. Feed your players information in short, easy bites they can easily swallow. Don't overwhelm them with too much new information at one time.

Part of your planning for practices will involve decisions about when to teach new skills and drills and when to reinforce what the players have already learned. Becoming a good teacher takes time and a focus on improving your skills. The more you coach, the better you'll be at it. Be patient. Just as it takes time for your players to learn to read the defense, it takes time for you to learn how to communicate with your team.

Director of Player Personnel

Handling players well is crucial to establishing team unity and cohesion.

Rule number one: *Be consistent.* You can't treat your players one way one day and another way the next. You can't enforce discipline one time but not the next. Mixed signals cause confusion. Girls respond to structure and consistency.

Rule number two: *Don't play favorites.* Though it's natural for you to enjoy certain personalities more than others, you can't show your team that you like one player more than another. You can't treat one player more favorably than another. Coaches who play favorites create big problems for themselves and the team. They cause negative feelings and a lack of trust in their leadership abilities. Though you should recognize and respect each player's unique characteristics, treat all players the same. (I'm not suggesting that you try to motivate every player the same way. That's a different matter.) No one should think she's a second-class citizen, that other players can bend the rules and she can't; nor should anyone think she has special privileges over the other players.

Motivator

Many books have been written on how to encourage and inspire a group of people to put aside their personal interests for the good of the group. There are no surefire methods for motivating players that ensure success. However, there are some team-building activities you can do and some principles to follow that will raise the chances that your players will be motivated. Perhaps the biggest coaching challenge you face will be how to motivate and inspire your players to do their best at all times. You'll find this aspect of coaching frustrating at times. If you find that you're good at it, your job will be much easier and your team will be well on its way to achieving a successful season.

Puzzle Master

Putting together a successful team is like putting together a complicated puzzle. It might seem that there are only a limited number of pieces (the number of players on your team), but the puzzle becomes difficult when, as the season progresses, the pieces change shape. Girls develop physically and emotionally at different rates. Your team might experience unexpected roster changes during the season. You might have players leave the team during the season for academic or personal reasons, and you're likely to have players who are sick or injured. What looks like a finished puzzle in December can look like a jumble of scattered pieces in January. Good coaches adapt to changing circumstances.

Grand Planner

Basketball is a difficult game to learn. Learning to handle the ball under pressure, for example, just one of the many skills a player must learn, must be worked at over a long time. Practice sessions provide only so much time for teaching the large number of things you need to teach. As a coach, you have lots of decisions to make regarding the use of that time. How much time should I spend on individual skills versus team skills? How much time on shooting and rebounding? How much time should I devote to offense versus defense? How much time to the fast break? What about special end-of-game situations?

No magic answers exist. What formula works for one team might not work for another team. Plan your practices based on the strengths and weaknesses of your players each season, the competition you'll face, and the preparation time you've allotted. And because some players will learn faster than others, you'll have to decide whether to accelerate the new things you teach or to slow the process so more players can absorb them. Be flexible. If your team needs more work on half-court defense, that means time on something else has to be reduced. Do you cut back on free throw shooting, press offense, or what? Making the best use of the limited time available is a tricky balancing act.

X's and O's Guru

This is part of knowing your subject, but it goes beyond knowing how to teach individual fundamentals into the area of strategies and tactics. You have critical decisions to make early in the season. Should our primary defense be man-to-man or zone? If zone, which one? How do I decide? What offenses should we run against the defenses our opponents will play? What inbound plays should I teach? How should we set up to break the full-court presses we'll face? How should we prepare for half-court traps? If we have a star player, how will we combat the box-and-one we may see?

There are as many X's and O's as there are coaches. The keys are to choose the ones that work well with your team and to not overload your players with more information than they can handle.

Bench Coach

By the time each game day arrives, your team's preparation is over. You've either done a good job of getting your team ready to play or you haven't. Over the next hour and a half, you'll find out if your players are ready to face defensive pressure, are in good basketball condition, will remember to run those special plays, and will attack the boards. You won't know how well prepared they are until the game is underway.

Who should start? When should you substitute and who should come in? When should you switch from zone defense to man-to-man? When should you press? When should you call a time-out and what should you say? What should you tell the team at halftime? The decisions a coach makes during a game often decide whether the team wins or loses.

Parent Handler

Someone once said, "If you want to please everyone, don't go into coaching."

Most parents are supportive, enthusiastic, reasonable people. They appreciate the unpaid time and effort you give to coaching their daughter (though high school head coaches are paid, the compensation is so low that they might as well be unpaid!). They understand that it's not the most important thing in the world, that it's just a kid's game.

However, if you coach long enough, you'll encounter your share of unhappy parents. Sooner or later, you'll have to listen to a parent who doesn't like something you've done. The usual complaint is playing time. Some coaches stipulate at the parents' meeting that they'll talk to parents about everything except the issue of playing time—that because the coach sees the players at every practice and the parents don't, the topic is not up for discussion. Other coaches will discuss the issue with parents. Regardless of how you decide to handle this issue, you'll have to develop a thick skin and an ability to defuse the situation.

Parents are easy to get along with when their daughter is happy. But when she's not, be ready to hear about it. Be ready to listen like a psychiatrist and talk like a diplomat. No matter what the parent says or how unreasonable he or she is, be calm and professional. Above all, don't take it personally. As the coach, you're the easiest target on the team.

The Assistant Coach's Role

If you're an assistant coach, you have several distinct roles:

Order Follower

If the head coach is the captain of the ship, you're the first mate. Your job is to carry out orders to the best of your ability. Hopefully, the head coach will give you lots of responsibility and say in how things are done, but if he or she doesn't, you still must work as hard as you can to fulfill the duties you're given.

Number One Supporter

As an assistant, you may hear players, parents, or fans express criticism of the team and the head coach. Your number one quality as an assistant is to be loyal to your boss. Even if you agree with the criticisms, you must keep that to yourself. Your primary task is to support the head coach, regardless of your opinions. On the court, you and the head coach should be a unified front. Off the court, in private, tell him or her what's on your mind. Good head coaches want their assistants to be honest.

Advisor

Presumably, part of why the head coach hired you was to hear your opinions. Provide all the input you can. Be honest. A good head coach doesn't just want a "yes man." Tell it like it is— the good, the bad, and the ugly.

Pinch Hitter

If the head coach gets sick or otherwise can't make it to a game, you will have to step into his or her shoes. If you watch, listen, and learn, you'll be ready for this eventuality.

Head Coach in Training

Many middle school assistants are parents with no aspirations to be head coaches. Many high school assistants, however, hope to be head coaches some day. If that's you, learn all you can while you're an assistant. Observe your head coach. Watch how other coaches do things. Read books, buy tapes, and attend coaching clinics. Keep your ear to the coaching

ASK THE COACH

Question: This is my first year as a Varsity assistant with our local high school. I'm frustrated because I know more than the head coach does. People have come up to me on the sly telling me I should be the coach, not the other guy. I don't want to be disrespectful, but I can do a better job. The trouble is, the head coach doesn't want to listen to what I have to offer. I think he's jealous. What should I do?

Answer: As long as you're his assistant, be loyal. Don't undermine him in any way. I'll take your word that you could do a better job, but he's the head coach, not you, and your responsibility is to him, above all. Stop listening to the critics. If you're cornered, stick up for your coach. Even if you can't stand working for him, it's your duty to stick out the season, do your best, and remain positive. After the season, you can look for another coaching job. If you join in with the criticism, not only will you be disloyal, you'll hurt the program. Keep this in mind—when you apply for another position elsewhere in the future, the athletic director or the head coach will call your current head coach for a reference. If you undermined him, you'll find that you also undermined your own reputation.

Question: I'd like to be an assistant, but have never been one before. How do I go about it?

Answer: I assume you have some kind of background in basketball. If not, it will be hard to find a job at a high school. It will help if you have some coaching experience, even at the youth level. Talk to as many coaches in your area as you can. Tell them to keep you in mind if they hear of any openings. The coaching profession at all levels has a lot of turnover. If you look around long enough and keep the word out, sooner or later someone is bound to offer you a job.

Question: How much does an average high school assistant make?

Answer: Nothing, or next to nothing. Most high school head coaches don't fare much better. People coach because they love it, not for the money.

Question: My daughter is a ninth grader on my JV team. She's the best player on the team and will play most of the time, but I'm leery about what other parents will think. What should I do about this?

Answer: A parent who coaches his or her daughter is in a difficult situation that often leads to problems. My first caution concerns your statement that your daughter is the "best player on the team." Are you sure? Would unbiased coaches agree with you? If you give your daughter more playing time than you give other players, and your players and other parents don't perceive her the way you do, you'll cause resentment, which will hurt team unity. Most parents are incapable of viewing their daughters through an objective lens. If you provide them with a basis for complaining (or even if you don't), some parents will be quick to conclude that you favor your daughter over theirs.

I can't state this firmly enough: *The best thing for you and your daughter is for you not to be her coach.* If that means you can't coach the JV team that year, so be it. As much as you want to coach, it's not in her or the team's best interests for you to do so. If you're determined to do so anyway, thinking you'll be smart enough to avoid the pitfalls, go out of your way not to favor her in any way. Of course, you don't want to overcompensate and treat her less favorably than you treat the other girls. That would be unfair to her.

Having your daughter on the team you coach is a tricky matter. Decisions you make regarding her will be under constant scrutiny, sometimes by unreasonable people. Again, my advice is to avoid this situation, if possible.

---

grapevine. Explore opportunities. Some day the right chance will pop up.

Coaching girls' basketball can be one of the most rewarding, exciting, and fun things you'll ever do, but make no mistake—it's a challenging undertaking. To a large degree, the extent of your success will depend on how well you learn the skills and roles listed above.

Good luck!

Developing a Philosophy and a Style

If you've coached for a while, you've already established your coaching philosophy and style. If you're a rookie, decide early on what kind of coach you're going to be. Do you prefer to coach an aggressive team that attacks on offense and defense, that gambles and takes chances, or do you prefer to control the action, to slow the pace, and to call specific plays every half-court possession? In other words, will you be a fast-break coach, a coach who emphasizes

defense to create offense, or will you be a half-court-oriented coach? Will your team play pressure man-to-man defense or a more passive zone defense where you wait for the other team to make mistakes? Will your team press all the time, only in some situations, or not at all? What style suits your personality and your players' skills and personalities best?

I like a running style. It's fun for the players to play and for the fans to watch. With my team, our goal is to have more than 100 possessions a game. If we get less, I'm unhappy. Other coaches prefer a slow-paced game. They like to control the action more and aren't comfortable with the helter-skelter aspect of fast-break basketball. That's not me, but that's OK. Every coach is different. Only you can decide what style of play is the most comfortable for you.

Part of your decision will be based on the skill level and experience of your players. You may want to play a running and pressing style, but if your team has slower players than your opponents do, this style probably won't work. Part of coaching is adjusting to the players you have. Two seasons ago, I decided to cut back our playbook because we had far too many offensive options and sets. I thought my team needed to spend more time concentrating on fewer things. Though you may stay with the same basic philosophy each season, you still have to adapt to the players you have. Good coaches adjust their playing style as needed to fit each new set of players.

Coaching Goals

If you ask most new coaches what their coaching goals are, you'll likely hear: "I want my team to win as many games as possible." As coaches gain experience, most realize that this goal is but one of several important goals.

Establish a clear set of coaching goals. Goals are your road signs. If you don't have road signs to keep you on track, you won't know where you're going, and you'll end up on a road you don't want to be on. Goals are the basis for the specific organizing and planning you'll do. It's fine to want your team to win all its games—what coach doesn't want that?—but there are many components to achieving success. Most have nothing to do with the number of wins and losses.

One of the main goals I have every season is to do what I can to help our team reach its potential. Every year is different, of course. Some years, I think we have the potential to be a Final Four team. Other years, I think making the NCAA Tournament would be a great accomplishment. I've had teams that won twenty-five games, but I've thought that we should have done better. We didn't reach our potential. On the other hand, I've had teams that won sixteen games, and I've thought we went far along the path to our potential.

Although you'll have to decide what coaching goals make sense to you, here are the goals I suggest you consider:

Make sure each player has a positive season. This should be your number one goal. If, at the end of the season, every player, from your star player to the last player at the end of the bench, had a season that made her feel good, you've done an excellent job. Accomplishing this goal isn't easy, but you should keep it at the forefront of your mind throughout the season. The season is all about the girls. It's not about you or a few select players. It's about every girl on the team.

Make basketball fun. This is important at every level, not just for teams with girls at the younger ages. If basketball isn't fun for the kids, it will become a chore, something they don't look forward to and enjoy. This will make it hard to have a successful season. If your style is one that insists on precision drills and a military-like atmosphere, and you give no respite from this atmosphere, you'll eventually lose the enthusiasm and goodwill of your players. Find a balance in practice between working hard and having fun. Every now and then, have the kids play fun drills like Knockout (Drill 42) and Dribble Tag (Drill 16). Or, for the last half hour of practice, divide them into teams and have them run relay dribble races and team shooting competitions. As the season goes on and players start to wear down physically, give them a day off now and then, or make every Monday a "Fun Day" at practice. If your players think basketball is fun, they'll look forward to practice and will continue to work hard. If they have a positive, fun experience on your team, they'll be eager to play again next year.

Emphasize fundamentals. Teach the team how to play the game, as opposed to a countless number of plays. Yes, you need to spend enough time on team aspects to prepare them for games, but spend at least half of each practice on the basics. All the top high school and college teams work on fundamentals throughout the season. As part of this goal, before the season begins, develop a list of skills you want your players to learn over the season (see the sample master practice plan in the Appendix).

Instill good work habits. Unless you coach a veteran team, it's likely that many of your girls won't know how to work hard physically. Part of your job is to teach them how to do that. Insist on a good work ethic from the first

Question: My players are in a funk. We've lost three games in a row, and no matter what I do, I can't seem to get them out of it. They don't look like they're having fun anymore. What can I do?

Answer: Your players take their cues from you. If you're overly disappointed or angry about losing, they'll hear it in your tone and see it in your body language. They'll think you're disappointed in them as people and as players. Review your coaching goals. Focus on fundamentals. Concentrate on team improvement. Go easier on them next practice. Have them play some fun team games. Take winning and losing out of the equation for now. Put the fun back into the game. The more they see you smiling, enjoying them, the better they'll feel about themselves.

practice on. Make sure that your players run to you when you raise your hand, call to them, or blow the whistle. If you allow them to dawdle, to keep dribbling, to saunter on over, it will take longer to move from one drill to the next. Too many coaches don't set the standards for efficient practice habits from the start. If you don't establish the right tone at the beginning, it will be hard to change your players' behavior later.

Coach individual and team improvement. Fans, players, parents, and coaches at all levels put far too much emphasis on wins and losses. It's popular to think that if a team wins a lot, it's because of great coaching, and if a team loses a lot, it's because of bad coaching. This view is narrow-minded. The real mark of good coaching isn't how many games are under the *W* column and how many are under the *L* column. It's how much the players and team improve over the season. Being a coach is like being dealt a hand of cards in a poker game. Sometimes you're holding kings and aces, and sometimes you'll be holding nothing but low cards. Depending on your coaching situation, you may be able to recruit some good players to your team, but most coaches have little or no control over the talent they get. The true measure of coaching is what the coach does with what he or she gets. As long as your players improve and the team improves, you've done a fine job. Whether your team loses more games than it wins is secondary (get used to the fact that not all the fans and parents will agree with you).

Teach sportsmanship. This goes back to you as the role model. Talk to your players about what good sportsmanship means. Teach them how to win and lose with dignity and grace. Teach them to treat their teammates, their opponents, the referees, and their coaches with respect. Teach them how to behave in a first-class manner. By doing so, you'll be teaching them far more than basketball.

Teach life lessons. Sports are a wonderful opportunity to learn life skills. Use your influence to teach your players skills far more important than how to shoot a free throw. Every season has ups and downs. Every team goes over bumpy roads. By your actions and your words, you show your team how to overcome adversity, how to stick together, how to never give up, and how to work hard for a common purpose. Sports are rich with life lessons. Don't get so wrapped up in the X's and O's that you forget to pass on important values and concepts. Basketball lessons last for a season. Life lessons last forever.

Win as many games as possible. Here it is, at the end of the list. Of course it's an important goal, but you'll find that if you achieve the other goals on this list, the wins and losses will take care of themselves.

Coaching Girls

Some coaches love coaching boys, some love coaching girls, and some love coaching no matter what gender their players are. Most coaches, however, would agree that there are significant differences in coaching girls versus coaching boys.

You might be surprised to know that these differences aren't based on the obvious physical contrasts. Most boys can run faster, can jump higher, and are stronger than most girls their age, but that doesn't change the individual and team skills you should teach. What makes coaching girls versus coaching boys different is that girls and boys have different emotional and psychological characteristics. Your chances of being a successful girls' basketball coach will improve when you learn how to adapt your approach so you can best relate to, motivate, and teach girls.

Most coaches who have coached boys and girls agree on the following generalizations (as with all generalizations, there are plenty of exceptions):

Most boys are naturally aggressive. Most girls aren't. This means you'll have to be patient. Many girls won't get that killer instinct you're looking for during the whole season. Some will never get it at all. You'll find that girls who play in the driveway with their brothers will be used to the physical contact that occurs in basketball (these girls are often your best players). For the beginners, however, it will take a while before they don't shy away from the rough nature of the game. Again, patience is the password to success.

Most boys think of themselves first. Most girls think of themselves last. With boys, a coach often has to tell the players to pass more and shoot less. With girls, a coach often has to tell the girls to pass less, because they're missing opportunities for high-percentage shots. This is a good thing. Because girls are (generally) selfless, a team of girls often becomes an excellent passing team.

Most boys think playing in games is the best part of the season. Most girls think being part of a team is the best part. Girls like the camaraderie, the closeness, and the group aspect of being on a team. They like working together and helping each other succeed. This provides you with a great opportunity to have a team that has good

chemistry. That's not to say all your players on your team will be close and that you won't have players who don't like one another, but if you handle it right, the odds are your team will have unity and cohesion.

Most boys don't mind if a coach yells at them. Most girls do. Most boys don't take constructive criticism personally. Most girls do. Girls are sensitive, and some are hypersensitive. Not many will respond positively to the marine sergeant approach. If you're too harsh in tone or content, or if you correct a particular player too much (in her mind, not yours), you may find you have an unhappy player on the team. This isn't to suggest you shouldn't raise your voice. There are times you'll need to raise your voice, such as during games, so your players can hear you. Shouting instructions from the sidelines, as long as you're not berating a player, won't hurt anyone's feelings. However, even if your intentions are good, negative shouting will hurt the player's feelings, may alienate that player, and may cause other players to perceive you in a negative way.

Most boys don't care if you get to know them beyond basketball. Most girls want you to do so. Here's one of the popular coaching axioms: to coach boys, you must reach the athlete first, then the person; to coach girls, you must reach the person first, then the athlete. Take the opportunity to get to know your girls as people, not just as players. Not only will they appreciate you for it, which will make them more receptive to your coaching, but you'll enjoy an extra dimension to your players you never knew existed.

How to Use This Book

This is a reference book, a how-to book packed with information, best read in small chunks. Use it to prepare for the season, to coach your team during the season, and to evaluate how you did after the season.

The book has more information than you'll need. If you coach younger girls, pick and choose carefully what to teach. Limit the information

Question: I'm a guy coach who has had good success coaching boys' teams. Would I be better suited to coaching a boys' team instead of a girls' team?

Answer: It depends. If you approach the emotional and psychological aspects of girls the same way you approach those aspects in boys, you might have a hard time understanding girls and relating to them. However, if you pay attention to the differences in the genders and adapt your approach, there's no reason why you can't be just as effective as a girls' coach.

Question: I'm a guy coach, and this is my first time coaching girls. I read in the paper about a high school girl player accusing a male coach of sexual harassment. The coach was fired, but it turns out the player made it up. What can I do to avoid any possibility of someone accusing me of doing something inappropriate?

Answer: Sadly, there are coaches who have abused their influence as coaches and players who have tried to ruin their coach's reputation. These instances are few and far between, but our society has changed to the point where, as a male coaching girls, you should go out of your way to avoid situations that might be misconstrued by others. My advice is (1) never go into a room alone with only one player, (2) don't touch your players (high fives are fine, as are hugs in public at the end-of-the-season party, but pats on the rear are definitely inappropriate), (3) don't drive your car with just one player in it, and (4) if one of your players flirts with you or behaves inappropriately in any way, talk to your athletic director immediately and decide what action should be taken to address the situation.

---

you give your players. They can absorb only so much.

The first six chapters cover all the basics to get you started, including the rules of the game, practice planning, teaching fundamental skills, teaching offenses and defenses, and game preparation and strategies.

Chapter 7 contains drills you can use to teach the various skills. Each drill is marked with a degree of difficulty designation so you can choose the ones that best fit your team:

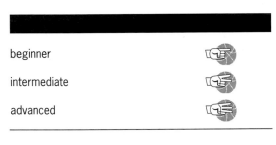

beginner

intermediate

advanced

To make it easy to understand the concepts, plays, offenses, defenses, and drills presented in the book, I've included many diagrams. The diagrams use the symbols shown at right.

Throughout the book, I introduce many basketball terms and phrases. Some are self-explanatory, but others require explanation.

Part of becoming a good coach is talking like a good coach. If you come across a term or phrase that you don't know, check the glossary in the Appendix. I also include a number of Ask the Coach sidebars to cover related topics.

The Appendix also includes a sample practice plan, a sample player-parent handout, and a guide to referee signals, among other things. The index will help you locate advice on specific topics.

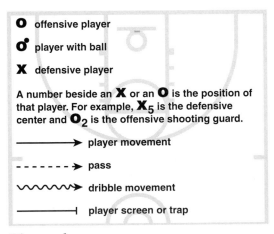

O offensive player

O player with ball

X defensive player

A number beside an **X** or an **O** is the position of that player. For example, **X₅** is the defensive center and **O₂** is the offensive shooting guard.

→ player movement

- - - → pass

⌇⌇⌇→ dribble movement

—— player screen or trap

Diagram key.

Chapter 1

PREPARING FOR THE SEASON

Before you can coach basketball, you need to have a basic knowledge of the rules of the game, starting with where it's played.

About the Game

The Court

Basketball is played on a playing surface called the *court*. Courts can be indoors or outdoors. The surface can be made of wood, concrete, or asphalt. Some courts are carpeted, and some have hard rubber surfaces. The best (and most expensive) courts are made of maple wood.

College courts are 94 feet long and 50 feet wide, but the dimensions of middle school and high school courts vary.

Basic Rules

Basketball is a complicated game with many rules. If you're a rookie coach, it will take some game experience before you learn everything you need to know. Here are the basics:

Object of the game. As with most other team sports, the team with the most points at the end of the game wins.

The ball. There are several sizes of basketballs, but for girls' basketball, you'll use the standard women's ball, which is 28.5 inches in circumference. All the major manufacturers, such as Wilson and Spalding, manufacture this size ball in both indoor and outdoor versions. You can buy women's balls at any good sporting goods outlet.

Number of players and substitutions. There are five players on the court for each team. The coach can substitute fresh players at any time, from one player up to five at a time. There are no limitations on how many times in the game substitutions can be made and how many times a player can come in and out of the game. Substitutions can be made only on a *dead ball*, when the referee blows the whistle and play stops. You can substitute after the first of two free throws and after the last free throw, but you can't substitute before the first free throw. The only player for whom you can't substitute is the player shooting at the free throw line.

Time. The length of the game varies, depending on the level and age. College games last 40 minutes, divided into two 20-minute

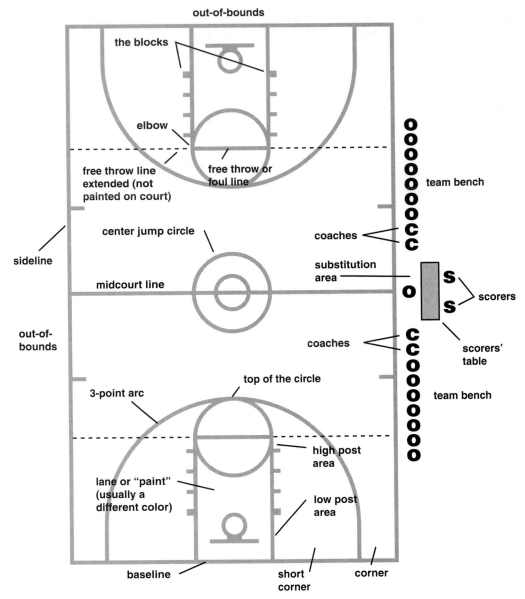

The basketball court.

halves. High school games last 32 minutes, divided into 8-minute quarters, but some high schools use 16-minute halves. The time between quarters is brief—1 minute is the norm—and the time between halves is no more than 10 minutes. Some high school leagues use a 30-second *shot clock*, meaning that the team with the ball must shoot within 30 seconds of the moment they gain possession, or the ball is given to the other team. Middle school leagues don't have a shot clock, though some use a *running clock*, meaning that the clock doesn't stop every time the referee blows the whistle. This is done to ensure that the game ends on time and the next game can begin when scheduled.

The baskets. Each basket consists of a rim with a net attached to a backboard, which is attached to a structural support, like a pole. Some baskets are fixed in place, and some can be raised to the ceiling to get them out of the way. Each team has its own basket at one end of the court. Both teams sit alongside one length of the court, each on one side of the scorers' table . At the start of the game, *your team's basket* is the near basket. For the first half, your players will defend this basket and will try to score at the *other team's basket* (at the far end). At halftime, the teams will *switch baskets*—your team will now defend the far basket and will try to score at the near basket. Prior to the start of the first half, teams warm up at the other team's basket.

Scoring. When a player shoots and scores from anywhere inside the 3-point arc, it counts as 2 points. Any shot made from outside the 3-point arc counts as 3 points. (In high school, the arc is 19 feet from the basket.) For the shot to count as 3 points, the shooter's feet must not touch the arc. If even her toe is on the line, it's considered a 2-point basket, not a 3-point basket. Two-point shots and 3-point shots are *field goals*. *Free throws* are awarded to a player who has been fouled. Free throws, shot from the free throw line, or foul line, are worth 1 point. The foul line is 15 feet from the basket. If a team mistakenly scores at the wrong basket (this sometimes happens with younger players!), the basket counts for the other team.

Moving the ball. When a team has possession of the ball, it tries to move the ball close to the other team's basket for a good scoring opportunity. Players can advance the ball by *dribbling* (bouncing the ball on the floor with one hand) and *passing* (throwing) it to a teammate, subject to certain rules. When they throw the ball at the basket to try to score, they are *shooting* the ball. As noted above, different kinds of successful shots *(made shots)*, result in scoring from 1 to 3 points.

Defending the basket. When a team doesn't have possession of the ball, it defends its basket. Players are allowed to gain possession of the ball from the other team at any time through stealing passes, stealing dribbles, and getting defensive rebounds, subject to the limitations regarding fouls. A good defensive team makes it hard for the offensive team to do what it wants to do. A good defender makes it hard for her player to catch, dribble, pass, and shoot.

Rules about Fouls

The rules about fouls are designed to keep the game from getting too rough and to penalize players who violate the rules. One of the referee's main duties is to enforce the rules about fouling. Each time a foul is committed, the referee blows the whistle and play stops. The referee uses a hand signal to indicate what the foul was and calls out the number of the player who committed the foul ("Number 32... blocking"). (See the referee hand signals in the Appendix.)

Personal fouls happen when a player makes physical contact with an opponent in a manner not allowed by the rules. Contact is the key component. If there's no contact, if the player didn't touch the other player, there's no foul.

A defender can foul a player with the ball or without the ball. When she fouls a player who is shooting, such as by hitting her arm or hand, it's a *shooting foul*. If the shot scores, the referee signals *and one*, which means the shooter gets to shoot a free throw as well. If the shot misses, the shooter is awarded two free throws in the case of a 2-point shot and three free throws in the case of a 3-point shot.

When a defender fouls a player without the ball, it's a *nonshooting foul*. A player (the *inbounder*) from the team that was fouled passes *(inbounds)* the ball to a teammate from a spot outside of the court boundaries. The spot is along the nearest line (baseline or sideline) to where the foul occurred.

Some of the most common nonshooting fouls are the following (most are self-explanatory):

Reaching across a player's body with
    your arm

Holding a player (any part of her,
    including her jersey)

That's a reaching foul every time.

Pushing a player (with any part of the body)

Tripping a player

Blocking a player who is driving to the basket by getting in her way and knocking her off her path

A player can also commit a personal foul if her team has the ball. She can commit a *moving pick* by moving too soon after she sets a screen. She can *push* a defender with her hands as she tries to get open. She can commit a *charging foul* when she dribbles into a defender who has established position and is no longer moving. When an offensive player *drives* (dribbles hard to the basket) and collides with a defender, this is one of the more difficult calls a referee has to make. Was it a charge by the dribbler or a block by the defender? The collision happens in an instant, and it's hard to know if the defender established good position prior to the contact. Whichever way the referee calls it, you can be sure half the fans in the stands and one of the coaches will disagree.

If the defender leans into the dribbler with her body, that's a block.

If the defender positions herself in the dribbler's path, sets her feet, and doesn't move, that's a charge. Sometimes, a little acting helps!

There are three other kinds of personal fouls:

An *intentional foul* happens when a player makes illegal contact with an opponent and is obviously trying to incur a foul (probably to stop the clock)—she isn't trying to steal the ball. Intentional fouls result in two free throws awarded to the player who was fouled.

A *flagrant foul* is called for excessive roughness, such as when a player punches, kicks, or fights with another player. It seldom happens, but when it does, the referee has the right to eject the offending player from the game.

A *technical foul* can be assessed to a player or a coach (this means you and your assistants!) at the referee's discretion for various unsportsmanlike actions, including using profanity, insulting the referee, and throwing the ball at a player. A technical foul is also assessed when the defender reaches across the imaginary plane of the baseline while guarding an inbounder or when a team's scorekeeper doesn't list the right player numbers in the scorebook. The penalty for a technical foul is that a player from the other team (any player the coach chooses) shoots three free throws without anyone standing along the sides of the lane. Regardless of how many shots she makes or misses, that player's team then inbounds the ball from their end of the court. Obviously, technical fouls can be costly to your team.

Each player is allowed a maximum of five personal fouls per game. When a player commits her fifth foul, she *fouls out* and, regardless of how much time is left in the game, must leave the game immediately. The coach must replace her with a substitute. A player who fouls out can't come back into the game.

Since you don't want to lose an important player before the game ends, know at all times how many fouls each of your players has. If a player accumulates fouls quickly or is in danger of fouling out, take her out for a while so she'll be able to play later in the game. A player with four fouls is a liability on defense, because she can't play aggressively for fear of fouling out. Good coaches will gear their team's offense to attack a defender in foul trouble. Throughout the game, keep track of the individual and team fouls for the other team. Depending on how the referees are calling the game, you might want one of your players to drive at a defender who is in foul trouble.

Team fouls are the totals of the personal fouls each team accumulates during a half. There's no limit to the number of team fouls a team can accumulate. At the end of the first half, the team foul total for each team resets to zero. Each team's scorekeeper keeps team foul totals. In addition to the points scored and the time left, some scoreboards also show the number of team fouls for each team.

ASK THE COACH

Question: Last game, I was given a technical foul after I complained about a call. I thought I was being nice and polite, but the ref obviously disagreed. I was flabbergasted and talked about it to the other ref, who just shrugged his shoulders. Should I have called a time-out to talk to the ref who gave me the technical?

Answer: No. All it would have done is aggravate an already aggravated situation. Part of being a good bench coach is reading the referees. Some referees have thinner skin than others. If you see that a referee isn't happy with being questioned (by you or the other coach), it's smart to keep quiet. The last thing your team needs is a technical foul, especially in a close game. It's your job to see that no one on the team, most of all you, gets a technical in any game. You want to teach your players about good sportsmanship with your own actions. I know there are coaches out there who try to get a technical foul called on them at a key time in a game as a way to fire up their team, but I disagree with that as a practical strategy. Not only that, the coach is teaching the wrong lesson to his or her players.

Once a team commits its seventh team foul in a half, the other team is *in the bonus*. They are awarded a *one-and-one free throw* for the next three nonshooting fouls that occur during the rest of the half. The player who is fouled shoots one free throw. If she misses, the teams fight for the ball. If she makes it, she shoots a second free throw (the *one-and-one* term means that if she makes one shot, she gets another one). Once a team commits its tenth team foul, it's penalized further. The other team is now awarded a *two-shot free throw* for every non-shooting foul. Every player fouled from now on gets to shoot a second free throw, even if she misses the first one.

Fouls are a huge factor in games. A team that fouls a lot puts itself at a disadvantage to the other team. It risks losing players and giving the other team extra points. Conversely, a team that knows how to play tough defense without fouling is tough to score points against. A team with good free throw shooters has an advantage over a team that shoots poorly from the line. Often, close games are decided by who wins the "Battle of the Free Throw Line." Your team should practice free throws every practice.

Other Rules

Here are the other basic rules of the game. If a player on your team violates any of these rules, your team immediately gives up possession of the ball to the other team.

- **10-second backcourt call.** Once a player inbounds the ball in the backcourt, her team has 10 seconds to advance the ball past the midcourt line. Some middle school leagues waive this rule.

- **5-second closely guarded call.** A player with the ball who is guarded by a defender standing within 6 feet of her must advance the ball within 5 seconds. This prevents a player from dribbling in one spot as a stalling tactic.

- **5-second call on the dribbler.** A player who *picks up her dribble* (stops dribbling) must pass or shoot within 5 seconds.

- **5-second call on the inbounder.** An inbounder must pass the ball within 5 seconds.

- **3-second lane violation.** An offensive player can't *camp out* (stay) in the lane for more than 3 seconds. She must keep moving in and out to avoid this call. However, once the ball has been shot and hits the rim, the 3-second count starts over.

- **Moving pick.** A screener can't move any part of her body after setting a screen.

- **Backcourt violation.** After bringing the ball over the midcourt line, a team can't allow the ball to go back over the line into the other half of the court.

A clear case of carrying the ball (palming). The referee will have to blow the whistle on this one!

- **Traveling.** A dribbler can't take more than one step without dribbling.
- **Double dribble.** A player can't dribble with both hands more than once.
- **Palming.** When dribbling, a player can't *carry the ball;* her palm must make contact with the top half of the ball. Referees call carrying less than they used to, so more dribblers take advantage of this.

A *held ball* occurs when a defender grabs the ball while it's in the hands of an offensive player, and both players hold the ball at the same time. This often happens when two players dive to the floor after a loose ball. The held ball is a unique rule violation in the way it's handled. While other violations result in an automatic change of possession, the held ball uses an *alternating arrow* or *alternating possession* system. Regardless of which team is on offense or which team is on defense, the ball is awarded to the team that is attacking in the direction of the pointed arrow. Most coaches dislike the alternate possession system because it doesn't always reward the defender for a good play.

Most scorers' tables have a box that displays a red LED arrow or a mechanical pointer used as an arrow. The arrow points to one basket or the other. The clock keeper is in charge of the arrow. At the beginning of the game, the arrow is neutral. If team A gets possession of the ball off the center jump, the rules consider that team A has used its possession, so the clock keeper points the arrow in the direction of team A's basket. That means that on the next held ball, team B gets the ball. Team B inbounds the ball along the nearest point on the sideline or baseline where the held ball occurred. As soon as team B inbounds, the clock keeper switches the arrow so that team A will get the next held ball.

The Positions

Basketball players fall into one of two general categories: *guards* (or *perimeter players*), who play away from the basket along the 3-point arc area, and *forwards* (or *posts*), who play near the basket and around the free throw line.

Each player is assigned a position to play. The way basketball coaches label the positions has changed over the past ten to fifteen years. The old terminology has evolved into numbers. For example, instead of talking about the *shooting guard*, many coaches now talk about the *two guard* or the *2*. This has come about because the distinctions between the traditional positions have blurred over the years. Today's players are more versatile and can play more than one position. Players like Magic Johnson (who played for the Los Angeles Lakers) showed that height no longer dictates where a player plays on the floor. He was 6 feet 9 inches and played point guard.

Whether you prefer the old designations or the numerical approach, here are the general characteristics of the positions you need to fill on your team.

Point Guard or 1. This is the most important position on the team. If you have a good point guard, your team will have a good chance of succeeding. If you don't, your team will

Held ball. Which way is the arrow pointing?

struggle offensively. Your point guard is your team leader on the floor. She directs the offense and knows where everyone is supposed to be. Put your best ball handler at the point. Ideally, she can dribble with both hands with her head up and is a good passer. She should have good *court savvy*—she should know when to pass, when to drive, when to shoot, when to slow things down, and when to speed things up.

The point guard is more important to a basketball team than a quarterback is to a football team. While the quarterback rests when his team is on defense, the point guard often has to guard the other team's best player. I'll say it again—the point is the most important position on the team. Most teams have plenty of *wing players* (players who play on the perimeter in the free throw line extended area), but many have no true point guard. The coach is stuck with trying to make a point guard out of a player not well suited to the position. If you have a true-blue point guard on your team, consider yourself lucky. If you don't, make it a priority to develop your best perimeter player into one and expect a lot of full-court presses.

Shooting Guard or 2. Put your best outside shooter in this position. She should be a good ball handler. This player should have the best shooting range of your players, ideally beyond the 3-point line, and should have confidence in her shot (balanced with good judgment on when to shoot and when not to shoot). She should be able to shoot not just when catching the ball but also when facing a defender and dribbling. If she can also fake the shot and drive, so much the better. As part of your offense, design ways to get your best shooter the ball in the spots on the court where she likes to shoot.

Small Forward or 3. Small forwards come in all sizes. This player may not be as good a ball

Great point guards are great floor leaders.

Wing players who can slash into the paint are dangerous.

handler as the other two perimeter players, but she should be able to protect the ball from quicker defenders. While any outside shooting ability is a plus, she should be a good *slasher*— able to slice toward the basket for close-in shots and offensive rebounds. If she's tall, she should look to pass over the defense whenever possible.

Power Forward or 4. This player should be your best inside scorer. She should shoot well from the short corner, as well as from the high post area. She should be an *inside-outside* offensive threat, able to score from the perimeter and close to the basket. She should be strong and an aggressive rebounder, someone you can count on for some offensive rebounds every game. As with all post players, she should be a good free throw shooter. If she's aggressive and the referee is blowing the whistle, she'll go to the line often.

Center or 5. This is traditionally the tallest player on your team. She should be the best rebounder and inside defender. She's usually assigned to guard the best offensive inside player on the other team. She should know how to play with her back to the basket and have at least one or two *post moves* (moves unique to playing in the low post area). She must know how to *post up* and establish position so she'll be

ASK THE COACH

Question: Help! I don't have any tall girls on my 14-and-under AAU team! Not one! What should I do?

Answer: First, don't panic. Second, you're not alone. Plenty of coaches find themselves with a team of guards. Height is a plus, but if you have only short players, you can still have a competitive team. Find your toughest, most aggressive rebounders and put them inside. Find your quickest players and put them outside. Find your best ball handler and put her at the point. Play to your strengths. A team of small players is usually quick and fast. Consider playing a pressing, fast-break style. Speed often trumps height. Minimize your team's physical shortcomings by tailoring your offenses and defenses to match your personnel.

Question: You talk about a "true-blue point guard." What does that mean?

Answer: A true-blue point guard thinks differently than the other perimeter players. Instead of focusing on shooting or slashing to the basket, she thinks about passing and making the offense run smoothly. Coaches talk about the point guard being the *general on the floor*. The point guard is the leader of the offense. She has to see the court well, direct players who are out of position to the right spot, and take action based on the best option that will result in a good shot. The point guard is multidimensional. She must be a good ball handler, a good passer, and a good defender. She thinks about assists more than shots. After a game, she asks, "Did I make my teammates better today?" not "How many points did I score?" She should be one of the quickest players on the floor, able to weather intense pressure with poise. If your point guard unravels, the team unravels. A great point guard can carry a team much further than any single other player. And yes, if she can also shoot well and slash to the basket, then consider yourself a lucky coach.

Question: I don't have a natural point guard on my team. I have a few players who can dribble fine, but none of them want to play the point. They say it's too much pressure. Our first game is two weeks away. How do I make a point guard out of reluctant players?

Answer: Not without a lot of patience and some luck. Playing the point requires a level of confidence few young players have. Developing confidence takes time. I suggest you focus on your two best dribblers, try them both at the position, and find out who has the most confidence. Talk to them together. Tell them that the team needs two people to start the offense, that they're going to share the duties. Tell them that neither will have to be out there for very long, that the other will soon come in. If they share the responsibility so that each girl isn't the only point guard shouldering the load, their anxiety and reluctance should decrease. As the season progresses, you may find that one of them decides playing the point is a good thing. The other player will become the backup.

open for passes. She should not mind the rough, physical play of the game. The center position is no place for timid players.

Before the First Practice

Team Equipment

If you coach a middle school or high school team, the school likely will have a certain amount of equipment available, including uniforms. AAU teams, however, usually have no uniforms and the parents must pay for them. Before the season starts, make sure the following items are on hand:

- **Balls.** Ideally, you want enough balls so each player can use one in the same drill at the same time. Like anything else, when it comes to quality, you get what you pay for. If you're in charge of buying balls, don't buy cheap ones. They don't last as long. However, there's no reason to buy the most expensive balls. Medium-priced balls bounce just as high.

- **Ball bag.** There are two types: see-through mesh bags with a drawstring and canvas bags with handles. Canvas bags look snazzier (especially with the team's name on the side), but the mesh types cost much less. Choices, choices!

- **Ball pump.** Balls lose air over time and with use. Electric pumps are expensive but easier to use than hand pumps. Assign the job of keeping the balls pumped up to an assistant or a manager. Have a supply of extra needles, because they break frequently.

- **Pinnies.** Buy three colors of pinnies (mesh-style sleeveless practice jerseys), at least six of each. Make sure they're washed often, because they smell after a few uses (you'll know when it's past time for the laundry . . . the girls will complain loudly). This is another duty to assign so you don't have to worry about it.

- **Medicine kit.** Most schools and AAU organizations provide a medicine kit, but if not, put one together. Buy an inexpensive hard plastic box with a carrying handle (a fishing tackle box or toolbox), along with bandages of different sizes, gauze, splints, antibacterial first-aid cream, scissors, non-aspirin pain reliever, and plastic bags for ice. If you don't have an ice machine where you practice and play, buy some ice packs (the kind you activate by snapping the pack). Most basketball injuries (twists, sprains, bruises) require ice to be applied right away. (See the sidebar on page 162.)

- **Scorebook.** These are available at any good sporting goods outlet.

- **Whistle on a lanyard.** Some coaches use whistles all the time, and some don't use them at all. It's a matter of personal preference and style. We use them in our scrimmages to make things more gamelike. All players understand that when they hear the whistle, they should immediately stop what they're doing.

- **Clipboard.** This can be purchased as the whiteboard type that has a diagram of the court on it or as the old-style pressed wood type. Buy the whiteboard type. You'll need it to illustrate plays during the games, you can clip sheets of paper on it (daily practice plan, roster, schedule, etc.), and you can use it to make notes. Buy extra dry-erase markers and pencils.

- **Rule book.** I've covered most of the rules of the game above, but there are other rules you need to know. The rule book comes in handy as a reference guide when you're unsure of a particular call.

- **Uniforms.** If you coach in a middle school or high school, your team will have uniforms, but if you coach an AAU team, your players will have to pay a fee for their uniforms. Players love to wear uniforms, and the snazzier, the better. Ideally, you'll have two sets of uniforms, home (white) and away (colored). Some

AAU teams have only one set. If that's your situation, the set should be colored. Be sure to have a couple of XL uniforms and one XXL uniform. It's embarrassing for a girl who is overweight or large for her age if she has to squeeze into a pair of shorts two sizes too small.

Player Equipment

Players should wear a clean T-shirt, clean shorts, and basketball shoes to practice. The latter are particularly important. Tennis shoes, running shoes, and regular sneakers don't provide the ankle support that basketball shoes do.

Players should also bring their own water bottle to practice (and games, if water bottles aren't provided), which helps protect them from any germs they might pick up from drinking at the gym water fountain or from sharing water bottles with other players.

Finally, your players should bring any medical equipment they need, such as an inhaler or ankle brace.

You should list these responsibilities in your player-parent handout (see the sample in the Appendix).

Tryouts: The Big Picture

Some schools are so small that the coach is glad to have anyone who shows up so there are enough players for a team. However, most schools have more players than spots available on their teams, and they must go through a tryout-and-cut process. Tryouts are always an exciting time for coaches and an anxious time for players. If you're responsible for setting up and running tryouts, keep these concepts in mind:

Be organized. This is no time to plan on the fly. Schedule everything by the minute, so tryouts will proceed in an orderly manner. Tryouts with lots of kids in the gym will be noisy. If you're not prepared, the proceedings will quickly slip into chaos. A well-planned tryout, like a well-planned practice, should march along like a Swiss clock.

Too much time is better than not enough time. If you anticipate that only a small number of players (fifteen to twenty) will try out, one tryout session might be enough, and two sessions will be the most you'll need. However, if you anticipate that a large number (twenty and over) will try out, you should have three days of tryouts at a minimum. If you have over thirty players, divide the players into two groups and hold sessions at different times. For high school, divide them according to grades. For AAU, divide them alphabetically. The benefits of having a minimum of three days of tryouts are enormous. After the first day, you and your assistants have time to share observations

ASK THE COACH

Question: I keep trying to pump up our balls, but the needles keep snapping off. Is there a trick to it?

Answer: Yes. Before you put the needle into the air hole on the ball, moisten the tip with a bit of saliva. That way, the needle will slide in easily. Also, as you pump, hold the needle in place so it doesn't wobble back and forth.

Question: How do I know when the ball has too much or too little air in it?

Answer: A simple test is to hold the ball in the palm of your hand with your arm outstretched. The ball should be head high. Let it roll off your fingers. If it's pumped up just right, it will bounce a few inches above your waist to the height of your elbow.

Question: I noticed that the numbers on our uniforms don't go over 5, meaning there's no 73 and no 86. What's wrong with having higher numbers like football teams do?

Answer: When referees call personal fouls, they use their hands to signal the player's number. For example, if a referee calls number 23 for a reaching foul, he or she will hold up two fingers with one hand and three fingers with the other. This is why 55 is the highest number you'll ever see on a basketball uniform.

and to reflect on who is a sure thing for your team, who is not, and who is in the middle. During the second and third days, you can focus on the smaller number of players who are "on the bubble," the kids you need more time to compare and evaluate. Another advantage of multiday tryouts is that after seeing the competition in the first session, some players might decide to withdraw. They might suddenly decide they don't like basketball after all or that it's "too much work." A three-day-minimum approach doesn't guarantee you won't overlook a promising player or won't choose a player who doesn't turn out like you expected she would, but it reduces the chances you'll make a mistake.

Get your assistants involved. Even if only fifteen to twenty kids try out, you'll need help to make the sessions run smoothly. Tryouts should include *stations* (see below). You can't run efficient stations without having an assistant at each basket, preferably someone with knowledge about the skill that's involved. Get enough help so you won't have to worry about the details. You want time to walk around the gym and watch kids doing different things in different areas of the gym. If you don't have enough help, you'll be stuck for 2 hours at one basket, and you won't see what you need to see to make good judgments about the players. You can't have too many assistants at tryouts.

Maximize use of the baskets. During each tryout session, the players should stand around as little as possible. When six players are on the court doing a drill or scrimmaging while twenty-five other kids are on the sidelines, the sideliners will become bored and fidgety and will turn into a distraction. If you plan it right, you and your assistants shouldn't have to spend much time engaged in crowd control. You'll be able to spend most of your energies watching and evaluating players. Use all the baskets available. If you have only two baskets, use the middle of the floor for nonbasket skills, such as passing and dribbling. The less the players stand around waiting their turn, the more effective the tryouts will be.

It's a tryout, not a clinic. Some coaches approach tryouts as they would a clinic. They take time to teach and demonstrate skills. At practice, this is what they should be doing, but at tryouts, teaching takes time away from watching and evaluating. Even three-day tryouts provide only so much time to see what each player can do. Use tryouts for their intended purpose. After tryouts are over and your team is in place, you'll have the whole rest of the season to teach.

Test fundamentals. You want to see how well each player dribbles, passes, shoots, defends, and rebounds. This sounds obvious, but you'd be surprised at how many tryouts don't give the coaches a good opportunity to see where each player is in terms of the basics. Some tryouts are nothing but scrimmages. This is a good way to see the top 10 percent and the bottom 10 percent of the players. In scrimmage situations, the strongest and weakest players stand out. However, the majority of the players at tryouts fall into a large gray area. They're not outstanding players, nor are they terrible players. Evaluating the kids in the middle group will be where you find your hardest decisions. A large number of players will be similar—not exactly the same, but with only slight distinctions. Scrimmaging tells you only part of the story, not the whole story. Specific skill-oriented drills should be part of tryouts. This is where stations come into play.

Scrimmage 3-on-3. The best scrimmage format for tryouts is 3-on-3, either half court or full court, with the players playing man-to-man defense. This makes it hard for any player to fade into the background. With 5-on-5 and even 4-on-4 scrimmages, some players won't touch the ball. On defense, they're not obvious unless their player has the ball, and their player might not touch the ball. In 3-on-3 scrimmages, where everyone plays man-to-man defense, each player is out in the open for you to see. If she plays good on-ball defense, it's apparent. If her man beats her with the dribble, it's apparent. If she doesn't block out or doesn't hustle back to the basket, it's obvious because someone scores an easy basket. You'll learn a lot about each player. If you don't have much time in your tryouts to scrimmage, forget scrimmaging 5-on-5, and scrimmage 3-on-3.

Tryouts: The Details

Assuming you have 2 hours per tryout session, break down the time you have along these lines:

Introductory talk and warm-ups:
15 minutes

Conditioning drills: 13 minutes

Water break: 2 minutes (use the time to set up stations)

Station work: 28 minutes (assumes 4 to 6 baskets)

Water break: 2 minutes

1-on-1 rotation: 28 minutes (start at last station basket)

Water break: 2 minutes (use the time to split players into teams)

3-on-3 scrimmaging: 20 minutes

5-on-5 scrimmaging: 10 minutes

Introductory talk. Your comments should be brief and enthusiastic. Introduce yourself and the other coaches or assistants. Explain what will happen during tryouts, how the teams will be chosen, and how cuts will be made. Reassure the players that they're not alone—everyone is anxious at tryouts. Encourage them to do their absolute best.

Warm-ups. The purpose of warming up is to get the blood flowing and to prepare the muscles for vigorous exercise. Just like in practice, you should have the players start off slowly with moderately paced drills. Players should never start off at full speed, no matter how fit they are. Not warming up properly can result in unnecessary injuries, like pulled muscles or twisted ankles.

Here are some good warm-up drills to use at tryouts:

Victory Dribbles (Drill 6)

Full-Court Passing (Drill 22)

Two-Line Layups (Drill 46)

Slide the Court (Drill 53)

After the players are warmed up, they should stretch for 2 to 3 minutes. It's important to stretch the muscle groups in the players' legs, arms, and backs. Stretching before warming up is another way to cause injuries.

Conditioning drills. Once the players are warmed up, they're ready for conditioning drills. This allows you to see who is in shape and who is not, which also tells you who prepared for tryouts and who didn't (on the Varsity level, your players should have been working on conditioning during September and October). Players who put in time preparing for tryouts are the kind of players who work hard in practice. They're serious about improving their skills.

Another benefit of putting the players through conditioning drills is to find out who understands that hard physical effort is part of playing basketball and who doesn't. If someone is lazy or doesn't like to work hard, you want to find out now, not at the first practice.

For that reason, make the conditioning part of tryouts strenuous. Don't make it grueling. There's no reason to make anyone sick, but push the players as hard as you expect to push them in practice. You'll find out a lot about the mental and physical toughness of the players. If some don't return for the second day of tryouts because basketball is "too hard," don't try to convince them otherwise. It's best for them and the team that they drop out. You won't waste time considering a player who probably wouldn't be happy playing on the team.

Here are some good conditioning drills to use in tryouts:

Victory Sprints (Drill 5)

Victory Dribbles (Drill 6)

Three-Man Weave (Drill 27)

3-on-2, 2-on-1 (Drill 71)

4-on-4 Recovery Transition (Drill 74)

The best conditioning drills involve the ball. Not only is each player getting in shape, but she's working on a skill at the same time.

Station work. Split the players into groups and assign them to a *station*, a basket where they will work on a specific skill. Before tryouts begin, assign an assistant to each station with instructions on how to run that station. Give him or her a clipboard, an evaluation sheet (see a sample in the Appendix), and a pencil.

On your signal, the players begin working on the skill required at their station. After 3 to 4 minutes, once each player has enough time to show what she can do, have the players rotate to the next station. When the players have rotated to every station, they should remain at the basket to begin the next activity, 1-on-1 rotation.

Station work is an excellent time to see how each player performs fundamental skills, particularly shooting, ball handling, and 1-on-1 offensive and defensive skills. The following activities are ideally suited for station work:

Free throws: best out of 10

Alternating elbow jump shots: number made in 1 minute

Right-handed layups from the right elbow: number made in 1 minute

Left-handed layups from the left elbow: number made in 1 minute

X Layups (Drill 48): number made in 1 minute

Mikan (Drill 49): number made in 1 minute

Dribble Drive (Drill 56): 1 point for score, 1 point for offensive rebound, 1 point for defensive stop

2-on-2 Defense (Drill 57)

1-on-1 rotation. Number the baskets 1 to 6. Tell the players they're going to play 1-on-1 until the offensive player scores or the defender gets the ball. Each group at each basket lines up at the top of the circle. The first player in line is the defender, and the second player is the offensive player. The offensive player *checks the ball*—that is, hands it to the defender; when the defender is ready, she hands the ball back to the offensive player. Then they play 1-on-1. After each contest, the winner goes to the next highest basket (e.g., from basket 3 to basket 4) and the loser goes to the next lower basket (e.g., from basket 3 to basket 2). When a player at basket 6 wins, she keeps playing there. When a player at basket 1 loses, she keeps playing there.

What happens is the best players rotate to baskets 5 and 6, the less-skilled players rotate to baskets 1 and 2, and the average players stay in the middle baskets. This drill is excellent for seeing who can drive and score, who can defend, and who blocks out. It allows you to watch each player match skills against players of varying abilities. It also separates the players on its own, which lets the players see where they stand in comparison to the rest of the girls trying out. In that sense, it's a "reality check" that helps set expectations. The less-skilled players clearly see where they stand. If they end up being cut, at least they have an inkling of the possibility.

Scrimmaging. As noted earlier, watching players scrimmage 3-on-3 is an excellent evaluation tool. To make it continuous and involve more players, have three teams of three players play 3-on-3-on-3 (Drill 72). If you have only two baskets, run the drill full court, which will occupy nine players. If you have six baskets, run two scrimmages across each half court, which will occupy eighteen players. You'll see who is aggressive, who is confident with the ball, who passes well, who turns the ball over, who dribbles with her head down, who knows how to protect the ball, who attacks the boards, who dives on the floor, and so on.

Though scrimmaging 5-on-5 isn't as informative, you can still learn a lot. Watch who shows leadership, who works hard to get open, who sets screens, who runs the fast break, who understands how to play help defense, and who hustles back on defense. The players who have played organized basketball before will stand out, as will those players who haven't. Fast players and the best athletes will also stand out.

When you set up scrimmages, try to match teams against teams with comparable abilities and experience. Watching a trio of experienced players wallop a trio of bewildered beginners doesn't provide you with useful information. After the 1-on-1 rotation, you should have a good idea about the relative skills of most of the players. An easy way to split the players into comparable teams is to say, "OK, everyone at baskets 1 through 3, go to this half of the court; everyone at baskets 4 through 6 go to that half of the court." In between tryout sessions, you'll have time to look at your notes and divide the players into teams that are more evenly matched.

Evaluating Players. Evaluating basketball players isn't an exact science. What you see a player do in one 2-hour period might be different from what you see her do in another 2-hour period. Some players don't play well in tryouts because they're so anxious. Most players relax as tryouts proceed, though some players won't. There's nothing you can do to change that.

Before tryouts begin, print out a one-page tryout evaluation sheet that covers everything you think is important to judge (see the sample in the Appendix). Make enough copies so you and the other coaches have one for each player. During tryouts, each coach and assistant should make notes. After each day, compare notes. If you don't write down your observations as they occur, you won't remember all of them later. Though it's inconvenient to pause during the action to jot something down, the effort will be worth it when it comes to recalling details about who did what.

There's a second reason to use an evaluation sheet. The upset parent of a player who doesn't make the team may call you to ask why his or her daughter was cut. There's no easy way to calm the parent, but it helps if you can say, "In the shooting drills, Sally shot only 22 percent, and she made only one left-handed layup in a minute." Citing statistics helps defuse the notion that you were haphazard or biased in your decisions. It also gives the correct impression that you're an organized, professional coach who takes the responsibility of choosing players seriously.

Cutting Players. If you're one of the coaches who is grateful to have enough bodies to make a team, you'll be spared one thing about coaching that no coach enjoys—cutting players.

There's no easy way to tell a player who has her heart set on making the team that she's not good enough, but some ways of giving her the bad news are better than others. I don't like the practice of posting a list in the hallway for everyone to see. There's no reason to create a situation where three players are jumping for joy next to the list, shouting "I made it!" while another player walks up to find out her name is missing. It's hard enough for many kids to put themselves on the line for everyone to see if they succeed or fail. Posting a list might be convenient for you, but it's not fair or necessary to put a kid through the personal embarrassment in a public setting.

Remember that every player gave her time and effort to try out. The ones who didn't make the team deserve to know why. Meet with each player in private and tell her why she wasn't chosen. Don't be critical. State your case in a positive manner. ("The other girls who play center have more experience than you do" is kinder than "You can't run, shoot, or dribble.") If she loves basketball, urge her to continue to work on her game. Give her ideas for other teams she can possibly play on (AAU, recreational team, etc.). If she's trying out for the Varsity team, hopefully she can make your JV team instead. Talking to the player in person won't erase her disappointment, but the player will understand that although her skills weren't good enough, you're interested enough in her as a person to take the time to talk to her.

In some cases, a face-to-face meeting isn't practical. Maybe you don't teach at the school where you coach. Maybe it's an AAU team. Maybe there were sixty players at tryouts, and you only took twelve. The next best approach is to call each player and give her the news over the phone. While it's not face-to-face, it's still personal. Another option is to write two simple form letters, one starting with "Congratulations for making the team" and the other starting with "We're sorry to tell you that you didn't make the team." Include an evaluation section at the bottom of the letter where you evaluate the player's skills. As in the personal meeting, the evaluation should be positive and informative. Rate her skills (excellent, very good, good, and fair) as well as the intangibles (hustle, court savvy, effort). See a sample end-of-tryouts rejection letter in the Appendix.

After you write a handwritten note on each girl's letter, put it in an envelope and seal it. After the last tryout session, after thanking the players for trying out and working hard, give each player her envelope (before sealing them, double-check to make sure each player is receiving the right letter!). Tell them not to open their letters until they're home. Though you can't avoid disappointing the players you cut, at least you gave them the news in private.

With some players, it might seem impossible to come up with something positive. Keep thinking. Every player did something well,

ASK THE COACH

Question: We have only fourteen girls trying out. I'd like to have no more than thirteen on my team, but I feel bad cutting only one player. Any advice?

Answer: That's an easy call. If you decide to cut only one player, that's a hard situation for that one kid. Would it work to make her a manager? If not, I'd keep her. One more player won't make much of a difference to you or the team. I'd also have an "expectations" conversation with her. Tell her you'd like her to be on the team, but that the other players at her position are more advanced. This means she probably won't play much in games. Tell her, "If you understand your role and will be happy with it, I'd love to have you on the team." Let her make the decision. If she decides she won't be happy not playing much, she'll decide to not play. If she decides she really wants to be on the team regardless of playing time, welcome her. She'll bring a great attitude, and you never know, maybe she'll develop into a fine player down the road.

Question: After two days of tryouts, I have filled all the spots on my team except for one more wing player. I've narrowed it down to five players, but they all seem alike. What can I do on the last day to make sure I'll pick the best one?

Answer: It's always hard to fill the last few spots on a team. The differences among the bubble candidates are subtle. Tomorrow, group the bubble players during the station segment. You'll make better comparisons when you see them performing side by side. Follow the group around to each basket so you can see and compare their individual skills. Pay special attention to their shooting skills and their 1-on-1 matchups. Then, put them in scrimmage situations against each other. By the end of the day, one or two will emerge ahead of the others. If the day ends and you still can't pick a clear favorite—if two players are neck and neck—consider taking one more player on your team than you originally intended to take. If that's not an option, take the player with the best attitude (hustle, enthusiasm, etc.). Everything else being equal, take the player who will work the hardest off-season. In a year, she'll be a better player than the other player.

Question: I have two players I'm considering for the last spot on my Varsity team. One is a senior who has been on the team for two years, and the other is a promising sophomore. The senior probably won't play much this year, but I hate to kick someone off the team. What should I do?

Answer: Varsity coaches often face this dilemma—do I keep a senior who won't play much or pick a younger player who has potential? Some coaches don't hesitate—they want the best players on their team even if it means they cut an established member of the team. In my view, this sends the wrong message. It doesn't reward the loyalty and hard work the player has given to the coach and the team in prior years. On the other hand, a high school team with a disgruntled senior sitting on the bench is a bad situation. I'd give the senior the "expectations" talk described above. If you're convinced that she'll be happy all season with not playing much, keep her. As for the promising sophomore, if she's clearly a Varsity-level player who can help the team this year, take her. Always take someone who can contribute to your team's success. However, if the sophomore will just sit on the bench, it would be better for her and your team next year for her to play a major role on the JV team this season.

whether it was performing a skill, hustling, or displaying a good attitude. Write an encouraging note at the bottom of each letter. If you like a player's attitude a lot and would like to have her participate on the team in some way, offer her the job of manager. Who knows—with your encouragement, she could try out next year and become a fine player.

Getting Started

Player-Parent Meeting

After you've picked your team, set up a meeting with the coaches, players, and parents. Require that at least one parent (or guardian) attend with each player. The meeting should be brief. Players, parents, and coaches have lots of other demands on their time, including dinner, homework, and family time. Limit your introductory comments to a maximum of 5 to 7 minutes, along these lines:

1. Introduce yourself and the assistant coaches. There's no need for an extensive personal history. Unless you played in college or in the pros, your audience will be interested in little more than how long you've been coaching.

2. Tell them how excited you are to have the chance to coach their daughters. Show enthusiasm and positive energy.

3. Describe your coaching philosophy. This shouldn't be a treatise on X's and O's, but a brief description of what you value as a coach, such as hard work, hustle, teamwork, punctuality, defense.

4. Talk about your approach to playing time. This is the time to mention the consequences of missing practice.

5. Describe the practice and game schedule.

6. Ask for money, if appropriate. As mentioned earlier, AAU teams require that parents pay a fee to cover the cost of uniforms and travel to out-of-town tournaments. If you coach an AAU team, part of your job is being the toll collector.

7. Ask for volunteers, if appropriate. If you coach a high school team, you likely won't need parent volunteers because you'll have one or more assistants and one or more managers to help with all the details, including keeping the scorebook at games and running the clock at home games. If you coach an AAU team, you'll also need someone to coordinate the logistics for tournaments and getting a gym to use for practice. Welcome anyone who offers to do anything.

8. Pass out forms: the handout with the team rules and expectations (see the sample player-parent handout in the Appendix), the season schedule, and the medical permission and release form. Pass this stuff out *at the end* of your talk. If you do it at the beginning, the parents will read it as you speak, shuffling pages loudly, and they won't listen to what you're saying.

9. Ask for questions. If someone has a lot of questions or has a concern that doesn't affect the rest of the people there, tell him or her that you'll be glad to talk further after the meeting is over.

10. Thank everyone for coming. Encourage them to talk to you whenever they have questions, concerns, or problems. Remind them that your contact numbers are on the handout.

Communicating with the Team

If you aren't organized, you'll have problems from the start. Coaching involves managing details that are often moving targets. The schedule established at the start of a season rarely stays the same. Snow cancellations, unexpected gym unavailability ("Hey, how come no one told us this was cheerleader practice?"), and last-minute game postponements are all part of the season. If you teach where you coach, you can announce a short meeting before or after school. But if you coach an AAU team and you're not set up to communicate on a timely basis, you're setting yourself up to be a one-person complaint department.

In the pre-Internet age, the traditional way coaches communicated with their teams was by bulletin board or by telephone. The *telephone tree* (a communication system in which you call a designated person—such as an assistant or a team parent—who then relays the information to the next person on the list), isn't fail-safe, but it still works. Many coaches have replaced that system with an e-mail list. You'll have to determine what works best for your team. If you use an e-mail list, include the e-mail addresses for the players and parents.

Rules and Expectations

Every team needs rules. Without clear guidelines, your players won't know what's right and what's wrong. Before the season gets underway, establish a set of team rules.

At the high school Varsity and college levels, some coaches let their players decide what the team rules are. Some coaches set all the rules. With my teams, I let my players decide certain minor rules, like what time curfew should be, but I set all the important rules. Middle school players aren't mature enough to set any rules, so they shouldn't be involved in the process. However you establish the rules, enforce them and don't make any exceptions. Part of being consistent in handling players means applying the same rules to all players, bar none, every time there's a violation.

With my teams, once the rules are set, I give my players a one-page contract that I ask them to sign. You don't need to go to that extent, but you should write down the team rules and expectations and list them on the handout you pass out at the meeting of players and parents. Explaining the rules before the season gets underway will avoid confusion and misunderstandings later on.

You don't need to discuss the penalty for every type of possible rules violation, but explain the penalty for violations that are more likely to occur, such as missing practice. That way, when a player doesn't play in a game because she missed the last practice, neither the player nor her parents will be surprised.

Enforce the rules. If you let a player slide by even with a minor infraction of the team rules, the other players will notice and think they can also slide by. It's easier to be tough in the beginning of the season than it is to turn tough as the season goes on. Make the rules and penalties clear at the beginning, stick by them the first time and every time, and you'll avoid problems with players and parents. Coaches who don't set firm rules and don't enforce them invite headaches.

Team rules and expectations should include the following areas:

Tardiness and absences. These will likely be the main problems you have to deal with as far as rules go. It will be an unusual season if you don't have players who are sometimes late for practice or who are absent, so determine what your parameters are beforehand. Every time someone is late or absent, find out the reason. There's a difference between an excused absence (the player had a doctor's appointment) and an unexcused absence (the player went skiing). Decide how you view it when a player misses a practice or a game because of another sport, because you'll likely have someone not show up because they're playing travel soccer or club volleyball. My view is that if a player takes up a spot on the team, she's committing to being there all the time (barring legitimate reasons for not being there, such as illness or injury). Only you can decide what's right for you. If your team is low on players, you might have no choice but to live with players not showing up because of other sports so you can field a team. When setting up the rules, let common sense guide you. You certainly can't hold a player accountable for being late when her mother is the driver.

Disruptive behavior. No player should disrupt practice. Some players have loud personalities. They like to talk and socialize, and they don't know when to stop. Some players who are new to being on a team need time to learn what's expected. Be patient with these players. They mean well and will soon learn when to be quiet and when to talk. Every now and then, you'll have a player who is disruptive because she's rebellious or maybe not accustomed to respecting adults. These players become problems if you don't enforce the rules. There are lots of ways of being disruptive without being obvious. In your list of rules, don't try to mention all the consequences for breaking the rules. There are many gray areas, and you don't want to box yourself in. A player you discipline may not agree with how you enforce the rules, but most everyone understands that coaching is a benevolent dictatorship and that how to enforce the rules is up to the coach.

Poor sportsmanship. You're not likely to have a problem in this area, but it should be part of what you teach and emphasize. Fighting, cursing, insulting the referee, and the like can't be allowed on your basketball team.

Expectations. List the expectations regarding effort, hustle, attitude, and so on. Also list expectations having to do with practicalities, such as bringing their own water bottle to practice.

Disciplining players. When a player breaks a minor team rule, like being late for practice or a team meeting, make her run five laps and do ten push-ups. If she breaks the rule a second time, add two more laps and ten push-ups, and have a brief talk with her. Tell her that you expect that she won't break the rule again, but if she does, it will hurt her playing time. If she breaks the rule a third time, penalize her by taking away playing time. She should miss one game, maybe more, depending on the circumstances. Talk to her and a parent or guardian in private about the situation. Listen carefully to be sure you know all the facts. If the problem persists, take away more playing time. That should remedy the situation. Of course, if a player is a constant problem and distraction, at some point you'll have to dismiss her from the team.

Assistants and Other Helpers

It's impossible to coach a basketball team without help. There are too many tasks for you to do all by yourself. You'll need help, so one of your first priorities is to find it. These are the roles you need to fill:

Assistant coaches. Assistants are invaluable. Without them, too much of your practices will be spent in crowd management, making the practices inefficient. With an assistant or two, the players will receive more individual attention, they'll stand around less of the time, your team can work on multiple skills at the same time, and you'll have one or two other

---

ASK THE COACH

Question: I have a player who is on the student government committee, which meets twice a week after school throughout the year. The meetings always run over, and she's late for practice every time. The player is a good kid, but I don't think it's fair to the other players that she comes late 40 percent of the time. I've heard some of the other players grumbling about it. Should I kick her off the team, or is that too harsh? What should I do about this?

Answer: First, talk to the teacher responsible for overseeing the committee. Most schools schedule their club and after-school activities at times that don't conflict with athletic activities. If the meetings run over, the player shouldn't be expected to stay after the scheduled end time. Hopefully, something can be worked out so the player won't be late. If nothing can be worked out and the situation stays the same, you have to decide what you can live with. If it were me, I'd have a hard time dismissing someone from the team for participating in something as worthwhile as student government. Part of your decision depends on how much of each practice she misses. If she misses, say, half the practice, obviously that's not acceptable. However, if she misses only 5 minutes twice a week, I'd have her run laps and do push-ups every time she comes late, just like anyone else who comes in late, but I wouldn't penalize her any other way. As long as you treat her tardiness no differently than how you'd treat another player's tardiness, I wouldn't worry about it. You can also require her to put in extra time in the gym or in the weight room on the weekend to make up for lost time.

observers with whom to share ideas. In games, assistants can provide important information and advice. They'll make you a better bench coach. The more your assistants know about basketball, the better.

Managers. If you coach middle school or high school basketball, find two or three students who are willing to be managers. They don't have to know a thing about basketball. What's important is that they're responsible and enthusiastic. As mentioned earlier, if you have a player whom you cut at tryouts but whose attitude and personality you like, ask her to be a manager. Managers do all the little things that make a team run smoothly, like getting the ball racks out, filling water bottles before games, running the clock during practice for certain drills, keeping stats in practice and in games, filming games from the stands, and so on. A good manager is an important part of your team's success.

Stat keeper. You need someone at every game who knows enough basketball to keep accurate stats. If you need to train this person, do so in advance of the first game. Have him or her get experience by keeping stats in a practice scrimmage. If you don't have assistant coaches or managers to fill this role, ask for a parent volunteer.

Scorebook keeper. Each team needs someone to keep the team's scorebook at the scorers' table during home and away games. When your team is the home team, your scorebook is the official scorebook for the game. Choose someone who knows how to *keep the book*, or lacking that, make sure the person learns what to do. If they make a mistake, it can be costly to your team. Unless you have an excess of assistant coaches, keep your coaches with you on the bench. Lots of teams use a manager to keep the book.

Clock keeper. *Keeping the clock* means being responsible for starting and stopping the clock during the games, adding points on the scoreboard as they are scored, and making sure the possession arrow is in the correct position. The clock keeper must always watch the action and, in particular, the referees, who signal when to start and stop play. Usually, the home team is responsible for the clock. Compared to the scorekeeper, the clock keeper has fewer things to worry about, but if he or she makes a mistake in a close game (forgetting to start the clock when the ball is inbounded or forgetting to stop the clock when the referee stops play), the coaches and fans will get testy. Make sure your clock keeper knows what to do.

Team parent. A team parent is a must for middle school and AAU teams but isn't needed for most high school teams. Some high school coaches like to have a team parent because this person takes the little organizational details off their shoulders (such as preparing the phone tree, setting up the end-of-the-year team party, running the concession stand, collecting medical release forms), but most high school coaches assign these duties to an assistant.

How to Run Effective Practices

Practices are the backbone of your season. Good practices guarantee that your players and team will improve. Bad practices guarantee that your team won't be prepared to compete in games. Coaches are fond of saying, "You play like you practice." I've found that to be true.

What makes a practice a "good" practice? First, you make every minute count. Second, the players work hard and are focused. Third, the players improve.

But, you might say, some players improved only a little bit, and some didn't improve at all. My response is—that's all you can expect. It's the rare player who makes a huge leap in improvement during a single practice. Basketball is a hard sport to learn. It takes time and many repetitions to develop shooting and ball-handling skills. If your players improve just a little bit every practice, you're doing a good job. Over the course of the season, the little bits will add up to a lot of improvement.

Here are the principles of running effective practices:

Question: I'm having trouble finding an assistant coach. I have a volunteer, but she doesn't know a thing about basketball. What should I do?

Answer: Don't think that because someone has little or no experience with the sport they can't do a good job. Is she enthusiastic? Is she smart? Is she organized? Is she willing to learn? Does she relate well to kids? If you answered, "Yes" to these questions, your volunteer should make a good assistant. It would be better to have someone like her as an assistant than someone who might know something about basketball but who lacks those more important qualities.

If you coach a high school team, you shouldn't have trouble finding an assistant unless you're in a small town. Lots of people want to get into coaching. Talk to as many coaches as possible and ask for leads. It won't be long before you have some candidates to interview.

Question: How much should I involve my assistant coaches in running drills?

Answer: A lot. Inexperienced coaches tend to underutilize their assistants. They let the assistants stand on the sidelines all practice long and rarely consult them during games. This is like having no assistants at all. Tell your assistants you value their input and advice. Follow their advice when it makes sense, and don't follow it when it doesn't. As part of each practice, split your players into two groups, maybe guards and posts, maybe first-string and second-string players, and send one group with your assistants to the other half of the court. This way, your players get more individual coaching. In games, confer with your assistants during the first 10 seconds of time-outs and before you enter the locker room at halftime. Always listen to them with an open mind. When addressing the team, ask your assistants if they have something to add.

If you use your assistants wisely, you'll be a better coach. In addition, you'll guarantee that they'll jump at the chance to help you in the future.

Question: When I volunteered to coach our eighth-grade team, a dad offered to help. Since I don't know much about basketball, I said yes. Now, we're two weeks into the season, and the dad is starting to take over. He interrupts me in front of the kids and has them do drills that he and I didn't talk about. I see the kids looking from me to him, not knowing whom to listen to. What should I do?

Answer: No wonder the kids are confused. You need to change the situation before it worsens. Take the dad aside and tell him that a ship can have only one captain and a team can have only one head coach. Remind him that the team already has a head coach and that you're happy to have his help, but only if he's willing to be an assistant. Hopefully, he's just an overeager dad and will understand he overstepped his limits. If he gets huffy and tells you he's quitting, thank him for his time and walk away before he changes his mind. The team will be better off.

Question: I've found a volunteer to keep the scorebook, but she doesn't have any experience, and I can't find anyone who has. What should I do?

Answer: Keeping the book isn't complicated. Every scorebook includes a sample game in the front. Look at it with your scorekeeper and make sure she understands how to record what happens during the game. Have her practice by keeping the scorebook during a scrimmage. Most people not only learn how to keep the book accurately the first time they do it, but they come to enjoy it.

Plan, plan, plan. As with running tryouts, you must be organized. Start with a master practice plan for the season (see the sample in the Appendix), which is a comprehensive list of all the things you want your team to learn and work on. Then, decide your priorities and make a weekly plan up to the time of your first game. If you want your players to learn zone defense, in what week do you want to introduce it? When do you want to teach press offense? What about sideline plays? In an ideal world, you'd teach the players everything they need to know about playing in games before the first game. In reality, this isn't possible. With a middle school team, you'll have at most four or five practices before the first game, and sometimes only one or two. With an AAU team, you won't have more than a half-dozen practices before the first tournament. Even with high school teams, given how long the fall sports seasons take to wrap up, you'll probably have no more than a dozen practices before the first game. The good news is that your competition is dealing with the same limitations you are. Recognize that you won't be able to teach your players everything they need to know by the first game. The most you can do is prepare them part way. This is where your master practice plan is so important. Sit down with your assistants before the season and list all the things you want the team to learn. The list should include individual skills (jump stops, pivoting, etc.) and team skills (man-to-man defense, fast breaks, etc.).

Then create daily practice plans (see the sample in the Appendix) for the practices leading up to the first game. After each game, prepare daily practice plans leading up to the next game. In your daily plans, make every moment count. Plan everything down to the last minute, even time for water breaks.

Start on time. Barring an earthquake or other natural disaster, start each practice on time. It sets the proper tone for how you intend to run the team. When you don't start on time, you send the message that punctuality isn't important to you. This becomes a self-fulfilling prophecy. Some players (and, in the case of younger players, the parents) will assume that it's acceptable to be late and will arrive late routinely. Then other players will start to come late. By the end of the season, you won't be able to count on anyone to show up on time. You can easily avoid this problem by starting practice on time the first time and every time thereafter.

Keep things moving. Insist that your players move quickly from drill to drill. Practices are like games in that they have a certain amount of momentum. If the players waste time moving from one drill to the next, their concentration will wander, and some momentum will be lost. You don't want to make practice a somber, funereal event, but you want every player to maintain her focus throughout. If you let things slow down, the girls will start to chatter. Keep up the pace. There's plenty of time before and after practice for chitchat and socializing.

Game speed and intensity. Insist that your players practice at game speed and game intensity. This isn't easy for some girls to do. They want to be nice to their friends and don't want to embarrass them, so their tendency is to play passively against their teammates. Explain to them that it's their job to practice as hard as they can, that when they don't, they're letting down their teammates. Emphasize that their teammates are counting on them to help them improve. This is a key concept for you and the players to understand. If your players don't practice at game speed and game intensity, they'll be unprepared to play against players who do. In theory, you want your practices to be harder than the games. In practice, if you lack talented players, this is sometimes impossible.

Condition with the ball. Running laps or sprints will condition your team, but why not work on basketball at the same time? Have your players get in shape while working on skills. Drills like Three-Man Weave (Drill 27) are perfect conditioners. As the players' cardiovascular endurance improves, so do their passing skills.

Stick to the schedule. When your team isn't doing well with a specific drill, it's tempting to stick with it until they get it right. Resist the temptation to be stubborn ("Girls, I don't care if it takes us until New Year's . . . we're going to do this until we get it right!"). The problem is this becomes a situation of diminishing returns. The players get more frustrated, which makes it harder for them to do the drill the way you want them to. Once the time is up, abandon the drill. Instead of sticking with something that's not working, stick with the schedule. Some days, not everything you want to run is going to work, no matter how hard the players try or how much you repeat yourself. That's the nature of coaching. When the allocated time for a drill is up, whether it went well or badly, have the team move on to the next one. There's always next practice.

When introducing a new skill or drill, demonstrate it. If you can't or don't know how, have your assistant or an experienced player demonstrate. Seeing what you're talking about helps your players learn faster.

Plan for maximum player participation. This is the same principle you used in tryouts. The fewer players you have standing on the sidelines, the better. Keep everyone as involved as possible. Stations are a great way to make sure no one stands around too long. This is when having assistant coaches is so valuable. Splitting your team into groups should be part of every practice. Assign one group to each assistant and send them to a basket to work on a specific task. Take a group yourself to another basket. Working with a small number of players is when some of your most effective coaching will be done. The players concentrate better and receive more individual instruction, which helps them improve faster. Relish the chances you get to work with only a few players.

Repetition, repetition, and more repetition. When you introduce a new skill or drill, repeat it at the next practice, maybe even the next several practices, depending on what it is. Everything you teach needs to be reinforced now and then. Without reinforcement and repetition, players will forget what they learned three weeks ago. It's your job not to let that happen.

Adjust your daily plans as you go. After each game, analyze what your team did well and what it did poorly (see the sample game sheet in the Appendix). Adjust your next practices to address the areas needing improvement. If the team had too many turnovers, work on passing under pressure. If the team couldn't score against man-to-man defense, work on man offense. If the players missed a bunch of layups, spend time on layup drills. If the team ran out of gas in the second half, conditioning becomes a priority. I'll say it again—good coaches adapt to changing circumstances.

Fundamentals. I've already emphasized how important it is to teach and practice fundamentals. At the beginning of the season, half of every practice should be devoted to individual fundamentals. As the season proceeds, you can cut this time back, but even at the last practice of the year, your players should work on fundamentals. Yes, team skills and game experience are important, but how much you practice fundamentals is the basis for how much your players improve.

Develop a list of core practice elements. Over the years, I've developed a list of a dozen aspects of the game I want my team to practice every day in one form or another (see next page). In my daily practice planning, I include at least one drill that addresses each aspect. I may choose a different drill for that aspect the next day, but I make sure to cover each aspect no matter what. Decide what your core elements are and practice them every time.

Vary the pace. Look at each practice as a whole. Mix up the drills to keep your players alert and interested. Don't schedule all your high-intensity drills to follow one after the other. After a slow-paced drill like shooting free throws, schedule a fast-paced drill like the 3-on-2, 2-on-1 (Drill 71). Conversely, after your team has run that drill for 10 minutes, shooting free throws is a perfect follow-up. This also has the benefit of having your players practice free throws when they are breathing hard, which is much more gamelike than having them work on free throws when they're fresh.

Scrimmages. Other than in the first few practices of the season, my teams scrimmage almost every practice. These aren't free-for-all scrimmages without rules, but *controlled scrimmages*, with restrictions. For example, a scrimmage might have the defense play a 2-3 zone, so we can practice our zone offense. Another scrimmage might start with a free throw shooting situation so we can practice fast breaks after a made or missed free throw. In another, I might say that the shots can come from only our post players, which forces the perimeter players to work on passing to the post. We also routinely practice *time and score* situations, where I stipulate that a

COACH HATCHELL'S DAILY DOZEN PRACTICE ELEMENTS

1. Fundamentals (dribbling and passing)
2. Shooting
3. Free throws
4. Rebounding
5. Half-court offense
6. Individual offensive skills
7. Press offense and fast break (this will work on conditioning)
8. Individual defense
9. Half-court defense
10. Presses and transition defense
11. Controlled scrimmages
12. Special situations

certain time is left in the game and the team is ahead or behind by so many points (e.g., the Blue team is up 3 points, only 30 seconds are left, and the White team has the ball). It's important to make your scrimmage situations as gamelike as possible, so your team will be better prepared for real games.

Keep a notebook with your daily practice plans. This is an essential practice tool. After practice ends, write down your thoughts on what worked well and what didn't. This will come in handy later in the season and even next year. As you become more experienced, your practices will become more effective and efficient.

As you gain experience, you'll determine and refine your own approach. Go over the plans with your assistants before each practice so they know what to expect and what role they'll play. See the Appendix for a sample daily practice plan.

ASK THE COACH

Question: How much time should I devote to each drill?

Answer: It depends on the drill, how much total practice time you have, how many players are on the team, and the ages of your players. If you have four to six baskets, shooting free throws shouldn't take more than 5 minutes. Wing Denial (Drill 54) shouldn't take more than 7 to 8 minutes, particularly if you use two baskets. Conditioning drills like 3-on-3-on-3 (Drill 72) and scrimmages can last longer, but the players will begin to lose their intensity after 12 to 15 minutes. Older players will have more endurance and can go longer. Regardless of how much time you allocate to each drill, plan everything down to the last minute, including the time for going from one drill to the next, for water breaks, and for a team talk.

Chapter 2

FUNDAMENTAL SKILLS

Warming Up

Bodies need to be warmed up before they do rigorous physical activity. The old way of thinking was to have players stretch before they began to exercise. It's now recognized that stretching cold muscles can cause injuries. The proper sequence to warm up your players at the beginning of every practice is as follows:

1. Have them get their bodies moving by jogging or running a drill at half-speed for 5 minutes. Two-Line Layups (Drill 46) and Three-Man Weave (Drill 27) work well for this. Use warm-up time to accomplish more than one purpose. Whatever you have the players do, don't let them go at full speed yet.

2. Gather the team for 2 to 3 minutes of stretching. Someone should lead the players through a sequence of static and dynamic stretches (see the Ask the Coach sidebar below) so every muscle gets stretched. Stretches should work on the major muscle groups: legs (quads, hamstrings, calves), arms (biceps, triceps), and torso (back, laterals, glutes). At the beginning of the season, you or an assistant coach should be the leader, but once your players know what to do, have one of them lead warm-ups. Choose a team captain or a player at random. Every player on the team should be chosen at least once during the season.

ASK THE COACH

Question: I've heard coaches talk about static stretches and dynamic stretches. What's the difference?

Answer: *Static stretches* are the traditional kind of stationary exercises, like torso twists and quadriceps stretches. *Dynamic stretches* are exercises done on the move, such as walking lunges and toe-and-heel walks. Both types of stretching provide benefits to athletes.

3. After this, the players are ready for intense physical activity. Right after stretching is a great time for a high-energy drill like 3-on-3 Recovery Transition (Drill 73).

Footwork

Ready stance. Basketball is a game of running and jumping, along with sudden changes of speed, sudden changes of direction, and quick hand and feet movements. The game is fast-paced, so every split second is important. Taking an extra split second to shoot the ball is the difference between scoring and having your shot blocked. Taking an extra split second to help a teammate on defense is the difference between preventing a layup and the other team scoring 2 points. Taking an extra split second to make a pass is the difference between an assist and a steal and layup at the other basket.

A good player plays the game low, always in the *ready stance*. Her knees are bent, her feet are shoulder-width apart, and her hands are up and out. Her back is straight and her head is up, centered over the rest of her body. She's balanced, ready to spring into action, not needing a split second to lower her body before running, sliding, jumping, or shooting. The ready stance is the foundation for all basketball movements.

Jump stops. Basketball players must learn how to come to a complete stop with or without the ball, their body under control and in balance. They must learn to make a *jump stop*. There are two kinds: a one-two jump stop, and a two-foot jump stop. The footwork in both is simple.

In a *one-two jump stop*, the player steps with one foot first and then the other, with both knees bent so her momentum is stopped. It's a natural movement for the player, but the disadvantage of this type of jump stop is that if she has the ball, she has no choice about her pivot foot. By the rules, her pivot foot was determined when she stepped with the first foot before coming to a stop.

This player is ready to play hoops!

From the triple threat position this player can dribble, pass, or shoot.

In a *two-foot jump stop*, the player makes a short little hop, landing on both feet at the same instant. Imagine a player dribbling to the basket. As she plants her right foot she decides she needs to stop. As she steps forward with her left foot, her right foot comes off the ground and she lands on the floor with both feet. To stop her momentum, she lands low, knees bent, back upright. If she does it right, she should be in the *triple threat position* (the ready position with the ball, called triple threat because the player is ready to dribble, pass, or shoot). With a two-foot jump stop, she can use either foot as her pivot foot.

Some coaches teach their players to use the one-two jump stop, and some coaches prefer the two-foot jump stop. I don't think it makes much difference which method you teach. If you coach younger players, my advice is to teach the two-foot jump stop and not worry about the one-two jump stop.

Pivoting

In *pivoting*, a player uses one foot as a point upon which to spin her body. The purpose is to protect the ball so defenders can't poke it away, steal it, or cause a held ball.

When a player pivots, she spins on her *pivot foot* and steps forward or backward with her *non-pivot foot*. As long as the player doesn't lift the ball of her pivot foot off the floor or drag it, she's allowed to spin as she decides what to do with the ball (she must get rid of it within 5 seconds).

Even if your players are experienced, don't assume they don't need to practice pivoting. All players should practice pivoting under pressure to make sure that they can protect the ball and not get rattled.

If you coach inexperienced players, this is how to teach pivoting:

Line up your players, facing you, and have them get in the ready stance. They should have a ball next to them on the floor.

Tell them to raise the heel of their right foot off the floor and to imagine that they're squishing a bug. They should rotate the ball of their foot, maintaining contact with the floor, as their heel swings from side to side.

Have them step forward with their left foot, again spinning on the ball of their right foot. As they swing their foot forward, their left arm and shoulder should also swing forward. This is a *forward pivot*.

Have them swing their left foot back to where they started, again maintaining contact with the floor with the ball of their right foot. This is a *reverse pivot*. Have them do this several times.

Once they're comfortable with pivoting on their right foot, have them practice pivoting on their left foot.

Have the players pick up the ball and hold it securely with both hands off their right hip in the triple threat position. Their elbows should be away from their body.

Then they should *rip the ball* across their body so it's off their other hip. This swinging motion should be forceful and sudden. Have the players hold the ball over their shoulder and swing it low so it ends up low by their

ASK THE COACH

Question: I'm a new coach coaching a sixth grade team. How should I teach the two-foot jump stop?

Answer: Line up the players on the baseline, facing the court. Have them step with their right foot, take a little hop, and land on both feet. Then, have them jog down the court and come to a jump stop every time you say, "Stop." Once they learn this, have them sprint down the court, again stopping on your instruction. When they've mastered this, have them practice jump stops with a ball. At first, they shouldn't dribble. They should carry the ball. When they have the footwork down, add the dribble. Last, have them dribble as fast as they can and jump stop.

Learning how to come to a jump stop with the ball and without the ball is an essential fundamental that beginners can learn quickly.

When pivoting, this player starts with the ball high (left) and rips it low (right).

opposite foot. Have them go from low to high. These sudden, forceful movements protect the ball from eager defenders.

Last, combine pivoting and ripping the ball. When the players combine forceful movement of the ball with the pivoting movement of their feet, they can keep the ball safe, even when guarded by two or three defenders. The key is to rip the ball, elbows out, combining forward pivots with reverse pivots, so the defenders can't get their hands on the ball without fouling.

Practicing pivoting and protecting the ball. Divide the team into pairs, each pair with a ball. Have one player practice pivoting and ripping the ball while the other player tries to snatch the ball away. The offensive player should keep her elbows out as she moves her body and the ball around. This will cause the defender to back away a bit. The sight of a flying

elbow will make her think twice about being too close. However, teach the pivoting player not to swing her elbows with her torso in place. That's a foul. Her elbows should swing around only as the rest of her body swings around. Emphasize that a player should never swing her elbows with the intent to hurt another player.

Catching the Ball

Before a player can learn to dribble, pass, or shoot, she must learn how to catch the ball. This is one of the most under-emphasized fundamentals.

When a player is open and in the passing range of her teammate with the ball, she should call out her teammate's name. She should give a good target to the passer, with her hands out in front of her, shoulders high, fingers open and pointing to the ceiling. Receivers who play

Question: My players have a hard time pivoting when a defender is right on them. They have no room to rip the ball. What should I teach about this?

Answer: Too many players pivot from side to side and don't use their pivot to make space for themselves. Have your players practice aggressively ripping the ball as they step into the defender. This will force the defender to back up a step, and the offensive player will have some space to work with.

with their hands low often fumble the ball because they can't raise their hands in time.

As the ball is in the air, the receiver should *jump to the pass*, making a two-foot jump stop as the ball hits her hands. This gives her the choice of using either foot as her pivot foot. She shouldn't jump high off the ground in an exaggerated manner. A low two-foot hop is all that's needed.

There are six things your players should remember when receiving the ball:

1. Be in the ready stance. Players should keep their body low, knees bent, feet about shoulder-width apart.

2. Hold their hands up, fingers apart, giving the passer a target. Players should let their teammate know exactly where they want to receive the ball.

3. Call for the ball. Players should yell their teammate's name, wave their hands, or clap, if they have to. They make eye contact with the passer. This shows they're ready to receive the ball.

4. Keep their eyes on the ball. Once the pass is in the air, players should take a short hop and watch the ball into their hands (see photo page 30). Taking their eyes off the ball results in fumbled passes and turnovers. When players rush before the ball is safely in their hands, they travel. They need to take their time catching the ball. Once it's in their hands, they'll have plenty of time to decide what to do with it.

5. *Backstop* the ball with their shooting hand. When players catch the ball, one hand

This player lets her teammate know she is open and wants the ball.

should block it and stop its momentum. The other hand should secure it.

6. Run to the pass. How many times have we all seen a receiver stop and wait for the pass to reach her, while a defender swoops by for the easy steal and layup? Even pro players do this. Teach your players to keep running to the ball until it's in their hands.

This player keeps her eyes on the ball, "seeing" it into her hands.

Once a perimeter player catches the ball, she should make a forward pivot toward the basket, using the foot nearest to the basket as her pivot foot. She stays low and faces the basket with the ball on her hip. She's in triple threat position, ready to dribble, pass, or shoot.

Your team should practice catching and getting into the triple threat position. Young players who aren't taught properly develop bad habits. Upon catching, they start dribbling for no reason or they stand up straight and yank the ball over their head, reducing their options to an overhead pass. It's easy to play defense when the player with the ball can do only one thing.

Dribbling

There is no more important fundamental skill to learn in basketball than how to dribble. When a player learns to dribble under pressure with either hand and with her head up, her confidence increases and her whole game improves. Your team should practice dribbling every practice, from the first practice to the last, no matter how experienced the players are.

Dribble with a purpose. Inexperienced players dribble too often and too long. They dribble without knowing where they're going or why they're going there. We've all seen young players dribble around the perimeter area, their heads down, while the other players stand around watching them. Even older players misuse the dribble. The dribble is a valuable skill, but if it's misused, it's a liability.

Players should dribble for only one of three reasons:

- to drive toward the basket
- to create a better passing angle
- to get out of trouble

Dribbling concepts. Here are the most important concepts to teach about dribbling:

Fingertip control. The dribbler must use her fingertips, not the palm of her hand, to push the ball down. This gives her much better control over where the ball goes.

Head up. The dribbler must keep her head up, her eyes focused on what's happening on the court. Dribblers who can't look up won't see open teammates, will miss good chances to drive, will dribble into traps, and won't see the clock. In other words, they'll have zero court savvy. Good defenders notice right away when a player can't dribble with her head up, and they'll attack her. This makes it harder for the dribbler to stay poised and do something positive with the ball. A player who can't keep her head and eyes up has no *court vision*. She's an offensive liability.

The natural tendency of the inexperienced dribbler is to stare at the ball. She wants to see where it hits the floor to make sure it bounces back to her hand. This habit is normal but should be discouraged from the start. During dribbling drills, have your players look up to the ceiling, even if the balls bounce off their feet. This is a necessary part of the learning process. They'll soon tire of fetching the ball, which will force them to learn how to dribble sooner.

If your players insist on looking at the ball while dribbling, consider buying a few pairs of *no-look glasses* that make it impossible to see the ball, even if they look down. Some coaches find such aids helpful. The glasses are inexpensive and available through the better sports equipment suppliers.

Keep the ball low. The dribbler should keep her dribbling hand lower than her elbow. Along

A good dribbler keeps her eyes and head up to see the court.

with bending her knees, this keeps her in an athletic stance, ready to move quickly in any direction, ready to make any of the various dribble moves she may need to use. Keeping the ball low also helps protect the ball by making it harder for the defender to poke it away.

Both hands. To be a good offensive player, a dribbler must become so comfortable with the ball that it's like an extension of her arm. The best players are so skilled that an observer can't tell if they're left-handed or right-handed until they shoot a jump shot.

Basic Dribble Moves

The first dribble moves your players should learn are the control dribble, the speed dribble, and the crossover dribble.

The *control dribble* is used when the dribbler is closely guarded. Protection of the ball is the top priority. The dribbler keeps her body between the defender and the ball, using her nondribbling arm as a shield, and dribbles the ball low for control (see top photo page 32). Players must learn how to protect the ball under defensive pressure when dribbling with either hand, always looking up to see the court.

The *speed dribble* is used to advance the ball quickly from one end of the court to the other, typically while attempting to run a fast break. When a player gains possession of the ball, either from an outlet pass thrown by a rebounder or from a steal, she should immediately look up the court to assess the situation. If a teammate is open ahead of her and she's able to throw the pass accurately, she shouldn't dribble but should pass the ball (the ball travels faster by the pass than by the fastest dribblers). However, if no one is open and she has room, she should use the speed dribble to advance the ball as fast as possible to the top of the opposite circle.

To start the speed dribble, the player tosses the ball 6 to 8 feet ahead of her so she can get a running start. She dribbles using alternating hands, meaning she pushes the ball ahead with one hand and then pushes it ahead with the other hand. This technique allows her to run up the court faster, because she swings her arms

This player uses a control dribble, keeping her body between the ball and the defender.

in a more fluid running style than when she dribbles with one hand only. As opposed to the control dribble, when she dribbles the ball no higher than her knees, in the speed dribble, she lets the ball bounce chest-high before pushing it ahead. She takes several steps between each dribble. Her goal is to take as few dribbles as possible to advance the ball. Skilled high school players should be able to use only three dribbles to advance the ball from the outlet pass area to the top of the opposite circle.

The *crossover dribble* is used to change the ball from one hand to the other, bringing it in front of the player's body in one dribble. This is done to protect the ball from a defender, to set up a defender for a screen, to improve a passing angle, or to change directions for a drive to the basket. Assume the dribbler approaches a defender dribbling with her right hand. Instead of continuing in the same path, she brings the ball in front of her with a short, hard dribble, over to her left hand. With the ball now on the other side of her body, the dribbler can explode to the basket before the defender can change her position.

The ability to execute a sudden crossover dribble gives the ball handler a big advantage over the defender. The defender will have to

When speed dribbling, the player pushes the ball ahead and lets it bounce chest-high.

The crossover dribble. The player dribbles with her right hand (top left). Then she dribbles low and hard in front of her feet (top right). The ball is now in her left hand, and the crossover is complete (bottom).

play off the dribbler to avoid being beaten, which creates more open shots and easier passes for the ball handler. So that the defender can't steal or deflect the ball as it passes in front of the dribbler, the dribbler must keep the ball below her knees. A dribbler with a quick crossover move is difficult to guard. Every good point guard has a good crossover move.

Advanced Dribble Moves

Once your players are comfortable with the basic moves, teach them more advanced moves. These are most useful in the open court in fast-break situations. They are also useful in half-court offense when a team is in a formation that spreads the defense.

The first move to learn is the *change-of-pace move* or the *hesitation dribble*. As the dribbler approaches the defender, she slows down (hesitates) and raises her body up as if she's going to pick up her dribble. The goal is to make the defender relax. When the defender stops backpedaling, the dribbler suddenly accelerates, pushing the ball past the defender before she can recover, and drives to the basket. Anytime a dribbler drives past a defender, she should brush by the defender's hip, following the straightest line possible to the basket.

The purpose of the *inside-out move* or *fake crossover move* is to fake the defender into thinking the dribbler intends to cross the ball to the other hand and change directions, when the dribbler intends to continue on her present path. Again, assume the dribbler approaches a defensive player, dribbling with her right hand. She hesitates, positions her dribbling hand on the top right side of the ball (the side she would use to begin the crossover move), starts to bring the ball toward the other side, at the same time stepping with her left foot as though she's preparing to cross over. Before the ball moves more than an inch or two, she rotates her hand so it's now on the top left side of the ball and pushes the ball ahead, in the same direction she was headed. She pushes off on her left foot, takes a big step with her right foot, and drives by the defender. If the dribbler adds a

head fake—if she looks in the direction of the fake crossover for a moment—the defender will be convinced the dribbler is changing directions. Like a good crossover move, a good inside-out move is an excellent offensive weapon.

Another move the dribbler can use to change directions and catch the defender off balance is the *between-the-legs dribble*. The dribbler approaches with the ball in her right hand, dribbles between her legs so the ball changes to her left hand, and drives to the basket. The advantage of this move over the crossover is that the defender has no chance of poking the ball away as it goes from one hand to the other. As with the other change-of-direction moves, the dribbler must push the ball ahead decisively after it changes hands. Without a big first step, the defender has time to recover and establish good defensive position again.

The *behind-the-back dribble* is what it sounds like. It has the same purpose as the crossover and between-the-legs moves, except that the

Between-the-legs dribble.

dribbler brings the ball around her back. To do it right, the player's hand wraps the ball around her back so the ball hits the floor on the other side where the other hand can easily dribble it. This isn't an easy move to learn. Players should first learn how to dribble behind their back from a stationary position without a defender. The drive can be added later, as can the defender. As with most basketball skills, dribbling is best taught in stages. Don't move on to the next stage until your players have learned the last stage.

Another effective move players can use to change direction suddenly is the *spin dribble*. Imagine a right-handed player driving to the basket. As she gets to the free throw line, she realizes that the defender is staying between her and the basket. She plants her left foot and does a reverse pivot, keeping the ball in her right hand as her body spins. When her body is three quarters of the way around, she dribbles again. When she turns all the way around, she dribbles with her left hand. Her new path is 45 degrees from before she spun.

This is a difficult maneuver. The hard part is keeping the ball secure in the player's right hand as she spins. It's against the rules to carry the ball or hold it next to your body. The trick is for the player to *lock the ball* at her wrist by bending her hand toward her elbow and cupping the ball. As she spins, the centrifugal force will help keep the ball from popping out. Once the spin dribble is complete, the player can

Behind-the-back dribble. To get the ball around her back, the player pulls her hand way back.

either shoot a jump shot or keep on dribbling. A guard who can spin dribble with either hand is a dangerous player.

The *pull-back dribble*, another advanced move, is used to create space between the dribbler and

ASK THE COACH

Question: What's a good drill to teach the behind-the-back dribble?

Answer: I can think of two simple drills to help learn that dribble. The first one is to line up the players along the midcourt line with at least 3 feet between each player, facing you, each with a ball. Have them use their right hand to dribble the ball on the line to the right of their right foot. They should pull the ball back behind them so it's directly behind their backside, their palm facing their backside, and bring the ball around their body so the next dribble is on the line to the left of their left foot.

The second drill is to practice figure-eight dribbles by dribbling the ball from back to front between their legs. This gets them used to reaching their hand far enough behind them so they can make the ball come to a spot level with their feet.

Question: I understand the reasons for spending time on dribbling with my guards, but why is it important for my post players?

Answer: Your post players need to be good ball handlers, too. Though you won't need them to break the press or master any of the advanced dribble moves, a post player who can't dribble limits her value to the offense. She'll be only a double threat player (only able to pass or shoot), won't be able to improve passing angles, won't be able to get away from pressure to make outlet passes, and will routinely turn the ball over. A post player who can't dribble is a plus for the other team.

---

her defender. Again, assume the dribbler approaches a defender dribbling with her right hand. She pulls the ball back a couple of steps, drawing the defender toward her. As the defender closes in on her, the dribbler switches the ball to her left hand, using a crossover or between-the-legs move, and drives by the defender.

It takes lots of repetitions to learn these advanced dribble moves, but the time is well worth it. When your ball handlers can change directions in an instant in a variety of ways, they'll create excellent opportunities to drive to the basket and take high-percentage shots.

Passing

The best way to beat any defense is with good passes. Good passing teams are good offensive teams. The ball travels faster up the court than the best dribbler can dribble it. If your players can pass well, they'll have much success on the offensive end of the court. Good passes keep the ball out of the hands of the opponent, make the defense work hard to stay in position, and create excellent opportunities for easy shots.

A team that handles the ball and passes well is hard to defend. Passing drills should be a daily part of your practices throughout the season. Here are the basics to teach.

Passing stance. The stance for passing the ball is similar to the stance for shooting. The player stays low, feet shoulder-width apart for good balance, with her knees bent.

Fingertips. The ball should be on the player's fingertips, which gives her more feel, touch, and ability to control the ball.

Passing lanes. The imaginary line from the passer to the receiver is called a *passing lane*. Obviously, a passer shouldn't throw the pass if a defender is in the passing lane or can get into the lane before the ball reaches the receiver. The four players on offense without the ball should always be working to create open passing lanes for themselves and their teammates.

Passing distance. The ideal spacing between players is 12 to 15 feet. This is enough distance so one defender can't guard two players at one time, yet not so far that a pass has to travel a long way through the air to reach its target. Passes longer than 15 feet must be thrown prudently. Many defensive guards are quick and have great anticipation. They can dart into the passing lane in an instant. The most dangerous pass to make is the guard-to-guard pass along the top of the circle. If a defender intercepts that pass, it usually means a layup for her team. Teach your perimeter players to be extra cautious when throwing this pass.

The 12- to 15-foot guideline doesn't apply to inbound and outlet situations. When an inbounder or a rebounder sees that a teammate is open ahead of the defense and has no one between her and the other team's basket, she should throw the *home run ball*—a long pass over the head of the defenders. Of course, she shouldn't attempt the pass unless she has the arm strength and accuracy to complete it.

Types of Passes

There are several passes to learn, each useful in a different situation. Every pass, other than the lob pass, should be thrown hard and crisp.

Defenders love soft, lazy passes, because they make for easy steals and easy layups. Bad passes account for the majority of turnovers in basketball. A great pass near the end of a game can result in the winning basket, and a bad pass can result in a turnover and a loss.

To throw a two-handed *chest pass*, the player passes the ball from her chest to her teammate's chest. The player should snap her hands so her thumbs point to the floor after the ball leaves her hands. Some coaches teach stepping with the pass and others teach not stepping. I think both methods have value. The step method's advantage is it adds extra velocity to the pass. However, there may not always be time to step, so we have our players practice not stepping as well. The chest pass is the quickest way to move the ball from point A to point B.

To throw a *bounce pass*, the player uses the same mechanics as in the chest pass, except she aims the ball at a spot on the floor two-thirds the distance to the receiver (see top photo page 38). The goal is for the ball to arrive chest-high to the receiver as in the chest pass. The bounce pass is ideal for passing from the wing to the low post because the post defender has a hard time defending it. The bounce pass also is useful when passing to a player cutting to the basket in the lane. Bounce passes shouldn't be used for passes longer than 12 to 15 feet, because the ball takes too long to arrive at its destination.

The *push pass* is a one-handed pass thrown with either hand. It's often used to get the ball by a defender who is closely guarding the passer, in conjunction with a pass fake (see bottom photos page 38). After faking low, for example, drawing the defender's hand to her knee, the passer brings the ball in front of her throwing shoulder and snaps it by the defender's ear. Players should learn how to throw push passes well with their weak hand, not just their strong hand. Emphasize snapping the wrist to increase the speed of the pass.

The *curl pass*, a one-handed bounce pass, allows the player to pass around a defender right in front of her (see left photo page 39). To throw a curl pass with her right hand, the player first makes a pass fake to her left. After the defender's hands have reacted, the player quickly steps with her left foot across the defender's body, wrapping the ball around the defender's left leg. She releases the ball with her arm extended, no higher than her knee. A well-thrown curl pass is nearly impossible to prevent. The curl pass is ideal for passing to the low post and passing out of a trap.

Chest pass. The player snaps her wrist to make the pass sharp.

Bounce pass. The passer (right) aims for a spot on the floor two-thirds of the distance to her teammate.

Push pass. The passer first fakes low (left) and then passes high (right).

Curl pass. The passer wraps (curls) the ball around the defender's body.

A quick outlet pass starts the fast break.

The *overhead pass* is thrown with two hands. The player brings the ball to a position slightly behind her head, extends her arms to the receiver, and snaps her wrists as she releases the ball. Encourage your players to step toward the target as this will help the accuracy and speed of the ball.

When an overhead pass is used to pass the ball over a defense (from one wing to the other) it's called a *skip pass*. Skip passes are a key part of effective half-court offense. The other situation when the overhead pass is ideal is to start the fast break. In this case, the pass is called the *outlet pass*. Quick outlet passes are essential in transition offense. They can be thrown after a steal but are usually thrown after a defensive rebound. An outlet pass begins when a defender rebounds a missed shot. She times her jump to catch the ball

ASK THE COACH

Question: What difference does it make which hand a passer uses as long as she makes the pass?

Answer: The difference is in making the pass or not. Just like players prefer to use their strong hands to dribble, they prefer to pass with their strong hands. When a right-handed player wants to pass to a teammate to her right, she makes the pass with ease, sharply and accurately. However, if she wants to pass to a teammate to her left and uses her right hand, she has to bring the ball across her body and will pass it from a position closer to the defender's hands. A good defender will deflect the pass or block the pass. This makes the right-handed player hesitant to pass to her left, which makes her predictable. For this reason, players must learn how to pass well using either hand.

at the height of her jump and catches the ball with her arms outstretched. As she comes down, she keeps the ball over her head, pivots in the direction of the outlet player (who is calling for the ball), steps toward her, and snaps the ball with two hands. She follows through with her fingers pointing to the floor.

As players become skilled at making the outlet pass, they should learn to turn their bodies in the air as they come down with the rebound, spinning away from the basket, so that when they land, they're already in position to throw the outlet. When your rebounders learn this skill, your fast-break game will improve. The key to a good fast break is moving the ball up the court as fast as possible.

The *baseball pass* is used to throw the ball a long way. It's the best pass when the inbounder wants to throw the ball as far up the court as possible. To throw it, the player starts with the ball in two hands. She turns her shoulders and feet perpendicular to the intended receiver, draws her throwing hand and the ball behind her head, and throws the ball one-handed as if throwing a baseball. As she brings the ball behind her head, her other hand points to the receiver. This keeps her balanced. As her arm comes forward, she steps toward the receiver with the foot opposite her throwing hand (if she's right-handed, she steps with her left foot). As part of her follow-through, her throwing hand turns to the outside so her palm faces the near sideline. This helps guide the ball.

Younger players may not have large enough hands to throw this pass, but with practice, most high school players will have no problem controlling the ball. A well-thrown baseball pass can often beat a full-court press for an easy score.

The *lob pass* is thrown when an offensive player near the basket is being *fronted*—when the defender positions her body between the ball and the offensive player. If the offensive player is at least 6 feet from the basket, this is an opportunity to throw the lob. It's up to the passer to make sure her teammate has enough room to complete the pass and is in proper position to receive the ball. If the post is too close to the basket, the passer shouldn't throw the lob. The margin for error is too small. The post should be at least as high as the block on that side. The passer should also check to be sure another defender isn't lurking

When throwing a baseball pass, the player points her nonthrowing hand at the target.

A lob pass should have the right amount of arc—not too high, not too low.

behind the post, ready to steal the lob or draw the charge.

The technique for throwing the lob is similar to shooting. The same motion is used. The passer aims the lob so it lands in front of the near corner of the basket. The arc of the ball has to be just right. If the arc is too high, the ball will be in the air too long. The offensive player may not be able to hold her position, or a help-side defender will have time to intercept the ball. If the arc is too low, the defender fronting the post can jump up and steal it.

Your perimeter players and low post players should be alert for chances to use the lob pass. Nine times out of ten, a successful lob results in an uncontested layup.

Passing Strategies

Passing to the post. Passing to the post (also called *feeding the post*) is an important part of team offense. It doesn't do any good for your post players to practice their post moves if your perimeter players can't get them the ball.

There are three principles involved in passing to the post from the perimeter:

ASK THE COACH

Question: What's the best pass for an outlet player to use on the fast break?

Answer: It depends on who is open and where they are. If a teammate is open beyond 15 feet away, the outlet player should throw an overhead pass or a baseball pass, depending on which she's better at. Another technique, if no defender is in between the outlet and the passer, is to throw a running chest pass. The player takes one hard dribble toward her teammate and throws a strong chest pass. Adding the momentum from the dribble gives the ball extra distance. Outlet players should practice this pass in fast-break drills so they know when it's useful and when it's risky.

1. The passer must recognize how the defender is playing the post player. She must see if the defender is playing directly behind her teammate, in front, on the *high side* (positioned toward the free throw line), or on the *low side* (positioned toward the baseline). Without knowing this, the passer won't know how to throw the right pass.

2. The passer must pass the ball to the target hand of the post. When the post's defender is behind, the post will be able to give a target with both hands, and the pass is relatively easy. When the post is defended on the high side or low side, the post gives a target with only one hand. The passer should pass away from the defensive pressure. The best pass to feed the post is a bounce pass, because it's harder to prevent than a chest pass. If the perimeter player is closely guarded, she uses a curl pass. A good ball fake helps set up the curl pass. If the defender is fronting the post, as explained above, the only pass that will work is the lob pass.

3. After making the pass, the perimeter passer should never stand and watch. She moves to take advantage of the attention the defense is giving to the player with the ball. She *relocates* (moves to an open spot on the perimeter), so the post can *kick the ball out* (pass back to the perimeter area). The post will have to kick the ball out if she's double-teamed. Or, the perimeter player cuts to the basket after the pass for a give-and-go situation. Teach your perimeter players to watch their defender's head after they feed the post. If the defender turns her head to follow the pass, the perimeter player cuts to the basket for a return pass and an open shot.

Passing off the dribble. Most every possession involves passing off the dribble, so this skill should be practiced daily. There are two things your players should learn:

First, players should communicate with the receiver before they throw a pass. They should call out her name or make eye contact. Too many turnovers happen because the passer assumes the receiver is ready, but the receiver doesn't expect the pass.

Second, players should pass the ball with the hand nearest the receiver. Passers who only pass with their strong hand limit themselves. They make good passes when the receiver is on

Feeding the low post gets your team great shots.

After feeding the low post, the passer looks for a give-and-go opportunity.

the side of their strong hand, but when the receiver is on the side of their weak hand, they have to bring the ball across their bodies. This is awkward, takes time, and often results in a tipped or stolen pass. Passing adeptly with either hand is just as essential an offensive skill as is dribbling with either hand.

When a dribbler drives toward the basket, and a defender who is guarding another player leaves her man to prevent the layup, the dribbler should come to a two-foot jump stop and pass to the offensive player who is now open (the offensive player should move to create an open passing lane). A pass made in this situation is called a *dish* and the player is driving and *dishing*. Your point guard and wing players should be adept at this.

Ball fakes. A *ball fake* or *pass fake* occurs when a player pretends to throw a pass in a certain direction but passes it elsewhere instead. Coaches like to say, "Fake a pass to make a pass." A player uses ball fakes to keep the defense off balance. For a fake to be believable, the player must turn her head and look in the direction of the fake. Many defenders watch the offensive player's eyes, and this will convince them a pass is about to happen.

Driving and dishing is a valuable skill.

A player who always fakes the same way becomes predictable. Players should learn to make different kinds of fakes. They should fake low, drawing the defender's hands lower, and make an air pass. They should fake high, drawing the defender's hands up, and make a bounce pass. They should fake to one side of the court and pass to a teammate on the other side.

Effective ball fakes aren't valuable just in deceiving the passer's defender. They work well to make all five players in a zone defense shift to the side of the perceived pass. This opens up momentary passing lanes to players inside the zone. Ball fakes also work well against aggressive man-to-man defenders who lunge into the passing lanes to intercept the ball. A well-executed ball fake will often draw an overeager defender out too far, resulting in an easy back-door basket for the offense.

Avoiding bad passes. More experienced teams throw fewer bad passes than the less experienced teams, but every team is guilty of at least a few bad passes in every game. Sometimes it's the passer's fault (the pass is rushed, thrown prematurely, or thrown carelessly), sometimes it's the receiver's fault (she took her eyes off the ball or stopped running to the pass), and sometimes it's a combination. Your team should practice reacting to bad passes.

Here's an effective drill that takes only a minute. Set up pairs of players, each pair with a ball. The players should be 12 feet apart. One partner has the ball, and the other has her back turned to her partner. On your signal, the latter player spins to face her partner. Before she completes the turn, her partner throws a bad pass, forcing her to react. The pass should be catchable, but not where a good pass would be thrown (at her feet, to one side, etc.). The partner should vary the bad passes. After 30 seconds, they switch roles.

Shooting

What basketball player doesn't like to shoot and score? In almost every neighborhood across the country, you see kids shooting every day at baskets in driveways, in church lots, in school playgrounds, on crowded city streets. Kids love to shoot!

Unfortunately, many do so with bad mechanics and form. All the time they spend shooting only reinforces bad habits, making it harder for them to become good shooters. The key to becoming a good shooter is developing good habits, so that every time the player shoots the ball, she shoots with the same good form, repeating the same ingrained muscle movements.

Teach your players the proper mechanics and form of shooting early in the season, so that every time they practice, they'll practice good habits, not bad ones. No matter how experienced your players are, spend at least 20 minutes of every practice on shooting.

Shooting Basics

Practice, practice. Good shooters are not born, nor are they created overnight. Making baskets consistently takes time, discipline, and countless repetitions. No basketball player has ever mastered the skill. The greatest players in the world miss baskets routinely. They understand that to shoot a good percentage—in college and the pros, 50 percent is considered excellent—they must practice shooting, not just in the season, but in the off-season, too. There are no shortcuts to good shooting. Your players will become good shooters only by practicing sound mechanics over and over.

A pet peeve of mine is players who walk out on the court, not warmed up at all, and immediately begin shooting 3-point shots. How do they expect to hit 22-footers if they haven't hit some 8-footers first, and then some 15-footers? It's no different than a golfer who practices putting. Good golfers begin with short little putts before moving out farther and farther from the hole. Part of it is grooving their stroke and part of it is developing confidence.

When your players warm up or when they begin shooting drills, insist that they shoot a number of short shots first, then middle-range shots, before practicing long shots. Players who don't start with short shots develop inconsistent mechanics and poor habits that are hard to break.

Patience, patience. Shooting a basketball so it drops neatly into a net requires an unusual combination of muscles working together. If one muscle strays out of synch with the others, the shot will miss. As noted above, becoming adept at shooting takes time and perseverance. Encourage your players not to get discouraged. Michael Jordan, maybe the greatest player of all time, made less than 50 percent of his field goals for his career, even though he worked on his shooting every day. Larry Bird, one of the game's best jump shooters, routinely shot 500 shots a day . . . even on game day! These players understood that patience is essential in developing shooting skills. So should your players.

Shooting Mechanics and Form

Balance and stance. The foundation of a good shot begins with the proper stance and good balance. The first thing to teach your players is the *ready-to-shoot* position.

Place your players (without balls) in two lines parallel to the baseline, one on the free throw line extended and one 6 feet behind it. Players should keep their eyes on the rim and stand with their knees bent and their backs straight. The foundation for a good shot begins with the feet. Players' bodies should feel balanced—their weight should be distributed evenly on both feet. Some players will be more comfortable with their feet farther apart, and some will feel more comfortable with their feet closer together. As long as the distance between their feet isn't exaggerated one way or the other, that's fine. The important thing is to feel comfortable and balanced.

Positioning the head properly is a key part of being in balance. The player's head should be centered over her body. If a shooter's head is too far forward, she'll tend to shoot the ball long. If her head is too far back, she'll tend to shoot the ball short.

Players should stagger their feet slightly—they should place their lead foot 6 inches ahead of the other foot. For right-handed players, their lead foot is their right foot. For left-handed players, it's their left foot. Check that your players'

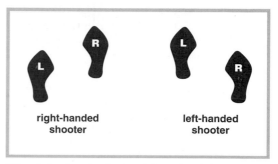

right-handed shooter   left-handed shooter

The right foot is the lead foot for right-handed shooters (left). The left foot is the lead foot for left-handed shooters (right).

shoulders line up perpendicular to an imaginary line running from the rim to them.

Once the players are in the proper stance, tell them to look at their feet and memorize how they are standing. Anytime they shoot, no matter where they are in relation to the basket, their feet should line up the same way with their shoulders perpendicular to the imaginary line, and their body balanced. When a player with the ball turns to face the basket for a possible shot, she is *squaring up* (also called *facing up*).

Many shooters forget to square up to the basket during the excitement of games. They shoot before their feet are set or with their bodies leaning to one side or with their shoulders out of line. As a result, they miss the hard shots and make the easy shots hard. Players shouldn't rush their shots. It takes only a split second to square up properly. Doing so increases the likelihood that the shot will be a good one.

Hand, arm, and elbow. Once your players are in the ready position (still without a ball), have them hold their shooting hand (for most players, the right hand) straight out from their body, toward the basket, palm pointing to the ceiling. Players bend their elbow, bring their shooting hand back to a spot over their shoulders, and twist their palms so they face up. In this position, the players should look like waiters carrying invisible trays of food to the table. The upper part of their shooting arms (the shoulder to the elbow) should parallel the floor, and the bottom part of their arms (from the elbow to the wrist) should be perpendicular elbow, and that when you say "Go," they should imagine that someone presses the button, causing them to release the shot. The first few times, have your players react in slow motion. Tell them to freeze when they need correcting.

Once a shooter's arm is cocked and ready, the shooter must do several things at the same time. As her legs straighten, her elbow rises, lifting the ball. As her arm extends, her wrist snaps, and her fingers direct the ball to the basket. Her index and middle fingers provide most of the force. If her wrist snaps properly, the ball should have a noticeable backspin as it travels through the air. Another common shooting flaw is a minimal wrist snap, which often results in the shot going too long. Also, when the ball has backspin, this sometimes creates what's called *shooter's roll*. This is when the ball doesn't go through the rim immediately, but bounces around softly for a moment before dropping through. Backspin helps soften the

The shooter makes an L with her shooting arm.

to the floor, creating a 90-degree angle. When viewed from the side, their arms should form a backward L shape.

Make sure the players' elbows point to the floor. One of the common shooting flaws is a *chicken wing* or *flying elbow*—when the shooter's elbow sticks out from her body at an awkward angle, making a proper follow-through difficult. Check each player's elbow. If her elbow is too low, the shot will be too flat. If her elbow is too high, she'll raise the ball high and behind her head, where she can't see it, and will throw the ball at the basket, instead of shooting it.

Lifting the shot. Once you have your players in the ready-to-shoot position, have them think of what happens next as *lifting* the shot toward the goal. Tell them to pretend that they have a *release button* under their shooting

The shooter extends her arm in a lifting motion, not a pushing motion.

shot when it hits the rim or the backboard, thus creating shooter's roll.

Follow-through. After the ball leaves the shooter's hand, her arm should be straight, her wrist bent, and her fingers should *wave goodbye to the ball* by pointing to the basket. Some coaches call the way a shooter's hand looks at the end of the shot a *gooseneck*.

Tell your players to hold their follow-through for a few moments after they shoot to make sure they have done it properly. Poor follow-through is a common cause of missed shots.

Eyes. The shooter's eyes should never leave the target throughout the shot. Too many young players watch the ball, which distorts their follow-through. If they're aiming at the basket (as opposed to the backboard), their eyes should be on the front of the rim. If they're aiming at the backboard, their eyes should be on the upper near corner of the painted box on the backboard. That's where they want the ball to hit on its way down.

Good follow-through is key to good shooting.

Arc. A common shooting flaw is to shoot the ball *flat*—without enough arc. This greatly reduces the chances of the ball going into the basket. A flat shot coming to the rim with a low angle has a slim margin for error. Shots with high arc have greater chances of success. Not many players know that the diameter of the rim is two basketballs wide! (Granted, on some nights, you'll swear it's no bigger than a coffee cup.) Encourage your players to shoot with high arc to give their shots a better chance. Tell them to make sure their shooting elbow is as high as their eyebrow after they release the ball. On jump shots more than 10 feet from the basket, when the ball is at the peak of its arc, it should be as high as the backboard.

Form shooting. Now your players are ready to use a ball. Have them repeat the same arm and hand movements they practiced without the ball.

Pair up each player with another player and have them shoot to each other from 8 to 10 feet apart, or each player can shoot the ball to herself so that it lands a few feet in front of her. If she snaps her wrist enough to give the ball good backspin, it will return to her each time.

Then have three players practice their form at each basket, keeping their guide hand by their side to focus on their follow-through.

Form shooting should be part of every practice. It only takes a minute or two of concentrated form shooting for your players to be ready to begin shooting drills.

Grip. The first time your players practice shooting with the ball, check the position of their hand. The fingers of their shooting hand should be spread apart, and the pads of their fingers should cradle the ball. Some coaches tell beginning shooters to *make a claw* with their hand to help them visualize the concept. However you explain it, the ball shouldn't touch the palm of their hand. When the ball is in the cocked position, examine your players' grip while standing in front of them. No matter how small their hands are, you should see space between the ball and their palm (see right photo page 48).

Guide hand. So far, your players have used only their shooting hand. Now it's time to

The best players regularly practice form shooting.

A proper grip. Notice the space between the shooter's palm and the ball.

add the nonshooting hand, which is called the *guide hand*. The term is misleading because the guide hand doesn't guide the ball. It only helps hold the ball in place. As the elbow lifts to shoot, the guide hand is of no further use and falls away slightly.

When your players have the ball cradled by their face and their body in the ready position, have them raise their guide hand to the side of the ball. They should not place their hand on top of the ball or in front of the ball. The fingers of their guide hand should point straight to the ceiling.

ASK THE COACH

Question: I have a senior on my Varsity team who has terrible shooting form. She throws the ball up awkwardly from several inches behind her head. The baffling thing is it goes in much of the time. She's shooting 43 percent from the field. Should I try to change her form or leave it as is?

Answer: Leave it as is. First, if she's hitting a decent percentage, there's no reason to fix it for style's sake. Second, by this stage in her basketball career, she's shot thousands of shots with the same motion. Changing her form will be difficult and frustrating for her. It might take all season for her to convert bad habits to good habits, and her confidence might never return. However, I wouldn't hesitate to change bad shooting habits with any freshmen and sophomores on your team. A player who is a junior is a tougher call. If the flaw in a junior's shooting form is minor, I'd change it. If it's a major flaw and the junior shoots a decent percentage, I'd leave it.

Note the guide hand before the shot (top) and after the shot (bottom).

Another common shooting flaw of younger players is that the palm of their guide hand turns toward the basket as they release the shot. This is a leftover habit from when they were smaller and had to shoot two-handed shots in order to reach the basket. Players who turn their guide hand often don't know they're doing so. Players whose guide hand influences their shots will shoot the

ball differently every time. As I said earlier, inconsistent shooting means poor shooting.

A good way to break this habit is to have the player shoot with her guide hand held behind her back. You can also buy a plastic shooting aid (it looks like a disc) that the player wears on her guide hand. It's designed so that if she uses her guide hand at all to influence the shot, the ball will miss the rim badly.

Stepping into the shot. It's important for players to get their shots off quickly. Players who take too long to prepare to shoot after catching the ball allow their defender to get into good position to block or alter the shot, or to take away the possibility of shooting at all.

To teach players to prepare to shoot quickly, coaches talk about *stepping into the shot*. The term is not technically accurate. What coaches really mean is stepping to the pass as part of preparing to shoot quickly. Open shooters are usually open for only a second or two, so the idea is to have them be ready to let fly the instant after they receive the ball. Without the proper footwork, the shooter will waste time setting up and won't have the chance to shoot or will shoot a low-percentage shot with bad form.

As the pass is in the air, the receiver steps toward the ball with her hands up, fingers out, ready to catch the ball. She steps with her *inside pivot foot*—the foot nearest the basket. For example, a player at the free throw line who is catching a pass from the left wing steps toward the pass with her right foot. She times the step so her foot hits the floor as the ball hits her hands. Then, she makes a front pivot with her left foot and squares up to the basket, ready to shoot.

A key element of stepping into the shot is keeping the knees bent. Too many players catch passes standing straight up and must take an extra split second to bend their knees to prepare to shoot. This results in their body having to go from an up position to a down position and back to an up position as they release the shot. A shooter who catches the ball already in the down position only needs to go up after facing the basket.

Using the backboard. Players should shoot a *bank shot* (a shot that hits the backboard

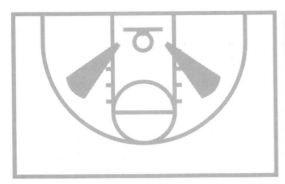

When players are in the 45-degree cone area on either side of the basket, they should shoot a bank shot.

first) when they shoot within a 45-degree cone on either side of the basket. However, once the length of the shot exceeds 12 feet, they should aim at the rim. At the longer distances, bank shots are more difficult to make than straight-on shots.

Why use the backboard? First, it's easier for a shooter to aim at a tangible surface with a painted box on it than it is to aim at an invisible plane stretching from the rim into the air. If this weren't so, everyone would shoot layups without using the backboard. Second, a shot bouncing off the backboard has a bigger margin for error than a shot bouncing off the rim. Third, using the backboard requires the shooter to aim the ball higher than if she were only trying to get the ball over the lip of the rim. The added angle helps players get their shots off against taller defenders.

When using the backboard, the ball should hit the surface on the way down, not the way up. The shooter should aim the ball so it hits the upper corner of the box painted on the backboard. The box is painted white on clear fiberglass backboards and black on white backboards.

Shot selection. Part of being a good shooter is having good *shot selection*—knowing when to shoot and when not to shoot. Encourage your players to take *good shots* (high-percentage shots), not *bad shots* (low-percentage shots). With my teams, I consider a good shot one that the

Players should use the backboard as often as possible; it's shooter-friendly.

player can make at least 60 percent of the time in practice (unguarded). You'll need to decide on your own parameters, based on the experience and skill level of your players. If your team has inexperienced players, you might consider a good shot to be any open shot taken within the free throw line.

There are three variables that make a shot a good shot:

1. The shooter must be in her range. She shouldn't take shots from areas of the court she's not good at shooting from. If a player can't make 10-foot shots consistently, she has no business taking a 3-point shot (save for a desperation heave as time runs out).

2. The shooter must be open. Even if a shooter is in her range, if she has a taller

player towering over her in good position to block the shot, the shooter should pass up the shot. This is a time to pass or dribble (or try a shot fake).

3. The shooter must be squared up to the basket and in balance. Just because the shooter is in her range and she's wide open, the shot won't be a good shot if she's falling backward and twisting sideways when she releases the ball. Shooters who shoot wild shots aren't likely to score.

Emphasize shot selection in your practice scrimmages. In certain drills, award a plus point to the offensive team every time a good shot is taken and a minus point every time a bad shot is taken. It won't be long before the players learn the difference.

Types of Shots

3-point shots. The adoption of the 3-point shot in basketball has revolutionized the game. Teams that are behind late in the game have a chance to catch up, and teams with less talent than other teams have a weapon that can keep them in the game.

At the middle school level, few players have the arm and leg strength to make a 3-point shot with any consistency. Even if they're strong enough, most of them still need work on short-range and middle-range shooting. If you coach middle school girls, unless you have experienced players, it would be better to wait to work on 3-point shots until they are older.

If you coach high school or an AAU team with high-school-age players, 3-point shooting should be a key part of your team offense. Your players should practice 3-point shooting every day as part of your shooting drills.

The fundamentals of 3-point shooting are no different than what you teach for 2-point shooting. However, because of the added distance to the goal, there are two slight modifications to teach:

More legs. A 3-point shooter should use her legs more—bend her knees more—than for a regular shot. This gives the shot added power to travel the extra distance.

Lower starting elbow. A 3-point shooter should lower her shooting elbow from its usual starting position. Since the shooting arm starts lower than before, it gives the shooter more power when the arm extends. Note that the shooting elbow lowers down toward the floor, not out and away from the body.

Too many players work on 3-point shooting before they become good 2-point shooters. I can't overemphasize this point—before you allocate much time in practice to long-range shooting, your players should learn to shoot well from short and medium distances. They should learn to shoot 8-footers before they move on to 12-footers, and they should learn to shoot 12-footers before they move on to 15-footers.

Layups. The layup is a simple shot when done correctly, but it's hard for new players to learn how to do it right. These are the key principles:

1. The player shoots the layup softly. She's only a foot from the basket. If the ball is put up too hard off the backboard, it has little chance of going in.

2. The player shoots the ball with an open hand—with her palm facing the backboard.

3. The shooter uses the painted square on the glass as a target. She aims for just inside the top corner of the side from which she's shooting.

4. The shooter extends herself up, not out. Too many players shoot *drive-by layups*. They run under the basket at full speed and fling the ball up, hoping it will go in. This has two bad consequences: first, since they're farther (lower) from the target than if they extended themselves upward, the shot has lower odds of going in; second, they run themselves out of position for the possible rebound.

The footwork for a layup is simple to understand, but inexperienced players struggle to

As the player extends her arm to shoot a layup, her knee comes up, as if a string connects her elbow to her knee.

make their arms and legs work together. The trick is raising the knee as the shooting arm extends. Players should imagine that one end of a string is tied to their shooting elbow and the other end is tied to the knee of the same-side leg. When they shoot a right-handed layup, their right knee must rise as their arm extends.

When teaching layups to beginners, approach it one step at a time. Start with strong-hand layups, as these will be easier to learn than weak-hand layups.

Place your players in a line away from the basket, each with a ball. Holding the ball in both hands, players raise their shooting arm so the string pulls their knee up at the same time. Have them shoot the ball in the air so it lands a few feet ahead.

Place them in a line that begins at the right-side block (left-side block if they're left-handed).

Have them shoot from a standstill, taking no steps or dribbles yet, focusing on the shooting arm and the knee working together. Their eyes should be on the upper right corner of the painted box.

Have them add a step. Back them up a step. They should step with their left foot (if shooting with their right hand) and put the ball up.

Once they're doing this well, back the line to the second hash mark along the lane. Tell them to repeat the sequence out loud: "left-right-left-and-up." Have them take three steps (left foot first) and shoot the layup.

Once they can do this fairly well, have them speed up their walk.

Lastly, have them add one dribble with their right hand. As they become better at layups, start them farther back and have them approach the basket with more speed. It won't be long before most of them shoot layups like veterans.

It's important to work on weak-hand layups at an early age. Too many high school players can't make weak-hand layups because they didn't learn them when they were in middle school. A player who can't make a layup with her weak hand will be limited offensively.

Power layups. Power layups are two-footed, two-handed layups used when the player anticipates contact during the shot. To make a power layup, the dribbler comes to a jump stop next to the basket and *chins* the ball (holds the ball under her chin, elbows out, squeezing the ball). This allows her to protect the ball in spite of being bumped by one or more defenders. She shoots the ball with both hands, aiming at the same spot on the backboard as if she were shooting a regular one-foot layup. Shooting in this manner gives the player a good chance of scoring 3 points (2 points for the layup plus 1 for the free throw), whereas if she shot a regular layup, she probably wouldn't score.

A good complement to a power layup is a shot fake (or *pump fake*). Before shooting, the player fakes with her shoulder and head as if to shoot, drawing the foul. The ball remains in the chinned position and her knees remain bent, ready to jump, but her head and shoulders

Power layup. The player comes to a jump stop (left) and puts the ball up with both hands (right).

move upward for a moment as if she's about to shoot. When the defender makes contact, the player goes up with the ball.

Foul shooting. The rules say that a player has 10 seconds to shoot a free throw after the referee hands her the ball. This allows her to take her time and not rush.

First, the player steps to the middle of the free throw line and sets her feet up as if to shoot a jump shot. When the referee gives her the ball, she takes a deep breath to relax. This is particularly important in the later stages of the game, when the shooter is likely to be tired.

Then, she goes through her *preshot routine.* Every player needs to develop a routine that helps her block out distractions and prepare her for taking the shot. There are as many routines as there are players. Some players bounce the

ball three times with both hands, some spin the ball, some shift their weight back and forth, some mimic the follow-through, some whisper special words to calm themselves, and some do combinations of these things. It doesn't matter what routine your players choose, as long as each player repeats her special routine every time when she goes to the line.

After the preshot routine, shooting a free throw is exactly like shooting an uncontested jump shot. All the principles of sound shooting form apply (balance, eyes on the target, lifting the shot, etc.).

In a two-shot foul situation, if the player makes the first shot, she should stay where she is on the line, in the hopes of repeating the same shot. If she misses the first shot, she should step off the line and regroup. She should try a players' names on the left and columns for dates across the top of the page works well. Over the course of the season, this tells you how each player is progressing.

Rebounding

A *rebound* is a shot that misses the basket and bounces off the backboard or the rim onto the court. An *offensive rebound* occurs when a player rebounds a missed shot at the opponent's basket. A *defensive rebound* occurs when a player rebounds a missed shot at her team's basket.

When a shot misses the basket entirely—hits neither backboard no rim—it's not technically a rebound. It's a pass (often followed by fans of the nonshooting team chanting "Air ball, air ball"). When a rebound lands in someone's hands or bounces on the court, the ball is still in play. When a rebound lands on the baseline or out-of-bounds, the ball is out of play. The clock stops, and before play starts again, the ball must be inbounded at the point at which it went out. The team that didn't shoot the ball inbounds the ball.

There's no more critical aspect of the game than rebounding. Statistics show that the team that *outrebounds* their opponent wins 75 to 80 percent of the time. That's not to say your team can't win a game in spite of poor rebounding—maybe your team shot well and the other team shot poorly, or maybe the other team committed a lot of turnovers—but, over the course of a season, no team at any level will succeed without being a good rebounding team.

Look at it this way. A rebound can mean a 4- to 6-point swing in the score. When your

Every player has her own free throw routine.

different train of thought so that, this time, the result will be different.

Charting Shooting in Practices

Have someone—an assistant, a manager, a parent volunteer, or an injured player—keep track of your players' shots in practice drills and scrimmages. They should note every made shot and every miss. A simple grid sheet with the team snares a defensive rebound, the other team loses the chance to score a 2- or 3-point basket, and your team now has the chance to score 2 or 3 points at the other end of the court. Conversely, when the other team gets a defensive rebound, the chance for your team to score 2 or 3 points vanishes, and the other team has a chance to score 2 or 3 points.

What does it take for a player to be a good rebounder? A lot of desire and some technique. A player doesn't need to be the best athlete on the team or even the tallest player to be the team's best rebounder. No special skill is needed. This is good news for young players and short players. Convince them how important rebounding is, that anyone who works hard at it can be a good rebounder, and you'll see some of your players develop into good rebounders.

Rebounding is one of the pillars of good basketball. You should devote part of every practice to it.

For a player to become a good rebounder, she must understand and learn the following principles:

1. The player assumes every shot will be a miss, including layups. Players miss layups all the time.

2. The rebounder gets into position as soon as she sees that a shot is about to happen. She doesn't wait until the ball bounces off the backboard—that's too late. When she sees the player with the ball set up to shoot, when she sees the shooter square up and her eyes fix on the basket, the rebounder doesn't wait for the shooter's arm to rise. She attacks the boards strong and hard.

3. The rebounder positions herself on the *help side* (also called the *weak side*), the side of the basket away from where the ball is. This is where a miss is likely to go. When a shot taken from one side of the basket misses, 75 percent of the time it will bounce off on the help side.

4. The rebounder positions herself at the optimum distance from the basket.

Much of the time, when a shot misses, it will bounce off the basket approximately half the distance compared to where the shot was made.

5. When the shot goes up, the rebounder steps into a defender with her body, getting between the defender and the basket. If she can't do that, she gets beside the defender. If she can't do either, she pins the defender underneath the basket. The rebounder doesn't just stand there, hoping the shot will fall into her hands.

Types of Rebounding

Defensive rebounding. The primary technique used in rebounding at a team's own basket is called *blocking out* or *boxing out*, when the defender positions herself between an offensive player and the basket so the offensive player can't grab the rebound. When a defender successfully blocks out her opponent, she's in the perfect position to catch the ball if the missed shot bounces in her direction.

Blocking out the shooter. To block out an offensive player who just shot the ball, the defender follows this sequence:

1. She steps toward the shooter (not toward the basket) and places one foot (it doesn't matter which) directly in front of the shooter's feet. Too often, a defender steps toward the basket, watching the ball, her arms raised, hoping the missed shot will magically fall into her hands. The chances she'll get the rebound are slim. If the ball does bounce her way, the shooter, with no one blocking her out, is free to dart in front of the defender and snag the ball.

2. The defender makes contact with the shooter by making a reverse pivot, using her lead foot as the pivot foot. As she turns, she swings her lead arm across the shooter's body, making it impossible for the shooter to move toward the basket, and puts her backside against the shooter's legs.

3. She pivots until she faces the basket. Her arms are up and wide, her feet are wide, and her body is low, in balance. With this strong base, she can keep even a bigger, stronger player *on her back* for the 2 seconds needed for the ball to come off the basket.

4. With a strong base as leverage, the defender uses her legs to push the shooter away from the basket. This allows her to maintain contact with the shooter and creates a bigger area where she can get the ball. If the shooter tries to get around her on one side, the defender makes short, choppy steps to maintain contact and keep the shooter on her back.

5. Once the ball comes off the basket, the defender releases from the shooter and goes to get the ball. Her hands are up and her fingers wide. She jumps and extends her arms, timing it so she catches the ball at the peak of her jump.

6. After she catches the ball, she *chins it*—brings it down to just below her chin with both hands, elbows wide.

7. She pivots away from the shooter (who is now a defender) and any other opposing players and looks up to see if she can throw an outlet pass. If she can't, she protects the ball and passes it to the point guard.

Blocking out the nonshooter. Blocking out the shooter is relatively easy, assuming the defender has established a good defensive position. The defender doesn't need to look around for the player to block out—she's standing in front of her, less than 5 feet away. Plus, the defender is already between her and the basket.

The rebounder's goal is to keep the other player on her back.

Chinning the ball protects it.

As long as she uses the proper block-out technique, the shooter can get the rebound only if the ball flies over their heads.

Blocking out a nonshooter presents a tougher challenge. Most of the time, a nonshooter grabs the offensive rebound, not the shooter. If the nonshooter is close to the shooter, the nonshooter's defender can easily make contact with her. However, the angle isn't the same as when blocking out a shooter. The defender is no longer directly between the offensive player and the basket (this assumes the defense is playing *pressure man-to-man* or *zone*, not *sagging man-to-man*—these terms are defined in Chapter 4). The nonshooter will often have an unobstructed line to the basket.

When blocking out the nonshooter, there are two keys for the defender. One is to anticipate the possible rebound before the nonshooter does. This allows the defender time to put herself between the player and the basket. The second is to take the proper angle. A defender who moves toward the spot where the nonshooter was before the shot went up will find that the nonshooter won't be there anymore. She'll be on her way to the basket. The defender must move to block out the nonshooter on an angle that allows her to cut off the nonshooter. If the defender anticipates the rebound early enough and chooses the right angle, she'll be in the proper position to block out the player.

When the nonshooter is two passes away, the defender has an even harder task. If she's in proper *help-side position* (see page 92), she may be 10 or more feet away from the player she's guarding. This puts more of a premium on anticipating the shot before the player does and choosing the right angle. When the nonshooter is in the far help-side corner, the distance is so far that the defender won't have time to cover the distance before the ball comes off the basket. The best she can do is stake out a position somewhere between the basket and the nonshooter and make contact if the player tries to cut inside of her.

As part of your rebounding drills, make sure to spend time on help-side rebounding. This is the most dangerous area in which to give up offensive rebounds because of the distance between the nonshooters and the defenders and the likelihood that a missed shot will bounce in that direction.

Offensive rebounding. A player who is a good offensive rebounder is valuable to your team. Offensive rebounders score easy baskets and are fouled in the process, which gives them a chance to make a 3-point play (this is called scoring 3 points the *old-fashioned way*—a reference to when the 3-point line didn't exist in basketball). A number of pro players who weren't good shooters had impressive careers by making offensive rebounding their specialty. Good rebounders work hard at both ends of the court on every possession.

Sometimes an offensive player is between the defender and the basket, so she blocks out

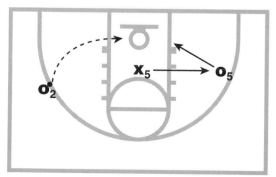
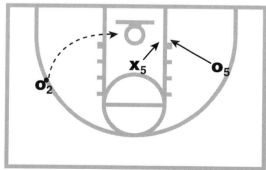

Bad block-out angle (left). Good block-out angle (right).

and shoot a *putback*—an immediate shot attempt after the rebound. Too many rebounders make the mistake of bringing the ball down to their waist, giving opportunistic players on the other team a chance to knock the ball out of their hands or to grab it and cause a jump ball. When a player grabs an offensive rebound next to the basket, she should always keep the ball over her head and go back up strong.

When a player grabs an offensive rebound that bounces far from the basket, she should look for the chance to shoot or pass to an open teammate right away before the defense has time to reset. If those options aren't available, she should pass to a perimeter player for a 3-point shot. If no one is open outside, she should dribble away from the basket so the offense can set up again.

The spin-and-go move.

her player no differently than if she's guarding her own basket. Most of the time, the defender is between her and the basket, so she must use different techniques to get to the ball.

The first technique is the *spin-and-go move*. When the defender makes contact and pivots, the offensive player does her own reverse pivot, ending up alongside the defender, which gives her an opening to go to the basket.

In the *fake-and-go move*, the offensive player fakes as if she's trying to get around the defender on one side. When the defender shifts her weight in that direction, the offensive player steps with her outside foot across the defender's body and cuts by her on the other side. The fake is made by pushing the defender's shoulder and side with her hands.

When a player grabs an offensive rebound next to the basket, she should keep the ball over her head and immediately jump back up

When a player hooks her arm behind the other player, that's a holding foul.

Question: In our last game, the referee called a foul on my post player when she was blocking out her player. Later, my post was called for a foul when she and another player were jumping up for the ball at the same time I didn't understand what she did that caused either foul. What are the rules concerning rebounding?

Answer: The battles between players fighting for a rebound are some of the most physical parts in the game. As long as it's done in a certain way, contact is allowed. I'm guessing the referee called the first foul for *holding* or *illegal use of the hands*. It's legal for the player who is blocking out to hold her arms and elbows wide, but she can't hook her arm behind the other player to keep her there (see bottom photo). It's also legal for her to pin the other player's arm between her arm and body, but she can't hold the player's arm with her hand. That's why you should teach your players to block out (and post up) with their hands open and out.

I'm guessing that the second foul was for *going over the back*. A rebounder is allowed to jump straight up for the ball, but she isn't allowed to jump forward, reach over the opposing player, and come down on the opposing player's back. This is considered an unfair advantage, so it's a foul (see photo page 60). Players who are taller than the player fighting them for a rebound tend to go over the back. They know they can get the ball because of their height advantage, and they can't resist the temptation to lean over and get it. Teach your players to go straight up and down when they rebound.

Question: I saw a player on TV who, instead of going for the rebound, jumped up and batted the ball to a teammate with one hand. Do you recommend this?

Answer: It's best to go after a rebound with two hands. That way, you can hold onto it and either go up for a shot or chin it, if it's a defensive rebound. There are times, however, when several players are jumping for the same rebound, and it's difficult to get both hands up and on the ball. Since most players jump a bit higher when they have only one arm up, it's better to try to tip the ball to a teammate, rather than not try anything at all.

Question: I can't seem to get my players to jump for the ball. They stand on the floor waiting for the ball to come down to them. Don't girls like to jump?

Answer: There's no reason why girls can't jump for rebounds. It's a matter of emphasizing it in practice and making it a habit. Have your players throw a rebound to themselves and go after it. Make sure they prepare to jump with their knees bent and their hands up. It won't be long before they learn how to time their jump to catch the ball at the peak of the jump. Don't just practice it once and assume they'll suddenly become great leapers. Practice it often, and you'll see results.

Getting Open: Moves without the Ball

A player can't score if she doesn't have the ball, and she can't get the ball if she can't get open. A player who can't get open is a nonfactor on offense. Your team might as well be playing 4 against 5.

To get open, a player must first be in the ready stance, with knees bent, body low, and feet shoulder-width apart. If she's standing upright, she can't make sudden changes of speed and direction, which are the keys to getting open.

Then, she must *read and react*—see how her defender is playing her and make a move based on that. Even the best defender gives the offensive player an opening of some sort. It's the offensive player's job to determine what that opening is. Lastly, the player must call for the ball when she's open. If the player with the ball is doing her job, she'll pass the ball at the right moment. I tell my players, "If you're open, the ball will find you."

Your players must work hard to get open if they're going to help the offense. In the rest of this section, I explain the various moves

A player can't reach over her opponent to get the ball. This is an over-the-back foul.

without the ball that you can teach. If you coach younger players, teach them what they can handle and nothing more. At first, don't teach inexperienced players more than V-cuts and backdoor cuts. Once they learn those, you can progress to the more advanced moves.

The *V-cut and swim move* is the basic move to use when a player wants to get open on the perimeter. Assume that a wing player wants to get open for a pass from the point guard who is at the top of the circle. The wing player goes toward the basket, drawing her defender with her. She goes at half-speed and can even walk her man in. When she's in the low block area, she plants her inside foot (the one nearest the baseline) and gets low, as she grabs the defender's arm with her inside hand (the one closest to the ball), holds the defender in place for an instant, and swings her outside arm (the one

away from the ball) over the top of the defender's head in a swimming motion. If she times this right, her head and shoulders will be closer to the ball than the defender. She then *explodes* (cuts as hard as she can) toward the ball. The path she takes going in and back out should form a *V*, not an *I*, meaning that she should cut toward the player with the ball, not back along the same path. If she cuts back to where she started, she probably won't get open. It's better to cut too close to the ball than to cut too far from it.

With the V-cut and every other move without the ball, your players should learn to change speeds when trying to get open. Players who play at the same speed all the time are easier to defend because their defender can adjust to that speed. However, if a player is always changing the speed of her cuts, as well as the direction of her cuts, she becomes unpredictable and will have the defender on her heels.

The *backdoor cut* is used when the defender *overplays* an offensive player on the perimeter—aggressively stays in the passing lane to deny her the ball. It's the opposite of the V-cut in that the backdoor cut first takes the defender away from the basket, not toward the basket. Before using this move, the perimeter player should signal to her teammate with the ball (by extending her fist) that she's about to make a backdoor cut so the passer can prepare. When the passer is ready, the perimeter player takes one or two steps away from the basket, hands up as if to receive a pass. At the same time, her teammate should fake a pass to further convince the defender. When the defender moves out to prevent the pass, the perimeter player plants her outside foot and explodes to the basket, cutting behind the defender for an easy pass and layup opportunity. When making a backdoor cut, even if the pass isn't thrown, the player should cut all the way to the basket so there's no confusion about her intent. Too many times, the perimeter player confuses the passer by only cutting for a step or two in an attempt to trick her defender into thinking she's not making the backdoor cut after all. Once your players take one step toward the basket,

After a player completes the swim move (top), she explodes toward the perimeter (bottom).

they should continue all the way. Even if they don't get the pass, at least they've not caused a turnover.

The *inside cut move* is more advanced. It's a great move to use if the offensive player has beaten the defender with the V-cut several times. Again, it's used when an aggressive defender overplays the offensive player. As the player walks the defender down to the low post area, as if about to make another swim move and V-cut, she instead cuts sharply toward the basket and circles around the defender's back for the pass. If she has a teammate in the low post, her teammate can screen the defender, allowing the cutter to be open for a quick pass.

The *reverse spin step-over move* sounds complicated, but it's not. The offensive player makes a V-cut as before, but this time, instead of "swimming" over the top, she plants her inside foot (the one closest to the basket), makes a sudden reverse pivot toward the ball, and cuts away from the defender to the short corner. For this to

A good fake sets up the backdoor cut (top). As the defender leans the wrong way, the perimeter player cuts hard to the basket (bottom).

work, the timing with the passer has to be just right. Again, a screen from a teammate in the low post can free her up even more.

In the *fake catch and explode move* the perimeter player walks the defender in toward the basket, raising her hands and calling for the ball as if wanting a pass. When the defender raises her hands and body to anticipate the pass, the offensive player cuts away from her to receive the ball.

The *flash move* occurs when an offensive player suddenly cuts into the lane straight to the ball. The player sets up her defender first with a step in the opposite direction. When the defender leans or follows, the player plants her foot and *flashes* (cuts) into the lane. Players should flash into the lane when there are holes in the defense. The flash is a good tactic against defenses that don't have defenders in the middle of the lane (like in the 1-2-2 zone).

When flashing to the ball, a player should let her teammate know she's open.

The *flash backdoor move* is the counter to the flash move. If the defender overplays the flash, the offensive player suddenly cuts to the basket at a 90-degree angle. For this move to work, the offensive player and defender need to be near the free throw line, or there won't be enough room for a safe pass.

Most teams don't practice enough how to get open without the ball. Don't practice these moves once or twice and consider them taught (that's a good rule for anything you teach). Getting open is essential to playing good offense, regardless of the formations and plays you use. Your players should learn not only the various moves you think they can handle, but these key concepts as well: changing speeds, changing directions, and convincing your defender that you're doing this when you're actually doing that. And remember, an offensive player has the element of surprise on her side. She should use it!

Getting Open: Moves with the Ball

Once an offensive player gets open and her teammate passes her the ball, that's only half of the story. The other half is she needs to know what to do from the triple threat position.

In this section, I'll describe various moves you can teach your players. Some are easy to learn, and some will take time and repetitions. Even experienced high school players won't be able to learn more than a few of these moves, so start slowly and choose the two or three moves you think are most important. Don't introduce more moves until your players learn to do the first moves with either hand and from both sides of the basket.

An important concept to preach to your players is *reading the defense*. All these moves are based on reacting to what the defender does or doesn't do. Just like with the offensive players without the ball, the element of surprise is the ally of the player with the ball. Once the defender reacts, the offensive player knows exactly what to do.

The first move to learn is the *shot fake*. The player pretends to shoot the ball to see how the defender reacts. When making a shot fake, the player remains low, ready to move quickly. As she fakes, her body doesn't rise up. She fakes by lifting her shoulders, head, and the ball. The ball shouldn't rise above her chin, so that if she drives or passes, she won't waste time bringing it back down. A critical part of an effective shot fake is for the player to look at the basket as if she intends to shoot. Many defenders watch the offensive player's eyes. If the player's eyes don't look at the target, the fake won't convince the defender.

This is key: don't rush shot fakes (and pass fakes). If the player fakes a shot (or a pass) too fast, the defender doesn't have time to react.

The *shot fake jump shot* is used when the defender doesn't react to the shot fake. If the defender doesn't rise up out of her stance to contest the shot or if she backs away, the offensive player should take the open jump shot (assuming it's a good shot for her—in her range).

The *shot fake drive* is used when the defender reacts to the shot fake by getting out of her low stance to try to block the shot. When the defender raises her body and her arms, the offensive player drives by, brushing the defender's hip and heading in a straight line to the basket. Too many players make *banana cuts* (wide, curving cuts) to the basket, which allow their

defender time to recover into a good guarding position again.

Another way the player can cause the defender to react is with a foot fake called a *jab step*. A jab step is simply a quick, short (6 to 8 inches) out-and-back step the player makes with her lead foot from the triple threat position. The direction of the jab step is at the defender's lead foot. The player has three options after making the jab step:

If the defender does nothing—doesn't move or lean in the direction of the jab—the

Shot fake (top) and drive (bottom).

offensive player does the *jab-and-go move*. She immediately takes a long, explosive step with the same foot in the same direction she jabbed, and drives by the defender. Her body should be low so that her head and shoulders drive by the defender's hip. The first dribble (with her right hand) should be beyond the first step. A common mistake is for the offensive player to make the first dribble by her side, negating the advantage she gained with the jab step. Once she gets by the defender, if she's inside the 3-point line, she should take no more than one dribble (two dribbles, if she's a middle school player) to get to the basket. If another defender comes over to prevent the layup, the offensive player should either pull up for the jump shot or pass to an open teammate.

Another option off a jab step is the *jab and shot fake*. As it sounds, the offensive player follows her jab step with a shot fake. Though the defender didn't react to the first fake, the second fake will often cause her to move closer to the offensive player to contest the shot. When this happens, the offensive player drives by her.

If the defender retreats in the direction of the jab step, the offensive player does the *jab-and-cross move*. She simultaneously rips the ball across to her left hip and steps with her right foot across the defender's body, keeping her head and shoulders as low as possible (see photos below and page 66). As with the jab-and-go, the crossover step should be long and explosive, and the first dribble (with her left hand) should be beyond the long step. Emphasize the importance of driving by the defender in as straight a line as possible. Too often players lose the advantage they gained by making a wide drive, allowing quick defenders to recover.

If the defender retreats more than a step to prevent a drive from either the jab-and-go or the jab-and-cross, the offensive player does the *jab-and-shoot move*. Since she has created enough space, she shoots the ball.

The *swipe-and-go move* is used when the defender overplays a perimeter pass and lunges out too far to try to steal the ball. The offensive player sees that her defender's momentum has taken her out of the play momentarily, so she *swipes* (rips) the ball low across her body, pushes it ahead, and drives toward the basket. Whenever a defender overplays the pass and lunges out of position, the offensive player should immediately drive to the basket.

The jab-and-cross move. This player jabs with her left foot . . .

. . . and then she crosses the ball and her left leg to the right side.

The *step-back shot*, an advanced shooting move, is used when the offensive player drives toward the basket but recognizes she can't get by the defender. The dribbler plants her inside foot (the one nearest to the basket), steps back with her other foot, pulls the ball back, and lands with both feet square to the basket and her body low, in the ready-to-shoot position.

The player should take a big step back so she'll create more space between her and the defender. Done properly, the footwork creates a triangle. The step-back shot is an excellent skill to learn for players who are adept at driving into the lane. It also allows shorter players room to take a close-in shot against taller players.

The *step-back counter* is another advanced move. If the defender anticipates the step-back and changes direction to contest the shot, the offensive player catches her off guard and drives by her. She can drive by on the side on which she has the ball, or she can cross over and drive by on the defender's other side. This move, like the other advanced moves, should not be taught to players who are still learning the basics.

Moves at the end of the drive. Players need to know more than how to drive to the basket. They need to know how to *finish*—how to end the play with a score. Sometimes they'll find themselves alone for a layup, but more often than not, one or more defenders will converge on them to try to stop them. They need to know how to finish with a strong scoring move.

The two-handed *power layup* (see pages 52–53) should be used when the player expects contact. Another good move is the *step-through move*. If the defender establishes good defensive

BASKET

1. plant inside foot, bend knees — dribbling ball in right hand

2. hop back at 45-degree angle, right foot first — pull-back dribble

3. land in ready-to-shoot position — ball in both hands

Footwork for the step-back shot.

Pulling the ball back quickly on the step-back (top) gives the player enough time and space for an open shot (bottom).

position, the offensive player comes to a two-foot jump stop to avoid a charging foul. She then pump fakes, more than once, if needed. When the defender raises her body and arms to contest the shot, the player steps across the defender's body with her leg (she can choose either foot because she made a two-foot jump stop), rips the ball, and finishes by stepping toward the basket and shooting a layup.

Another move is the *reverse spin move*, which is simply a spin dribble (see pages 35–36) that turns into a layup. The offensive player sets it up by driving toward the basket at an angle. If her defender stays with her, the player plants her inside foot and makes a reverse pivot, bringing the ball around as in a spin dribble move. She finishes the play with a layup or short jump shot.

An on-ball screen.

Screens

A *screen* occurs when a player positions her body as a temporary wall to block a teammate's defender. Screens are an essential part of team offense. Though many coaches teach screening as a routine part of their man-to-man offense, screens are just as valuable against zone defenses.

There are two basic types of screens. An *on-ball screen* (or *ball screen*) is set on a defender guarding the player with the ball to create an open driving lane or an uncontested shot. An *off-ball screen* (or *player screen*) is set on a defender guarding a player without the ball to allow the player to get open for an uncontested pass.

Screens have other names, depending on where they are set. A *cross screen* occurs when a player comes across the lane to screen for a player. The screen can be from block to block or from elbow to elbow.

An off-ball (player) screen.

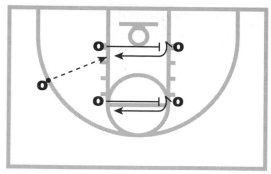

Cross screens.

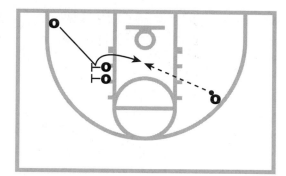

Double screen.

In a *down screen,* a player comes from the perimeter or high post area to screen for a player in the low post area. In an *up screen,* a player comes from the low post area to screen for a player in the high post area. This is similar to a *back screen,* when a player from the low post area comes out to screen for a player on the perimeter.

Finally, a *double screen* occurs when two players line up next to each other to set simultaneous screens. If two players who aren't next to each other set screens at the same time, it's called a *staggered screen.* All screens present problems for the defense, but double screens and staggered screens are particularly hard to defend.

Practice using and setting screens at every practice. The principles and mechanics of screening can be learned in one or two sessions, but integrating them into your offense takes time. Some players think that screens are only for the less-skilled players, that the best players

on the team shouldn't have to worry much about screening. Nothing could be further from the truth. The best pro and college players understand the value of screening. Tell your players that great screeners create great shots for themselves, not just for their teammates.

Setting a Screen

The technique for setting a screen is simple. The player first locates the defender she intends to screen. She runs straight at the defender and comes to a two-foot jump stop next to her, timing her jump stop so she makes slight contact with the defender. (There is one situation when the screener can't make contact—when the player is setting a *blindside screen*—a screen directly behind the defender that the defender can't see. In that case, the player must set the screen a foot away from the defender.)

Once the screener comes to a jump stop, her feet should be wide and her knees bent, so she's balanced, ready for contact if the defender

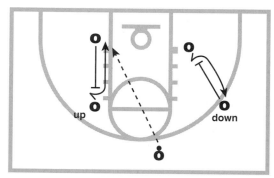

Down screen and up screen.

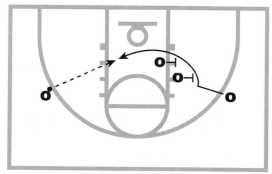

Staggered screen.

runs into her. Her arms should be held in an X across her chest to protect herself and to cushion the physical contact.

Emphasize the following principles to your players:

Proper angle. For a screen to be effective, is should be set at the proper angle, which depends on where the screener is in relation to her teammate's defender. She should visualize the path her teammate would like to use to dribble or cut unguarded and set the screen with her back facing that direction. Usually, the best angle to set the screen is right off the defender's nearest shoulder. The screener's arms should touch the defender's shoulder. Often, but not always, her back will face the basket.

Communication. As the player runs to set the screen, she lets her teammate know she's about to screen for her. She calls the other player's name or raises a fist to signal her intention. This gives her teammate time to prepare to use the screen.

Presence. As the player sets the screen, she *makes herself big*. She plants her feet wider than her shoulders so she has a strong base, gets low, and gets her arms up.

Freeze. Once the player sets the screen, she freezes. She doesn't move until her teammate cuts or dribbles by the screen, or until it's obvious that her teammate is going in another direction. Inexperienced screeners are so eager to screen their teammate's defender that they move after setting the screen, which is a foul. Any movement—leaning toward the defender, taking a small step, or holding their arms away from their body—is a foul. It's a minor mistake not to set a screen well, but it's a big mistake to give the other team possession of the ball.

Opening up. After the screen has been used, the screener *opens up to the ball*—turns to face the ball. This is especially important in an on-ball screen, where the screener is often wide open after the screen for a pass from the dribbler.

Screeners make excellent receivers. After a screen is set and used, the defenders become so focused on the dribbler or the cutter that they often forget to guard the screener. If a dribbler who has used a screen doesn't have a good drive or shot available, she should look to see if the screener is open. A screener who opens up to the ball should then *roll* (move) to the basket. An on-ball screen where the screener rolls to the basket looking for the pass is called a *pick-and-roll*. This two-player play is an excellent offensive strategy against a team that plays man-to-man defense. Isolate your two best players on one side of the court and run a pick-and-roll. Many college and pro teams use this tactic as a staple of their offense.

Using a Screen

Using a screen properly is just as important as setting one properly. If a player doesn't use the screen a teammate set for her, she's missed an opportunity to get open for a pass, drive, or shot. The principles to teach about using screens are the following:

Waiting for the screen. If the player with the ball moves before her teammate gets there, the screener won't have time to screen, and the defender will have no problem staying

---

ASK THE COACH

Question: Some of my players understand how to open up to the ball after they set an on-ball screen, but others don't get it. They never know which way to turn. How can I best explain it?

Answer: Tell each screener to imagine she has a strip of Velcro on her shoulder, as does the cutter or dribbler using the screen. As her teammate uses the screen, their shoulders will rub, and the Velcro strips will pull the screener in the proper direction. If this imagery doesn't help, practicing screens often will help even your most confused players learn how to turn the right way.

with the ball carrier. The screener's efforts are wasted, and the player with the ball won't get open. Worse, when the screener sees her teammate moving before she gets there, in her eagerness to help she might commit a moving violation. It's far better to wait too long for a screen than to rush.

Setting up the defender. As the player waits for the screener, she should give the defender the impression that she's going in the opposite direction. If the player doesn't have the ball, she should take one step away from the screener and cut hard back toward her when she's set. She should begin her move just as the screener freezes. If the player has the ball, the principle is the same. As the screener heads toward the defender, the player pass fakes away from her. Then, as the screener sets up, the player rips the ball across her body and dribbles by the screener, again leaving no room for the defender to follow.

Rubbing the screener's shoulder. As the player cuts or dribbles by the screener, her shoulder should rub the screener's shoulder. This leaves no space for the defender to follow.

Reading the defender. As the player with the ball rubs shoulders with her teammate, she should read the defender and should keep her head up to see if she has open space ahead of her. If the defender has been effectively screened, the player should take advantage of this before the screened player recovers or another defender slides over to guard her.

When a player without the ball uses a screen, she also needs to read the defense. As she cuts by the screener's shoulder, she should note how the two defenders involved (her defender and the screener's defender) play the screen. What the defenders do determines what the cutter using the screen does.

If the player's defender is *hung up on the screen* (the screen has momentarily blocked her), the player cuts to the basket for the pass before the defender recovers.

If her defender *goes under the screen* (moves behind the screener to regain good position on the other side of the screener), the player makes a *popout cut*—comes straight to the ball. Or she

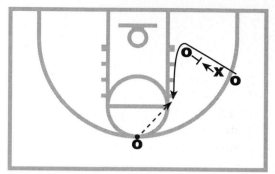

Popout cut.

makes a *fade cut*, in which she cuts away from the basket (instead of cutting to the ball), creating space between her and the defender for the pass and an open shot. Good shooters like to use this move to get open for 3-point shots.

If her defender *goes over the top of the screen* (follows her by chasing her around the screen), she makes a *curl cut* (see top left diagram page 72). She curls around the screener and cuts to the basket to receive the ball. The defender won't be able to stop the pass because the offensive player will be in between her and the ball. Curl cuts often lead to easy shots.

If her defender *cheats* on the screen (prematurely goes under the screen to prevent her from cutting off the screener's shoulder, she makes a *back cut* (see bottom left diagram page 72). She plants her outside foot when she's next to the screener, and instead of cutting where the defender is waiting, she cuts hard to the basket by the screener's other shoulder.

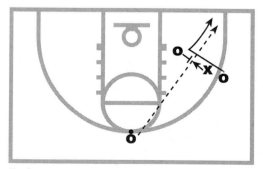

Fade cut.

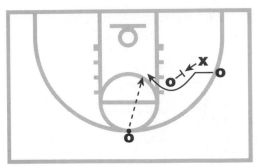

Curl cut.

Pick-and-roll.

Using Ball Screens

One of the most popular offensive plays is the *pick-and-roll*, which, as noted above, is nothing more than a ball screen. A pick-and-roll happens when a screener *picks* (screens) for the player with the ball, that player dribbles around the screen, and the screener *rolls* (cuts) to the basket for a pass or a rebound. To become effective at running pick-and-rolls, your players must know what to do when any of these tactics are used.

1. When the dribbler's defender tries to fight over the top, the screener's defender will often *hedge*, or step into the path of the dribbler so the dribbler has to hesitate, which gives her defender time to get around the screen. When the defender hedges, this is a good opportunity for the screener to roll to the basket for an open pass. The dribbler should look for this. Also, if the defender hedges more than an arm's length away

from the screener, the dribbler often has room to dribble through the opening. Another opportunity the screener should be alert for is *splitting the screen*—suddenly cutting to the basket before the screen is set.

2. When the defender goes under the screen, the dribbler should look to step back for a shot or to pass to the screener

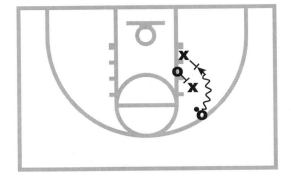

When the screener's defender hedges (top), the screener rolls to the basket (bottom).

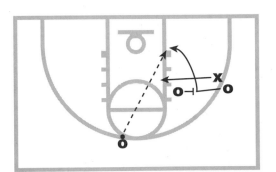

Back cut.

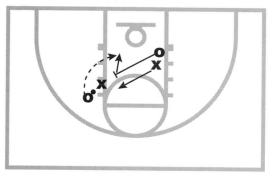

Splitting the screen.

rolling to the basket. The screener will often be open right at first, so the dribbler should be ready to pass the ball after one dribble. The screener won't be open for long.

3. When the defenders switch whom they're guarding, this is a good opportunity for passing to the screener. The screener *seals the defender* after setting the screen, which allows her to stay between the sealed defender and the ball. Sealing a player is exactly like blocking out. The player makes a reverse pivot, stays low and balanced, and keeps the opponent on her back for as long as possible. All your players should practice sealing the defender after screening.

4. When the defenders trap the player with the ball, she should look to pass to the screener, who will be wide open for a moment. Good defensive teams that trap the dribbler in pick-and-roll situations practice having another defender ready

to prevent the pass to the screener rolling to the basket. In that event, the dribbler should look to see which of her other teammates has been left open (somewhere, one of them is wide open).

Although your players will learn the basics of screening in short order, reading the defense and deciding what to do after using a screen comes only after repetition and game experience. Once your players become skilled at setting and using screens, your team will be hard to defend.

Post Play

A basketball team that has a strong inside game to complement its outside game is hard to beat. Teams that lack post players who are threats to score are easier to defend. One of your tasks is to identify players who can develop into good *posts*—power forwards and centers (4s and 5s)—and to spend sufficient time at practice for them to improve their post skills. Playing the post is different than playing a position on the perimeter.

The saying in basketball is "You can't coach height." Coaches at all levels love to have tall players on their team in hopes the players will be good rebounders and good close-to-the-basket scorers. However, not every tall player will be a good post player. Height is an asset when trying to snare a rebound, but it's only one ingredient of what makes a successful post. Desire, aggressiveness, anticipation, and technique are more important elements.

For years, Dennis Rodman led the NBA in rebounds per game, though he was "only" 6 feet

---

ASK THE COACH

Question: I have a question about screening and sealing a defender. It sounds like the player who is sealing is trying to block the defender in an illegal way, no different than holding. Why isn't this a violation of the rules?

Answer: Sealing has to be done a certain way, or it *is* a violation of the rules. As long as the player has her hands up in a pass-catching position, it's legal, no different than if she's posting up. If it looks like her only purpose is to impede the movement of the defender, or if she tries to use her hands to grab or hold the defender, that's a foul.

7 inches. That may be towering to you and me, but in terms relative to post players in the NBA, he was short. Every game, Rodman battled players who were 6 to 10 inches taller and 20 to 50 pounds heavier, and most every game, he outrebounded his opponent. He approached rebounding as a science. He studied the great rebounders like Bill Russell and Moses Malone, watched their techniques, and made it his goal to grab every missed shot at both ends of the court. He developed a knack for knowing exactly where the ball would bounce off the rim or the backboard after a miss. He knew when to time his fight for position and when to go after the ball. Your best rebounders may or may not be your tallest girls, but they'll understand the importance of blocking out and going hard after the ball every shot.

Another important factor in becoming a good post is the ability to handle and even enjoy the rough physical nature of post play. Players who don't like contact won't like playing inside. That's not to say their attitude won't change over time, but as you decide who will play the posts for you, look for players who think nothing of diving into a pile on the floor for a loose ball, players who are good at jockeying for position, and players who don't mind getting bumped and shoved. You'll find your posts in that group of players.

Girls gain control over their bodies at widely varying rates. Often, tall girls develop more slowly than short girls. It takes time before they can run without an awkward or gangly style. You can't expect them to learn back-to-the-basket moves when they have trouble making layups. Don't rush your tall kids too fast. Be extra patient with them, as they can only do so much of what you ask of them.

Most middle school coaches don't teach *post moves*, or back-to-the-basket scoring moves. Maybe they believe it's too early to teach this part of the game, or maybe, given practice time limitations, they believe other fundamentals are more important. In my view, this is a mistake. If players are old enough to learn how to play basketball, they're old enough to learn post moves. Making a post move is no more complex or difficult than shooting a jump shot. Just as you'll want to have your guards practice shooting jump shots every day, have your post players spend time every practice working on their specialties.

The right mental approach is required to be a good post player. A post should:

- want the basketball
- be aggressive
- want to score every time she touches the ball
- play without fear
- be in good basketball condition
- enjoy physical contact
- be a hard worker
- know how to communicate in the post
- be a good foul shooter
- be strong and play strong

Posting Up

There are several ways to use your post players when running your half-court offenses: to set screens for other players, to fight for offensive rebounds, and to score. Some coaches limit their posts to the first two roles, but I urge you to teach all your posts how to get open, no matter how skilled they are. Even a player who isn't athletic or smooth can learn to post up. She can learn a couple of basic scoring moves and at least draw a few fouls. She can also learn how to kick out the ball to open perimeter players when the defense collapses.

The primary technique for getting open in the low post is *posting up*. The purpose of posting up is for the offensive post to maneuver herself between her defender and the ball so the defender is behind her. The goal of the player posting up is to get the defender *on her back*—that is, shielded so she can't prevent the pass to the post.

A player can post up in the high post area as well as in the low post area. The difference is that once she gets the ball in the high post, she plays facing the basket. In the low post, after the player receives the ball, she plays with her back to the basket, which requires a different set of moves and considerations.

Most half-court offenses begin with a pass from the point to the wing. The first thing a wing player should do after receiving the ball is square up and look inside. If the post player on the near block is able to post up, this is an excellent chance to get the ball close to the basket for a high-percentage shot and perhaps a foul.

To post up, the player faces her defender with her knees bent, places one foot in between the defender's feet, and makes a reverse pivot with her arms out. As she pivots, she swings her arm into the defender's body, making contact to hold the defender in place. When she completes the pivot, her feet are wider than her shoulders, and she's low and balanced, which gives leverage to keep the defender on her back. Her arms are wide, and her elbows are wide and locked in place. Her fingers point to the ceiling,

and her palms open to the passer to let the passer know she's ready for the ball. Her goal is to have her shoulders and feet square to the passer—perpendicular to the imaginary line from her to the ball. Tell your perimeter players, "When you can read the letters on her jersey, she's open. Get her the ball. When you can't read the letters, she's not open, so don't pass it to her."

The key to posting up is making contact with the defender, or the defender can easily slide around her, in good position to deflect or steal the pass. Staying low and wide are essential to creating the leverage necessary to hold the defender in place. Tell your players to *sit on the defender's knees*. This will help them understand how low they must be. Sell your players on the concept that if you're lower than your defender, you can post up much bigger, stronger players.

This post is open (left); pass her the ball. This post is not open (right); don't pass her the ball.

Of course, post defenders aren't going to stand there and allow players to post them up. They'll fight as hard as they can to get around the player to prevent or steal the pass. As the defender tries to get around her, the post should use short choppy steps to maintain contact and keep the defender on her back. If the defender steps over one of the post's legs with her leg, the post should step over the defender's leg so she can stay in front of her. If the defender continues to step over, the post should continue to step over.

If the defender defends her on the *high side* (the side toward the free throw line), the post uses choppy steps and *walks her up the lane*. She gives a target with the hand away from the pressure. Though she's farther away from the basket than when she started, if she's able to keep the defender on her back, she's in excellent position to receive the ball for a power dribble and a layup.

If the defender defends her on the *low side* (the side toward the baseline), the post should step over the defender's leg and walk her along the baseline. If the passer sees her, she'll be open for an easy layup. Players feeding the post should always pass away from the defense—make the pass to the side opposite from where the defender is.

The post is allowed to use her arms to keep the defender on her back, but only in a certain manner. The rules prohibit her from hooking her arm around the defender or holding any part of the defender (including her jersey) with her hand. Teach your players to post up with their hands out and open, their palms facing the ball. As long as they do this, the referees will allow a lot of contact. Posts can pin their defender's arm in between their arm and their body, again, as long as their hands are outstretched and open to the ball.

Many post players post up too early or too late. Only the most accomplished post player can keep someone on her back for more than 2 or 3 seconds. If the post establishes a good post-up too early, by the time the wing is ready to make an entry pass, the defender will recover, and the post will no longer be open. If the post establishes position too late, the wing will have already passed or shot the ball, rendering the post-up useless. Practice posting up and feeding the post so your players' timing will improve.

Another mistake post players make is posting up too low—too far under the basket or too close to the baseline. Receiving the ball in these areas reduces their options when they catch the ball and places them at a poor angle for a shot. They

Players feeding the post should always pass away from defensive pressure.

As long as the offensive post player keeps her hands out and open, pinning the defender's arm is legal.

also risk the referee calling a 3-second lane violation. Posts should post up between the block and the first hash mark on the lane, outside of the paint. When they receive the ball, depending on how the defense is playing them, they'll have the option of making a baseline scoring move, a move to the middle, as well as pivoting to face the defender to shoot a jump shot.

Getting Open in the Post

Besides posting up, there are several other ways to get open in the post. The first (and best) way is to beat the other team's post players down the floor. After gaining possession of the ball, your team should always sprint down the court, looking for fast-break chances. Sometimes, teams develop the mind-set that a fast break is meant only for the guards, and that if the guards can't score an easy basket, the team

should pass the ball back up top to set up the half-court offense. Teams that understand that posts are very much part of fast breaks often get high-percentage shots close to the basket.

Your posts should practice sprinting hard to the opposite basket every time the team steals the ball or gets a defensive rebound. The first post down the court should run down the middle of the floor, looking over her shoulder for a pass. If she doesn't receive one, she should cut to the ball-side block, midway up the lane line, and call for the ball. Posts who do this will often find themselves wide open for several easy baskets a game.

A second way to get open in the post is to use the same V-cut and swim move players use to get open on the perimeter (see page 60). Assume the post is on the help-side block. If the defender plays her low—positioned near the baseline—the post cuts to the defender's baseline side, taking her even lower. She plants her foot nearest the baseline, makes a swim move, and cuts hard to the ball-side block. If she succeeds in faking out her defender, she'll be in a great position to receive the ball. If the defender plays her on the high side, the post cuts toward the free throw line, taking the defender higher. She then plants her high-side foot, makes a swim move, and cuts hard for the ball-side block. Again, if she makes a good fake, she'll be open for a pass.

A third way is to use the *spin-and-pin move*. This is similar to the basic post-up move and starts with the post facing the defender. She pretends that she's setting a screen, arms in front of her chest, and makes contact with the defender. Then, she makes a quick reverse pivot, maintaining contact, and spins to face the ball, putting the defender on her back.

A fourth way to get open is the *go-away-and-come-back move*. If the post is on the ball-side block but can't get open, she can *go away* from the ball (walk toward the other side of the lane for two or three steps, pretending she's no longer trying to post up on the ball-side block). As the defender follows, the post suddenly spins and cuts hard back to where she started. If she catches the defender off guard, she'll be open for an easy score.

Question: You recommend teaching all my players how to post up, but I don't get why. What good does it do to teach my guards how to post up when they're always out on the perimeter?

Answer: If you coach a middle school or an AAU team, I agree. The practice time is too limited, and there's too little time to teach skills as it is. However, if you coach a high school team and practice five to six days a week, you have the time to teach posting up to all your players. Having your guards know how to post up can be an effective tool in your half-court man-to-man offenses, particularly if you have strong, aggressive guards. Isolating these players in the low post and getting them the ball can mean easy baskets or fouls. You'll be surprised how effective a guard posting her defender up can be, because few coaches teach their guards how to play post defense. You should also teach your guards how to defend the low post because, as sure as sneakers squeak, some of the teams you play will have their guards posting up.

Teach all your players to post up, but don't teach them too many post moves. If you coach younger players, I'd teach only one post move that they can use on either side of the basket. If you coach a high school or advanced AAU team, pick at most two post moves to teach and leave it at that. If all your posts learn is how to post up, they'll be hard to defend 1-on-1.

Lastly, every time a post scores off a good pass from a perimeter player, she should point to the passer, acknowledging the assist. This small gesture recognizes unselfish play and fosters team unity.

Catching the Ball in the Low Post

Encourage your posts to *demand the ball,* to call for it with their hands and their voices. When a post gets open, she should yell her teammate's name or "Ball, ball!" and hold her arms out. Her hands should face the ball with the fingers pointing to the ceiling. As the ball is in the air, the post makes a short two-foot jump stop so that when her feet land on the floor, she can use either foot as her pivot foot. The passer should aim the ball at the post player's chest. Unless the post is wide open and her defender is directly behind, the pass should be a bounce pass.

After the post catches the ball, she *chins* it, just like when she grabs a defensive rebound. She brings the ball under her chin with both hands, sticks out her elbows, and squeezes the ball. Chinning the ball protects it and prevents

a defender from grabbing the ball or knocking it out of her hands.

Next, the post *reads the defense.* She pauses for a split second to peek over her shoulder. Is her defender favoring the low side, the high side, or right behind her? Is there another defender behind her ready to stop a move to the middle? Is a guard dropping down from the wing to trap her? Is one of her teammates wide open for an easy jump shot? Is the player who passed her the ball cutting to the basket for an easy give-and-go situation?

Too many post players rush when they get the ball. They don't take a moment to see where the defenders are, and they end up trying to make a scoring move that isn't open, resulting in a bad shot or a turnover. When they hurry, they don't recognize when they're double-teamed and when they should kick out the ball to an open teammate. Tell your players, "Don't hurry in the post. Read the defense before you decide what to do."

Post Moves

Once the post has the ball and reads the defense, she must decide if a good post move is available and, if so, which one. As your back-to-the-basket players gain experience, this decision will become more and more instinctive.

The first post move to learn is the *getting-a-piece-of-the-paint move.* As the pass is in the air, the post steps into the lane and hooks her leg around the defender's leg. This establishes that foot as her pivot foot. She makes a forward pivot with the other foot and spins to face the basket, ready to shoot the ball. Which foot she steps with into the lane depends on how the defender is playing her.

The next move is the *turnaround jump shot*. The post catches the ball, makes a forward pivot so she faces the basket, and shoots a jump shot. This move is most effective when set up with a fake as if the post intends to move in the other direction. If the post wants to pivot toward the baseline, she first takes a small step toward the middle of the lane, looking in that direction (very important), and spins quickly the other way for the turnaround shot.

The *up-and-under move* is for advanced post players. Teach this only to players who have learned the turnaround jump shot move. The up-and-under move starts out like a turnaround jump shot. However, instead of shooting, the post player pump fakes, steps toward the basket with her nonpivot foot, and finishes with a layup.

One of the most effective post moves is the *drop step*. Assume the player has posted up on the right-side block and has the ball. She reads the defense and sees (and feels) her defender guarding her on the low side. She decides to drop-step to the middle. She *shows the ball* (brings it up toward her left shoulder so the defender can see it) and, at the same time, *drops* (steps with) her right leg over the defender's leg nearest the middle. As the defender leans toward the fake, the post brings the ball down in front of her body for a two-hand power dribble and pivots toward the middle for a close-in shot. Done properly, the drop step allows the post to position herself between her defender and the basket for an uncontested layup. Your posts should learn how to drop-step from both

Up-and-under move. First the up (left) and then the under (right).

Players should use a power dribble when making a drop step.

Another move is the *step-back move*. It's similar to the move you teach your perimeter players (see page 66), except it starts with the post having her back to the basket. After she reads the defense, she steps toward the basket with her closest foot. This time, instead of the power dribble and power layup, she takes one dribble toward the basket, then steps back for an open jump shot.

The last move, the *jump hook*, is partly a post move and partly a shot. This move isn't usually taught to younger players, but it's an excellent shot to use against a taller defender. Assume a post has the ball on the right-side block. She steps with her right foot toward the middle, keeping her shoulders perpendicular to a line to the basket, and brings her left foot so it's next to her right foot. The ball is in both hands in front of her left shoulder. She shoots a left-handed shot, bringing the ball up with

sides of the basket and toward the middle and the baseline (that's four offensive moves).

A move done from the high post area uses a *step-dribble-hop* and finishes with a two-hand power dribble. Assume the post catches the ball in the high post area on the right-side elbow. After she chins the ball and reads the defense, she steps toward the baseline with the low side foot (in this case, her left), makes a strong two-handed power dribble, plants her foot, and takes a big hop toward the basket, landing with both feet in a jump stop. She then lays the ball up on the backboard with both hands. This is an excellent move to use when the post has only one defender between her and the basket. Since she uses a power dribble and a power layup, this move often results in a 3-point play (the 2-point score and one free throw).

A good jump hook is impossible to block without fouling.

both hands in a straight line toward the ceiling. As her left arm extends, she snaps her wrist toward the basket, as if she's patting the top of her head. She holds her nonshooting arm up and away to protect the ball from the defender.

Emphasize to your players to use the backboard on all shots close to the basket (other than short jump shots along the baseline). Using the backboard gives the shooter an easier target to aim for and more room for error.

Emphasize the following additional principles:

- Be a scorer. Unless a player is double-teamed, she should look to score.

- Get a piece of the paint. Players should try to post up with a foot in the lane.

- Feel the defense and move toward the pressure.

- Players should maintain contact until they catch the ball.

- Players should keep their back straight and head up when making a post move.

- Make a head fake when making a shot fake.

- If a player catches the ball near the basket, she shouldn't dribble and shouldn't bring the ball low where a defender could strip it away.

- Don't be a pig in the post. If a player can't post up to get the ball, she clears out from the area.

- Above all, rebound, rebound, rebound. A player can be a good post player if she doesn't score much, but she can't be a great post player unless she's a great rebounder.

Playing the High Post

To become complete players, your posts need to know more than how to play near the basket. A back-to-the-basket player who can also play in the *high post* area will be a dangerous offensive weapon. To play the high post, your posts will need to learn how to get open. Besides posting up, posts can flash from the help side or come

High post players should square up to the basket before deciding what to do.

off down screens from the low post. As the pass is in the air, they should step into the shot (see page 49) and square up to the basket. Then they'll have some options.

The first option is the basic *jump shot*. All the fundamentals on shooting apply to all jump shots, regardless of where on the court the shooter is. If a post can consistently make an elbow jump shot, she forces her defender to guard her tightly, which creates opportunities for other moves, as well as space for teammates to drive into the low post. As a regular part of shooting drills, your posts should practice shooting from the elbows.

In the *punch dribble move*, the post quickly dribbles once, either to take advantage of an open lane or to drive by a defender who is closely guarding her, and shoots the jump shot. Posts need to learn how to do this using either

The punch dribble.

hand for the dribble. They must keep the dribble low. As the ball returns to their hand after it bounces, they don't hesitate. They continue smoothly into the shot. Practice this from both elbows. Of course, if the ball is passed from the opposite end of the court, the post will use her opposite pivot foot.

The *step-back move* is an excellent move to use in the high post area. The key is to dribble decisively at the defender so she backs up in anticipation of a drive to the basket. With the defender's momentum taking her in the direction of the basket, if the post player steps back quickly, she'll have plenty of time to set up for a well-balanced shot attempt.

The *reverse dribble move* is only for advanced post players who can handle the ball well. After the post catches the ball, she dribbles toward one side of the basket. After one or two dribbles, when the defender is backing up in one direction, the post suddenly stops, plants her

inside foot, spins in the other direction, and shoots a jump shot. As with the step-back maneuver, if this is done right, the player will have time to shoot an uncontested jump shot.

The *give-and-go move* is one my players use a lot. After receiving a pass at the high post from one wing, the post quickly passes the ball to the opposite wing, thereby reversing it, and cuts to the basket for the return pass. If the pass to the opposite wing is quick enough, the post player's defender will be momentarily out of position, and the post will be open as she heads toward the basket.

The same easy shot can be achieved on a skip pass, so let's call that the *skip-and-go move*. Assume the post player cuts to the free throw line area but isn't open. If the wing throws a skip pass over the defense, the post's defender will again be on the wrong side for a moment, creating a nice opening for the post to slice to the basket for an easy score.

The last concept of playing the high post has to do with *fake-and-drive moves*, where the post player catches the ball and fakes a pass to the right or left corner. After the defender reacts, the post pulls the ball back and drives past the defender to the other side of the basket. As with any drive within the 3-point arc, the dribbler should dribble only once, so the defender won't have enough time to recover after the fake.

As noted earlier (see pages 40–41), a successful lob pass usually means 2 points and maybe a foul. Teach your posts to set up to receive a lob pass when their defender fronts them and they're at least 6 feet from the basket. The technique is simple. Assume a post player is on the right-side block, fronted by her defender. The post turns her body so her right shoulder and right arm press against the middle of the defender's back. Her feet are perpendicular to the defender's back. As she leans into the defender to hold her in place, she raises her left arm as a target to the passer. When her teammate lobs the ball, the post doesn't move until she sees the ball directly over her head. She then releases from the defender and catches the ball in front of her with two hands, like a football

This post player puts her shoulder into the defender's back to hold her in place (left) and waits for the ball to be overhead before releasing the defender (right).

receiver catching a pass. If the pass is thrown right, the post will have an easy layup.

Post play is a key part of the game. It should be on your list of core aspects you practice every day.

Handling Traps

A *trap* occurs when two defenders guard an offensive player by forming a V with their bodies and preventing her from dribbling. The best way to handle a trap is to avoid it. The player with the ball should have her eyes up, seeing what the defense is doing at all times. If she sees a trap coming at her, she should pass to an open player before the trap is set or dribble away from it (this is where the pull-back dribble comes in handy). Offensive players should

realize that traps represent opportunities: if two players are guarding one player, someone somewhere is wide open.

When a player is trapped, she shouldn't panic (this only comes with practice and experience). She pivots forcefully and rips the ball in a wide range of positions. Too many players pivot timidly, using small steps and swinging the ball a short distance. This restricts their options and allows the defenders to tie up the ball or even strip it from the offensive player's hands.

As the player pivots, she looks for her teammates, who should be working hard to get open for a pass. One of them should approach from the point of the V made by the defenders. When she does, the player with the ball should *split the trap*—step in between the defenders

Splitting the trap.

with her nonpivot foot, putting her head, shoulders, and arms between their bodies, and pass the ball. This maneuver allows her to make the pass and sometimes draws a foul from one of the defenders.

Individual Defense

Regardless of the type of team defense you decide to play, there are certain principles about individual defense you should preach to your players. If they buy into them, they'll be well on their way to becoming a strong defensive team.

Defense wins games. Most coaches understand that good defense (rebounding is part of good defense) is the foundation for winning games. If you have good offensive players who can score, consider yourself lucky. However, basketball is a fickle game—sometimes the shots go in and sometimes they don't, and nothing you or the players do can change that fact. While you can't depend on your offense to outscore the other team, you can depend on your defense to keep the other team from scoring too many points. If you make it hard for the other team to score, your team can compete in every game.

Anyone can play good defense. A player doesn't need to have great skill, athletic ability, or experience to become a good defender. Defense is 10 percent technique, 10 percent smarts, and 80 percent sweat. Any girl on your team can learn to play good defense. It starts with her making it a goal and working hard at it.

The defense never rests. Playing defense requires nonstop energy and intensity. The instant a team relaxes on defense, the offense finds an easy shot. Even if the offensive team is patient with the ball (most aren't), your players should never stop working hard on defense. Eventually, someone on offense will lose patience and force a bad pass or a bad shot. If your high school league uses a shot clock, the clock becomes your ally as the seconds run out. If you can motivate your players to play defense with high energy for as long as your opponent has the ball, your team will be tough to score on.

Know where the ball and your man are at all times. Some players focus only on the player they're guarding. They follow this player all over the court, sticking to her like glue, and lose track of the ball. This results in them not being available to help their teammates when the defense breaks down. Other players focus so much on where the ball is that they lose sight of their man. This results in their man getting open for easy shots. Coaches say "See ball, see man" for good reason.

Keep moving. Playing good defense means being in good position. Staying in good position means constantly making adjustments. A defender rarely stands in one spot for more than an instant. Every time the ball moves or her man moves, she changes her position. If the movement is slight, she makes a small adjustment. If the movement is large, she makes a large adjustment. She also changes the way she guards her man, depending on where her man is in relation to the ball.

Play defense with your feet. When players get tired, they tend to stop moving their feet as much as they did early in the game. They start standing around, playing defense with their arms and hands, which allows offensive players open passing and driving lanes, as well as uncontested shots. Defenders who don't move their feet get beat and aren't in position to play help-side defense. They're easy to spot—they wave their arms as dribblers go by, they commit unnecessary reaching fouls, they arrive too late to get in front of a player driving for a layup, and they commit blocking fouls. If you see a player playing *lazy defense*—not moving her feet on defense—it's time to take her out of the game for a rest. She's either physically or mentally tired.

Have active hands. The role of a defender's hands is to *stay active*—to move constantly and try to distract the player with the ball. Defenders with active hands poke the ball away from dribblers and *deflect* the ball (tip it with their hand, causing it to change direction). Deflections are an underrated statistic. They often result in the defender's team gaining possession of the ball. Everyone notices players who get steals, but not many people notice players who consistently deflect the ball. Deflections are as important to good defense as assists are to good offense.

Anticipate. Great defenders have great anticipation. They sense when and where a pass will go, that the dribbler is about to make a crossover move, that the passer is about to attempt a lob, that their man is about to make a backdoor cut, and that the wing player is about to cut for a give-and-go after feeding the post. This is partly due to *court savvy* (basketball intelligence), partly due to good instincts, and partly due to experience. It's easy to talk about anticipation, but hard to teach it.

Take away what your man does best. As a game progresses, it will become apparent which player on the other team is the most dangerous offensive threat (ideally, if you're a high school coach, you've scouted the team and won't have to wait until you're behind by 15 points to learn this). The defender assigned to guard her tries to keep her from touching the ball. When the offensive player has the ball, the defender tries to make it hard for her to do her favorite thing. If an offensive player likes to shoot, the defender guards her closely and make her put the ball on the floor. If the player likes to drive, the defender plays off of her to try to prevent a drive.

Don't "get beat." The top priority of every defender is to prevent easy scores—shots close to the basket. It's far preferable to let a player shoot from 15 feet away than it is to give her a layup.

Drop to the basket. When the ball enters the lane, all five defenders drop to the basket—leave their man or area to protect the basket. The goal is to force the ball out to the perimeter. When that happens, the defenders return to their proper positions.

Talk on defense. No player has eyes at the back of her head. There are five offensive players on the court, each doing something at the same time, some far away from the other players. It's impossible for one defender to know what all the offensive players are doing. Good teams communicate on defense (and offense) all the time. The players let each other know when an offensive player does something they should know about. Emphasize the importance of communication. Teach your players words and phrases to use when playing defense:

"Shot!" alerts everyone to block out for the rebound.

"Cutter!" tells everyone that someone is trying to get open in the lane and that she should be bumped (see pages 93–94).

"Screen!" warns the defender that she's about to be screened, which allows her time to decide what to do and helps her avoid colliding with the screener.

"Ball!" tells the other four players that a player is taking responsibility for stopping the player with the ball so they can focus on other offensive players. This is essential when the other team is running a fast break.

"Wing!" tells the other four players that the player is guarding an offensive player cutting down the sidelines.

"Dead!" tells everyone that the dribbler has picked up her dribble and that here's a great opportunity to steal a pass being made under pressure.

These are some of the basic words and phrases teams use on defense. You will no doubt add others to this list.

Never ever give up on the play. Until the ball goes in the basket, there's always a chance to stop the offense. A lazy defender, seeing her man dribbling ahead of her on the way to a surefire layup, stops playing defense. She stands and watches the player miss the layup, get her own rebound, and make the next shot. If the defender had continued pursuing her, maybe she wouldn't have been able to stop the first layup attempt, but she would have been in position to prevent the next one. Her assumption that the play was over cost her team 2 points.

Use man-to-man principles. It's important to teach your players man-to-man defensive principles, even if you plan to play zone, because the principles apply to all defenses. If you don't, your players will be passive and confused when playing zone offense. They'll think they're guarding a space on the floor instead of guarding players who are in that space, they won't understand the difference between guarding someone near the ball and someone far from the ball, and they won't know how to help when a teammate gets in trouble. In other words, without learning man-to-man principles, your players won't know how to play good team defense.

Types of Individual Defense

There are three basic ways a defender plays defense, depending on where her player is in relation to the ball: on-ball defense, denial defense, and help-side defense. Each of these has different techniques, stances, and guidelines.

Before understanding how to teach each of these defenses, you must understand the difference between the *ball-side* half of the court and the *help-side* half of the court (the latter is also called the *weak side*). Imagine a line that runs from the basket, bisecting the lane area, to the center of the midcourt line. This is the *ball-side/help-side* line. If the ball is anywhere to the left of the line, as viewed from midcourt, that half of the court is the ball side, and the other half is the help side.

Defenders must understand this concept to know which kind of defense to play. If they guard the player with the ball, regardless of where the player is, they play *on-ball defense*. If they guard someone who is on the ball side, but who doesn't have the ball, they play *denial defense*. If they

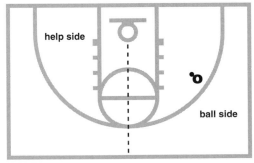

Ball side and help side.

guard someone who is on the help side, they play *help-side defense*. These concepts also apply to man-to-man full-court defense.

On-Ball Defense. On-ball defense occurs when a defender guards the player with the ball 1-on-1. The stance used is similar to the *ready stance*.

The defender's feet are spread slightly more than shoulder-width apart, her knees are bent, her back is straight, her head is centered over the body, her arms are out from her body, and her palms point up. One foot should be positioned ahead of the other 6 to 8 inches, depending on which way she wants to force the player with the ball. If she wants the player to dribble to her left (to the defender's right), her left foot should lead. If she wants to force the player to dribble to her right (the defender's left), she should lead with her right foot. Most players are right-handed, which means they are less skilled in dribbling with their left hands. Most of the time, when the dribbler is at the top of the circle, the defender should force the dribbler to go to her left. When the ball is on one of the wings, however, it depends on your defensive philosophy—do you want them to *fan the ball* (force it toward the sidelines) or *funnel the ball* (force it toward the middle)? This determines how your wing defenders will set their defensive position.

The on-ball defender positions herself between the offensive player and the basket at an arm's length. If the offensive player is quicker than the defender, the defender might need to back up a bit so the dribbler can't drive by her. If the offensive player is slower than the defender, or isn't a good ball handler, the defender should stand closer to pressure her more.

In a proper defensive stance, the defender can react instantly to the offensive player. The footwork used is a *step-slide* motion where the first foot steps in the intended direction and the second foot slides until the feet are the same distance apart again. If the offensive player backs up, the defender uses an *advance step*. The lead foot steps toward the player and the back foot slides forward. In a *retreat step* the opposite happens. The back foot first steps back from the offensive player and the lead foot slides in place. When the defender wants to switch her lead foot, she takes a *swing step*—does a reverse pivot by swinging her lead foot back until it's 6 to 8 inches behind the new lead foot.

This on-ball defender forces the right-handed dribbler to use her left hand.

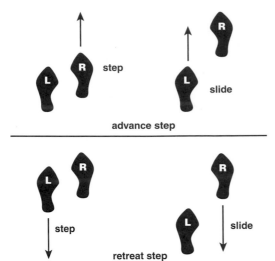

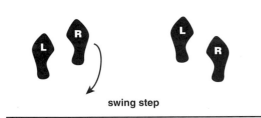

Advance, retreat, and swing steps.

When a defender guards a dribbler, she uses the same step-slide motion to stay in front of her. If the dribbler is dribbling to the defender's right, the defender pushes off with her left foot, steps with her right foot, and slides her left foot quickly so she's in the defensive stance again. As she step-slides, her arms remain wide, her palms up, and she should point her right foot in the direction she's headed. She shouldn't cross her feet, or she'll get tangled up, and she shouldn't take very long steps.

The defender's lead hand is waist high, palm up, and ahead of the ball to discourage a pass. If the dribbler is sloppy about protecting the ball, the defender can try to poke it away, being sure to keep her palm up. If she swats at the ball in a downward motion, even if she doesn't touch the offensive player, the referee is likely to blow the whistle. The defender's other hand is knee high, ready in case the dribbler

crosses over. The alert defender can deflect the ball as it hits the floor.

The defender's primary goal is to stay between the dribbler and the basket. She shouldn't lunge too far to try to poke at the ball, pulling herself out of balance and out of the play. Good ball handlers will quickly take advantage of defenders who commit themselves too much. The defender should have good balance at all times, making it difficult for the dribbler to dribble where she wants to dribble, to pass where she wants to pass, and to shoot. She stays in her low defensive stance unless one of three things happens:

The offensive player drives by her. In this case, the defender must get out of her defensive stance, turn, and sprint to catch up with the player. If the dribbler is far away enough from the basket, the defender will have time to run to a spot in the dribbler's path. The defender should be careful not to foul the dribbler as she tries to catch up (unless her team is in a must-foul situation).

The offensive player picks up her dribble. Now the defender doesn't have to worry about getting beat on the dribble. She immediately closes in on the offensive player and goes belly-to-belly with her, trying to distract the player and disrupt her court vision. Her hands *mirror* (or *trace*) *the ball*—they follow the ball as the offensive player pivots. She must not swipe at the ball. She might be able to knock the ball away, but more likely, she'll be called for a reaching foul. When she's forced the player to pick up her dribble, she's done only part of her job. The rest of her job is to force the player to make a bad pass or get a 5-second call.

The offensive player passes the ball. The defender immediately *jumps to the ball*—switches immediately from an on-ball stance to a denial stance when her man passes the ball. She jumps toward the ball several feet, not just slightly. If she remains facing the player or doesn't jump far enough, her man will cut to the basket for an easy return pass.

When the offensive player raises the ball to shoot, the defender must *contest the shot*. If the player hasn't dribbled yet, the defender extends

Mirroring the ball makes it hard for the offensive player to pass.

her lead arm (the one on the side of her lead foot) to distract the shooter and impair her vision of the basket. She stays low, her knees bent, still ready to prevent the drive. Savvy offensive players are only too ready to drive by her in a flash if she raises up in her stance. She must stay low and not react to shot fakes.

If the offensive player has picked up her dribble, the defender no longer is concerned about defending the dribble, so she immediately goes belly-to-belly with the player, raising her hands to discourage the shot and obscure the shooter's vision, but she keeps her arms straight up (see photos page 90). Inexperienced players think they should jump up and try to block the shot and end up swatting down at the ball. This is a foul, which bails the offensive player out of a bad situation. Referees are often out of position to see whether the defender's hand only touched the ball or hacked the shooter's arm. Tell your players to assume that if they don't keep their arms straight up, they'll get called for a foul even if they made a clean block.

Denial Defense. When a defender guards a player who is one pass away from the ball, she plays *denial defense*—she *denies* the player from receiving a pass.

Contesting the shot when the player with the ball can still dribble.

Assume the ball is at the top of the circle and the defender is guarding a player on the left wing, as viewed from the basket. The defender stands in the *denial stance*, a three-quarters-closed stance to the ball. Her back is at a 45-degree angle to the ball and the basket. Her nearest arm is out and in the passing lane. Her palm faces the player with the ball. She holds her other arm out, chest high, bent at a 90-degree angle to the player (this is called an *arm bar*). Her nearest foot is also in the passing lane. Her other foot is closer to the basket than the offensive player's feet. If the offensive player is close to the ball (12 feet or less), the defender is within 3 feet of her. If the offensive player is farther from the ball, the defender is farther away from her (5 to 6 feet). All the time, she's low, knees bent, ready to react to the player's movement, and she's looking over her shoulder at the passer. Inexperienced defenders look at their man and lose sight of the ball. Teach your players that this isn't necessary. Even looking over their shoulder, they can use their peripheral vision to see where their man is. In this position, if a pass is thrown, the defender can bat it away with her hand (that's why the palm faces the ball) and can pick it up for the steal.

Contesting the shot after the player with the ball has used her dribble.

Active hands deflect passes.

Denial stance.

If the player tries to cut to the ball, the defender moves her foot to stay in the denial position. She *bumps the cutter* (see pages 93–94). If the player cuts away from the ball, the defender stays with her, using a step-slide motion, keeping her hand up and staying low the whole time. If the player gets more than one pass away from the ball, the defender switches to a help-side stance (see next section). If the player makes a back cut to the basket, the defender uses a step-slide motion, pushing off on the foot nearest to the ball. To see the ball, she must turn her head quickly, now looking at it over the other shoulder. The defender will be ready to defend if the cutter goes through the lane to the other side.

This player is doing a great job defending the back cut.

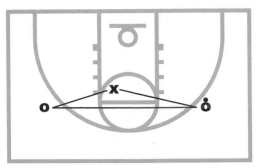

Help-side defensive triangle. The defender can easily see her man and the ball.

One of the elementary defensive drills to practice is Wing Denial (Drill 54).

Help-Side Defense. Help-side defense occurs when the defender guards a player two passes away from the ball—her player is on the help-side half of the court.

The help-side stance is different than the on-ball stance and the denial stance. The defender stands in an *open stance* (also called the *pistol stance*), her feet apart, her body balanced, her knees bent, and her arms out. She points her hands (this is the pistol part), one at her man and the other at the ball, which helps her know where both are at the same time. She stands where she can easily see the ball and her man by using peripheral vision or turning her head quickly. The spot where she's standing will form a shallow-angled triangle with her man and the ball. Her body is square to the other basket, ready to move when either her man or the ball moves.

When a defender plays help-side defense, her primary responsibility is to make sure the player with the ball can't drive into the lane for a good shot if she beats her defender. This dictates where she stands. If the player with the ball is above the free throw line extended, the help-side defender stands with one foot in the paint—again, always able to see her man and the ball. If the player with the ball is below the free throw line extended, the help-side defender stands in the middle of the lane, straddling the ball-side/help-side line. The defender is deep enough in the lane so that if the player with the ball suddenly dribbles to the basket, the defender can stop her from entering the lane.

Closing out. When a defender plays help-side defense and the player with the ball passes it to her man, the defender must sprint to get in good defensive position. This is called *closing out* on the offensive player. Many defenders close out incorrectly. They either run right at the player, taking the wrong angle, and allow the player to drive by. Or, they run at the player in an upright position, waving their arms excitedly. The savvy offensive player waits for the right moment and drives by them with ease. The defenders' forward momentum doesn't allow them to recover in time.

Closing out properly is easy to learn. First, the defender runs to a spot where she thinks the offensive player is headed (if the offensive player is standing still, the defender runs straight at her). Second, the defender sprints only part of the way. When she's 6 to 8 feet away from the player, she lowers her body, gets in the on-ball stance, and uses short choppy steps (advance steps) the rest of the way. Her lead hand is up to discourage the shot. Her

Help-side stance.

weight is on the back of her feet, not the front. She expects the drive and is ready to react to it. She's in perfect position to step-slide in front of the dribbler and maybe draw a charge. She doesn't jump up to try to block the shot. She'll either foul, or once she's off her feet, the offensive player will drive by her. Closing out properly is a matter of being in control, ready to react to anything the offensive player does.

Bumping the cutter. When an offensive player on the help-side cuts into the lane, she becomes an immediate scoring threat. If she's allowed to catch the ball, she'll shoot a high-percentage shot. Good defensive teams

Closing out. Players who sprint to close out . . .

. . . will be ready to play tough on-ball defense.

don't allow cutters to enter into the paint without a fight. Your defenders should make it hard for anyone to cut into the lane. They should *bump the cutter*—step in front of her and keep her from going where she wants to go.

Yes, bumping means making contact with the player. However, there's a way to do it that's within the rules and not a foul. The key is to understand the concept that the defender has as much right to be on a certain spot as the offensive player does. If the defender beats the offensive player to the spot, no foul exists. The first point to teach is that the defender should arrive at the cutter's destination before the cutter does.

The second point is to make contact properly. As the cutter approaches, the defender holds out her arm bar and assumes the denial stance. An offensive player in the lane, being in the center of the half court, is one pass away from the ball no matter where the ball is. As the cutter arrives, the defender steps in front of her in the denial stance, low and balanced, making contact with her arm bar against the player's chest. She should be careful not to push with her arm or grab with her hand, which are both fouls. As long as she keeps her arm bar stiff, she's allowed to make contact. She tries to force

the cutter away from the ball. If the cutter continues through the lane, the defender stays with her, continuing to bump her, keeping her arm and her leg in the passing lane.

Players trying to screen should be bumped, when possible. So much of team offense depends on exact timing. If cutters and screeners are delayed for a second or forced to alter their paths slightly, this will usually disrupt the offense.

Not enough coaches emphasize bumping the cutter. Teams that play man-to-man should always bump cutters coming from the help side. This shouldn't be hard because every defender has an assigned player, so no one should be caught off guard. Teams that play zone, however, have a harder time bumping the cutters, because the defenders aren't assigned specific players to guard. Also, by nature, zones have gaps and holes that attract cutters. For both reasons, if you play zone defense, teach your players to communicate and bump the cutters. A zone defense that doesn't see or bump cutters will give up some easy points.

Trapping. A trap occurs when two defenders converge on the player with the ball so the player can no longer dribble. The players form

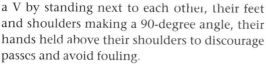

Players shouldn't let their man cut to the ball without bumping the cutter!

The player with the ball is trapped and in trouble.

a V by standing next to each other, their feet and shoulders making a 90-degree angle, their hands held above their shoulders to discourage passes and avoid fouling.

Traps can happen anywhere on the court, but several spots are ideal for trapping (see diagram page 96). When the defenders trap along one of the court boundary lines (the sideline, the baseline, or the midcourt line after the ball has been advanced over it), the line becomes an extra defender, reducing her options. When the defenders trap the player in a corner formed by two lines (the baseline corners or the corner formed by the midcourt line and the sideline), the two lines act as two extra defenders. Teams that press like to trap players in the far corners and along the sidelines, partly to force a bad pass, but also to delay the advancement of the ball and cause a 10-second backcourt call.

Trapping can occur out of man-to-man defense and zone defense, notably the 1-2-2 and 1-3-1 zones, though all zones offer trapping possibilities. Good defensive teams use traps to force turnovers, ratchet up the tempo, create confusion, and disrupt what the offense is trying to do. If your team has quick and aggressive players, make trapping a staple of your defense. If the other team has shaky ball handlers, have your players trap them as often as possible.

Post Defense. Playing defense in the low post is different from playing defense away from the basket (including the high post area), because the offensive player plays with her back to the basket.

When the ball is at the top of the circle, the post defender uses a denial stance, guarding on the high side, because her man is one pass

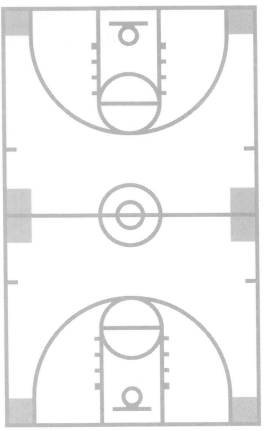

Ideal trapping areas.

Defending behind the post.

away. When the ball is at the ball-side wing, the post defender can play the offensive post one of four ways:

Behind. The defender can guard the post from directly behind, her body between the offensive player and the basket. This is a conservative approach, because it allows the wing player to pass the ball easily to the post. The advantage is the post will have to shoot over the defender to score. If the defender is taller than the offensive post, this might be a good tactic, but if the post is no taller than her counterpart, this won't be effective.

On the low side. In this case, the defender is in the three-quarters-closed denial stance with her back to the near corner. The advantage of this tactic is that if the offensive post gets the ball, she won't be able to make a

baseline move and will have to make a move to the middle, where (in theory) help defense is waiting. This works well against right-handed posts who like to drop-step toward the baseline but doesn't work well against left-handed (or ambidextrous) posts.

On the high side. The defender is in the denial stance, but with her back facing the free throw line. This works well against a good passing post who likes to kick the ball out to the opposite wing or to the player at the point. The disadvantage is it gives a good right-handed player an opening to use her strong-hand move. Your defender should play her man on the low side when the ball moves from the wing to the corner area.

In front. This is called *fronting* the post. The defender stands directly in between the

Defending the post on the low side.

offensive post and the ball, with her back to the post, low and wide, her arms out, trying to push the post closer to the basket. It's like posting up, except her hands are up to discourage the lob, not as targets for the pass. The advantage of fronting is that it's difficult to complete a pass, and the only pass that will work is the lob. Fronting won't work, however, if the offensive post is much taller than her defender. Also, if the post is stronger than the defender, she'll be able to push the defender away from the basket, making the lob pass more likely.

When the ball enters the lane, all five defenders should drop to help. If the offensive post is an excellent player and too much for one player to handle, double-team her when she touches the ball. In addition to everyone dropping (or *sagging*) toward the basket, designate a player to *double down* if the post catches the ball. It can be the ball-side wing defender,

Defending the post on the high side.

Fronting the low post.

the point defender, or the help-side wing defender. Don't let a good low post scorer take shots at will. Make her pass the ball, even if it's to a perimeter player who is wide open. If the game is near the end, and your team has *fouls to give* (the other team isn't in the bonus), foul the low post so she misses the shots and has to earn her points from the line. You'll find that post players who are unstoppable terrors near the basket are often poor shooters from the free throw line. Shaquille O'Neal (currently with the Miami Heat) is a prime example of this.

Chapter 3

TEAM OFFENSE

Principles of Team Offense

Basketball coaches have so many offenses to choose from that they're often unsure of what to do. In this chapter, I present a few simple offenses and a few advanced offenses. If you're interested in considering other options, they're available in the dozens of books and tapes you can buy. The key is to choose an offense based on the strengths and weaknesses of your team. Choose an offense suited to the abilities, tendencies, and experience of your players.

Coaches sometimes are overly concerned about what offense is the "best." They become enamored with the offense used by the last NBA or NCAA champion, thinking that it will make their team unstoppable. They forget that it's more important to run an offense well than which offense it is. These coaches overload their players with too many X's and O's. It takes time to learn and hone any offense, so keep things simple. Resist the temptation to add things just because this or that famous coach runs it. You coach young kids, not college or professional players. I can't overemphasize this

enough: the simpler you keep things, the more your team will accomplish.

If you coach a Varsity high school team, the most you should teach is the following:

- two man-to-man offenses
- three special man-to-man plays (designed to get the ball to your best players)
- two zone offenses (one for *one-guard fronts*, one for *two-guard fronts*— explained on pages 113 and 115–18)
- three special zone plays
- two press offenses (one for zone, one for man)
- one delay offense
- one sideline play (with multiple options)
- four baseline out-of-bounds plays (two for man, two for zone)
- two last-second plays (one for 1 to 3 seconds left, one for 5 to 10 seconds left)

Note: This is the *most* you should teach, and only if you coach a high school team with

Question: I coach a middle school team with mainly beginners. What is the minimum number of offenses I should teach?

Answer: One offense for man and two for zones (one-man front and two-man front), two special plays (one for zone, one for man), one sideline play, and two baseline out-of-bounds plays (one for man, one for zone). Use one of your primary offenses as your delay offense and one of your special plays as your last-second play.

experienced players who have been in your system before. If you coach a JV team, ratchet this number back, and if you coach middle school, ratchet it back significantly.

Regardless of what offenses you decide to run, the following principles apply to every offense:

Spacing. Good offensive spacing spreads out the defense, so one defender can't guard more than one player at a time. As mentioned earlier, the ideal passing distance between offensive players is 12 to 15 feet. If the distance

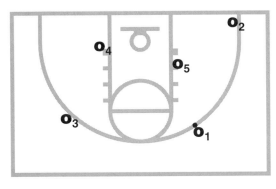

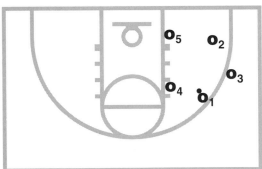

Good offensive spacing (top) spreads the defense. Bad offensive spacing (bottom) clogs the court.

is shorter, there are too many defenders in a small area, which clogs the court and makes it difficult for the player with the ball to find room to pass, shoot, or drive. If the distance is longer, the pass is riskier. The ball is in the air too long, allowing a good defender the chance for a steal or a deflection. Remember—good spacing means good offense, and good offense means good spacing.

Player movement. Four players standing around watching the dribbler is like no offense. A player who stands still is easy to guard and will rarely touch the ball. Good offensive players don't stand still unless they're wide open or setting screens. The four players without the ball should always be moving. They're cutting toward the ball, cutting to set screens, cutting to use screens, cutting to open spots, or cutting to replace themselves. Random movement has little value. Just as it's important to dribble with a purpose, it's important to move with a purpose.

Patience. Inexperienced players tend to play too fast. They dribble without a purpose, they pass before the receiver is open, they cut before the passer is ready to throw the ball, they don't wait for the screener, and they shoot before they're squared up. Good players play fast, but they don't rush. It takes time for players to learn to play with patience on offense. Emphasize it from the start.

Take what the defense gives you. This concept is basic to all offenses. The purpose of offense is to break down the defense, to find holes, seams, and weaknesses that players can exploit. Playing good defense is hard work. Most teams can do it for 15 to 20 seconds, but if you make them play defense for 30 seconds, the defense breaks down. Defenders tire of changing positions and don't move their feet as fast as they should. They get lazy, thinking they don't need to slide all the way back to where they just were. If the players on offense are patient enough, even when there's a shot clock, on most possessions, they'll have a chance for a high-percentage shot.

Shot selection. No matter what the offense is, your players must strive to take *good shots* (high-percentage shots), not *bad shots* (low-percentage shots). The primary goal of every offense is to attack the defense until someone has a good shot opportunity. Learning what differentiates a good shot from a bad one is a key component of achieving that goal. When you run your half-court offenses in practice, praise good shot selection.

Ball reversal. Ball reversal occurs when a team passes the ball from one side of the court to the other (from one wing to the other). Too many teams play offense in only one quarter of the court (half of the half-court area). Adding to their predictability, they play only in the right quarter (as viewed from the top of the circle), because most point guards are right-handed. As soon as the point guard dribbles to the top of the circle, she passes to the right wing or dribbles to the right wing, each and every possession throughout the game. This makes the defenders' jobs easy. Defenders don't need to worry about any other options and can cheat over to that side. Predictable offense is bad

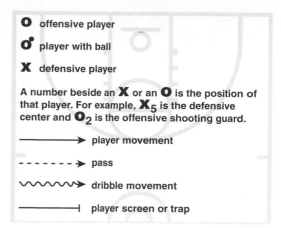

Diagram key.

offense. Playing only in one quarter of the court is bad offense. Ball reversal is good offense. It makes the defense move and shift, which creates openings and gaps. Practice ball reversal every time you practice half-court offense. Have your point guard initiate the offense by going to the left side as much as she goes to the right. Have the team practice ball reversal by passing to the point, by passing to the high post, and by using a *skip pass* (a pass from one wing to the other).

Offensive balance. Teams that always shoot from the outside or teams that always pass to a post player are one-dimensional. One-dimensional teams are easy to defend. Avoid these tendencies. Even if you have a star player who is clearly your best player, don't fall into

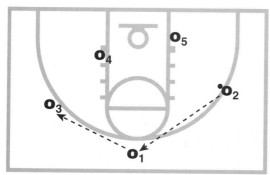

A. Ball reversal through the point.

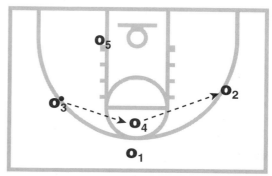

B. Ball reversal through the high post.

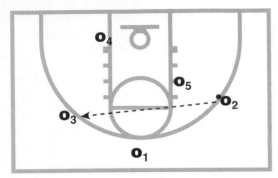

C. Ball reversal using a skip pass.

the trap of being a *one-man team*. One-man teams struggle because the defense knows exactly where to put their best defenders. On one-man teams, the other offensive players tend to stand around and watch the star try to score. Have a few special plays geared to your star, but as a rule, make sure everyone on the floor touches the ball on offense. If the defense double-teams the star, someone is wide open for a pass. Practice double-team situations so the star learns to find and pass to the open player. Make sure the ball goes inside to the post players as well as to the perimeter players. Watch that everyone on the perimeter and in the high post area squares up to the basket and looks like an offensive threat.

Inside-outside balance. This is a corollary to the previous point. The best teams score points in the lane and from the perimeter. This forces the defenders to play *honest defense*. The defenders can't *pack the lane* (drop back so they're all close to the basket), because if they do, the offensive team will score easy jump shots. They can't come out too far to guard the

perimeter players, because the team will make easy passes to the posts for close-in shots. Part of good offensive balance is having a good *inside-outside game*.

Transition opportunities. When a team switches from defense to offense (for example, on a steal or a rebound), this is called *transition offense* or *fast-break offense*. The easiest way to score is when your players beat the other team down the court for a layup. Even if you don't have fast players, your team should practice a fast-break offense. When one of your players gains possession of the ball, she should immediately look up the court, and her teammates should sprint for the other basket (how to run the fast break is covered on pages 120–24). Who knows . . . the extra two baskets your team scores in transition just might be the difference in a close game.

Safety. Regardless of what offense you're in, at least one player (usually the point guard) should be at the top of the circle to serve as a *safety*, a player whose job is to be ready to sprint back and stop the other team from scoring on a fast break. If you're playing against a team that plays good transition offense, particularly if their players run faster than yours, designate two players to be safeties.

Continuities and Set Plays

A *continuity offense* is a specific sequence of player and ball movement that repeats itself until a high-percentage shot is created. If your league has a shot clock, obviously your team will have only so much time allotted for continuity action. If your league has no shot clock, a continuity offense can be run, in theory, until time runs out in the half. Because the player and ball movement is nonstop, the main advantage of a continuity is that you won't have to issue instructions from the bench. All that's needed is patience and good execution until a good scoring opportunity opens up. A secondary advantage is it provides scoring chances for all five players. This makes it hard for a defense to focus on your best players.

A *set play* is a sequence of player and ball movement that doesn't automatically repeat itself. If a set play doesn't result in a shot, the offense *resets*—players must go back to a specific alignment so they can run another play. The advantage of set plays is that you can design them to put the ball in your best players' hands where they have a good chance of scoring or getting fouled.

As seen from the list above, you should teach your team one or more continuities, along with some set plays. I've included a number of continuity offenses and set plays to choose from. Decide which ones match your players' skills and experience. If you're interested in learning about the many other offenses out there, you can find them in other books and tapes on the subject. There are dozens of offenses to choose from. You can tweak them to fit the players on your team or you can make up an offense of your own design.

Keep the following in mind as you teach team offense:

1. **Keep offense simple.** This bears repeating—if you're not careful, you'll overwhelm your players with too much information. It's better to do two things well than six things poorly.

2. **Teach offense in stages.** When teaching a new offense or a new play, start without defenders. Place your players in the designated spots and walk through everything slowly. When they get it, they can run through it at half-speed, then at game speed. Only at this point should you introduce defenders. Inexperienced players will find offenses confusing at first. Some players will catch on fast, but others won't. Just as you stress patience to them in running a half-court offense, stress patience to yourself as they learn.

3. **Reinforce the fundamentals.** As your players practice team offense, reinforce all the fundamentals. Remind them to make pass fakes, to catch the ball in a jump stop, to change speeds when they're trying to get open, to call for the ball in the post, to give a target with their hands, and so on.

4. **Correct mistakes when they happen.** Stop play to point out whenever someone makes a mistake. Don't go overboard and stop play every 10 seconds, or they'll never learn the offense, but part of your job is to correct players when they need correcting. If you wait until later to point out mistakes, the value of the lesson is gone.

Basic Plays

Over the years, several plays have become standard elements of good offense. You'll find these plays a part of some of the offenses in this book, but teach your players to use them during any offense, whenever the right situation occurs.

Give-and-go. In the simplest two-man play in the game, the *give-and-go*, a player *gives* (passes) the ball to a teammate, *goes* (cuts) to the basket, and receives the ball back from her teammate (see left diagram page 102). Opportunities for give-and-go plays happen often. Teach your players to look for give-and-go opportunities when they make a pass and their defender turns her head to watch the receiver. If the defender doesn't *jump to the ball* (see page 143), the passer should immediately cut between the defender and the ball, calling for the ball.

Backdoor play. In a *backdoor play*, a player without the ball makes a backdoor cut (takes a step away from the basket and makes a

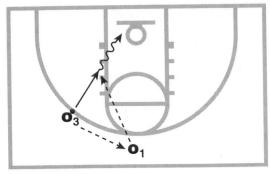

Give-and-go play.

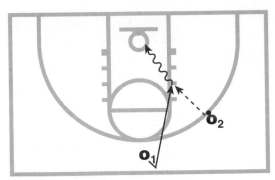

Backdoor play.

sudden cut to the basket behind the defender), and the player with the ball passes it to her. Teach your players to make backdoor cuts when their defenders overplay the passing lanes. What helps set up a successful backdoor play is for the player with the ball to make a good pass fake.

Pick-and-roll. As explained in Chapter 2, in a *pick-and-roll* a screener *picks* (screens) for the player with the ball, who dribbles around the screen, and then the screener *rolls* (cuts) to the basket for a pass or a rebound. Pick-and-roll plays have been an offensive tactic for many years. They're easy to run and hard to defend.

Isolation play. An *isolation* play is designed to get the ball to a particular player so she can play 1-on-1 against her defender. It's a good play to run when one of your players is much better than her opponent. It's also a good play to run when a defender is in foul trouble. Isolation plays involve setting one or more screens for the designated player. When she gets the ball, the other four players *clear out* (vacate her area) to leave the player on one side of the court. If their defenders decide to help, the designated player can pass to her open teammates.

Pick-and-roll. First the pick . . .

. . . and then the roll.

Man-to-Man Offense: Continuities

Give-and-Go Offense

This simple half-court offense, ideal for middle school players, is based on repeated give-and-go action and on players *filling* open spots on the floor by moving to an open spot on the perimeter when they make a cut and don't get the ball. This offense is best suited to attack man-to-man defense but works against zone defense, too.

Start this offense with your players in a *3-out, 2-in* formation. Three players start on the perimeter: 1 at the top of the circle, and 2 and 3 each at a wing. Players 4 and 5 start near the basket, each on one of the blocks. It doesn't matter which side 2 and 3 are on, or which side 4 and 5 are on, but I prefer to start 5 on the right-side block (as you face the basket) and 2 on the right-side wing.

The offense starts when 2 and 3 make V-cuts to get open, and 1 passes to one of them. Players 2 and 3 should try to get open 12 to 15 feet from 1. After passing to 2, 1 cuts to the basket for a give-and-go, looking for the pass from 2. When 3 sees 1 vacating her spot, she *fills the open spot* by replacing 1 at the top. The post player on the ball side (5) tries to post up.

If 1 doesn't receive the pass, she cuts away from the ball to the opposite wing to fill the open spot vacated by 3. Player 2 has three options:

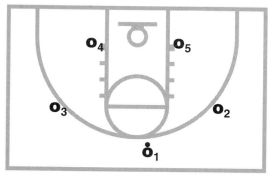

A. 3-out, 2-in formation.

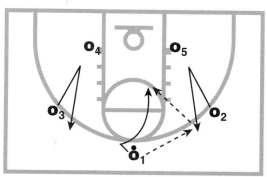

B. Initial movement in the Give-and-Go Offense.

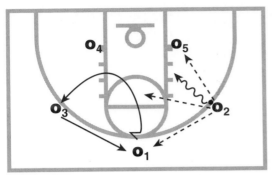

C. Options for 2 in the Give-and-Go Offense.

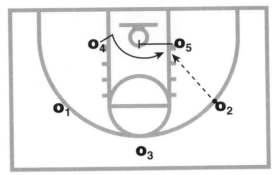

E. Cross screen in the Give-and-Go Offense.

- pass to 1
- pass to 5 posting up after 1 clears the area
- drive to the basket, if she has an opening

If 2 can't do any of these things, she passes to 3 at the top. Now 1 and 2 make V-cuts to get open. If 3 passes to 1, she cuts to the basket, looking for the return pass, while 2 replaces her at the top. The ball-side post players should post up every time the ball goes to their wing.

A variation of this offense is to have the ball-side post player set a cross screen for the help-side post once the cutter from the top has cleared out. The player on the wing with the ball should wait to see if the cross screen frees up the post before she passes back to the top.

If 2 and 3 have trouble getting open, start them in a *double low stack*, where two players stand next to each other at one of the blocks. Players 2 and 3 line up on the baseline side of a

post player, facing 1. As 1 enters the top of the circle area, 2 and 3 each use a screen by their post player to *pop out* (cut) to the wing.

Screen-Away Offense

Another simple continuity offense, the Screen-Away Offense, has the perimeter player at the top of the circle *screen away*—pass to one wing player and set a screen for the opposite wing player. This action, combined with a cross screen from post to post, creates good opportunities for players to get open.

The initial formation of the Screen-Away Offense is the same 3-out, 2-in as in the Give-and-Go Offense. The play starts when 2 and 3 get open on the wing. After 1 passes to 2, she runs at 3's defender and sets a screen. Player 3 waits for her and sets up the screen by stepping toward the basket. As with any other screen, 3 must read her defender and react with the proper cut (for how to read screens, see pages 70–71).

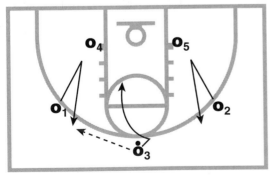

D. Continuity in the Give-and-Go Offense.

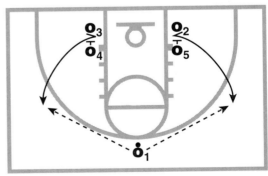

F. Double low stack and popout.

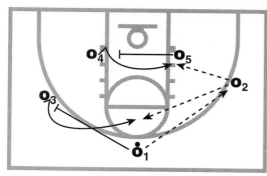

A. Screens in the Screen-Away Offense.

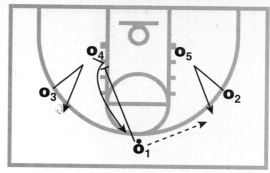

A. First down screen in the T-Game Offense.

After posting up for a count of one, if the ball-side post (5) doesn't get the ball, she sets a cross screen for the help-side post (4). If your players are patient and good screeners, they will find themselves open for high-percentage shots.

T-Game Offense

This continuity offense is a little more complicated since it has two down screens. Some coaches call this a *motion offense,* but I call it the T-Game Offense. This offense is best suited to play against man-to-man defense.

The setup is the same as in the two previous offenses. Player 1 initiates the offense by passing to 2 or 3. After a pass to 2, 1 cuts diagonally to the help-side block and sets a down screen for 4, who cuts to the top of the circle. As soon as 1 sets her screen, 3 *screens the screener* (sets a screen for a player who just set a screen)—that is, screens for 1. When 2 receives the ball, 5 posts up on the ball-side block. If 5 is open, 2 passes her the ball. If 5

isn't open, 2 reverses the ball by passing to 4, who passes to 1, or by making a skip pass to 1. At this point, 1 is often open for a shot or a drive.

If 1 can't drive or shoot, she looks for 3 to post up or cut across the lane to set a cross screen for 5. Cross screens are difficult to defend, but they take time to set up, so it's important for 1 to be patient. If nothing develops at this point, 1 passes to 4, who is now at the top of the circle, and the sequence begins again. After 1 and 2 make V-cuts, 4 passes to one of them. If 4 passes back to 1, 4 sets a diagonal down screen for 3, who now cuts to the top. Player 1 can pass to 5 posting up, if she's open, or to 3, who reverses the ball to 2.

One thing I like about the T-Game Offense is that every player is a potential scorer. This makes it hard for the defense to focus on defending one or two players, since anyone is a threat to score when she gets open off a screen.

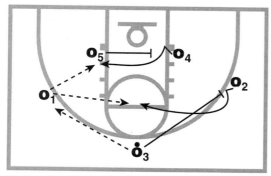

B. Continuity in the Screen-Away Offense.

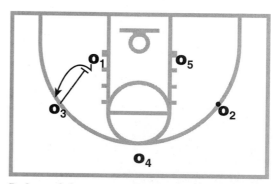

B. Second down screen in the T-Game Offense.

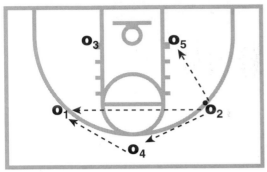

C. Options for 2 in the T-Game Offense.

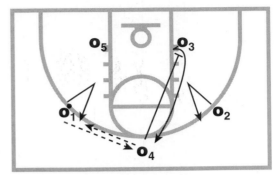

E. Continuity in the T-Game Offense.

1-4 High Offense

This is another more advanced continuity offense with a lot of motion and screening. Whenever my teams play a team that uses this offense, we find it difficult to defend.

The 1-4 High Offense begins with 1 at the top of the circle and the other players lined up on the free throw line extended as follows: 2 and 3 are at the wings, as in the T-Game Offense, but 4 and 5 start out on the elbows. Again, it doesn't matter which wing is on which side or which post player is on which elbow, though I prefer the setup shown in the diagram.

To begin the offense, 1 passes to 2 or 3. If she passes to 2, 4 and 5 move to the side of the lane away from the ball, midway between the high and low post areas, and set a double screen, facing away from the ball. They should be careful to set the screens outside of the lane area to avoid a 3-second violation.

When 2 receives the ball, she first looks to see if a driving lane is open. If it's open, she drives before 3 uses the double screen to take advantage of the open area between her defender and the basket. In other words, a *clear out* is created—the players without the ball leave the ball-side part of the court so the player with the ball can play 1-on-1 against her defender. If 3 sees 2 driving to the basket, she stays on the wing to keep the basket area open.

If 2 doesn't drive, 3 cuts on one side of the double screen, depending on how her defender plays her. She rubs shoulders with her teammate as she cuts by. If she doesn't receive the ball, she stops midway up the lane on the other side.

After 3 uses the double screen, 1 comes down and sets a down screen for 5 (the post nearest to the basket), and 5 cuts across the lane. After 5 uses the screen, 1 pops out to the wing vacated by 3. If 5 doesn't receive the ball from 2, she and 3 set up a double screen on that

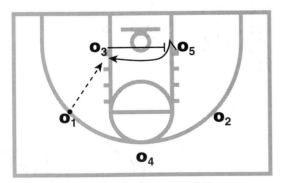

D. Cross screen in the T-Game Offense.

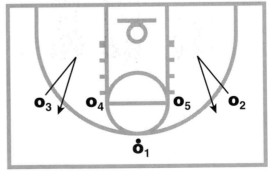

A. Setup in the 1-4 High Offense.

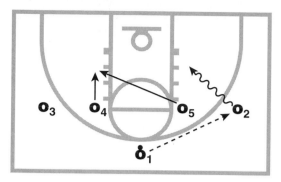

B. Clear out in the 1-4 High Offense.

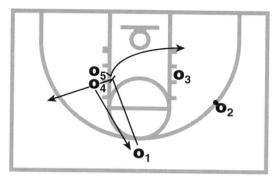

D. Screen for 5 and popout in the 1-4 High Offense.

side of the lane, facing out. As this happens, 4 comes to the top of the circle.

If 2 can't drive, she waits for 3 to come off the double screen and 5 to come off the cross screen. If neither are open, 2 passes to 4 at the top. This marks the beginning of the sequence again. Player 4 passes to 1, 2 cuts off the double screen set by 3 and 5, and the sequence starts again.

In addition to featuring a double screen, which creates problems for the defense, the 1-4 High Offense has 5 moving from one side of the lane to the other. In the T-Game Offense, 5 sometimes moves out to the perimeter. This is fine if your 5 handles the ball well, but many 5s don't. In that case, the 1-4 High Offense is better suited for your team. It keeps 5 near the basket where she can rebound and where she doesn't have to handle the ball.

As with the T-Game Offense, this offense is designed to give all five players the opportunity to score if they get open.

UCLA-Cut Offense

This is an advanced man-to-man continuity offense that features a pick-and-roll and a double screen. Like the two prior continuity offenses, this offense swings the ball from side to side and can be run repeatedly until a good shot is available.

The offense starts out in the 3-out, 2-in formation. Player 1 initiates the offense by passing to either wing. If she passes to 2, she steps away from the ball to set up her defender and cuts hard toward the ball-side elbow. As she does, 5 comes up from the block to set a back screen. This is called a *UCLA screen*, made famous by legendary UCLA coach John Wooden years ago. Player 1 cuts off the screen (the cut off a UCLA screen is called a *UCLA cut*), and 2 passes to her if she's open. If 1 doesn't receive the ball, she stops on the low block.

As 1 makes her cut, 3 goes next to 4 and sets up in a double screen, facing the ball. After 5

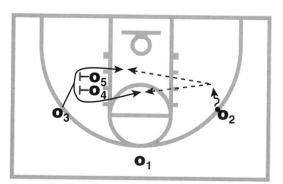

C. Double screen in the 1-4 High Offense.

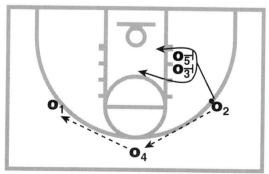

E. Continuity in the 1-4 High Offense.

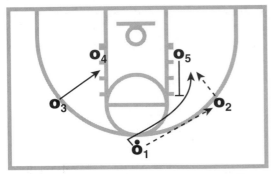

A. Initial movement in the UCLA-Cut Offense.

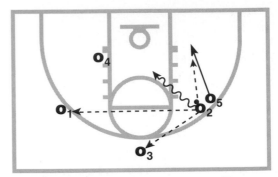

C. Options for 2 in the UCLA-Cut Offense.

sets the UCLA screen, she watches 2. If 2 doesn't pass to 1, 5 sets a ball screen for 2, creating a pick-and-roll situation. As 2 dribbles around 5's screen, 1 cuts away from the ball, uses the double screen on the other side of the lane, and pops out to the opposite wing.

After 2 dribbles around the screen, 5 rolls to the basket, opening up toward the ball. If 2 can't drive into the lane, she looks to pass to 5. If 5 isn't open and 2 can't penetrate into the lane for a jump shot, she passes to 1 on the opposite wing. If 2 can't do any of these options, she passes to 3 and the sequence starts over.

Man-to-Man Offense: Set Plays

Set plays are designed and run for two purposes: to get the ball into the hands of your best players, and to attack the other team's weakest defenders.

1-4 Low Play

This is an easy play to teach, and it's excellent if your point guard is a good 1-on-1 player. Player 1 begins at the top, and the other players spread out along the baseline, with 4 and 5 on the blocks and 2 and 3 in the corners.

Player 1 picks a side and drives on her defender. If she dribbles to the right, 2 moves to get open for a 3-point shot, and 3 comes up to replace 1 and become the safety. When 5 sees 1 driving in her direction, she steps out to the short corner. This forces her defender to decide whether to stick with her or to stay on the block to help stop 1's drive. Player 4 steps up the lane above the block, forcing her defender to make the same decision.

Player 1 has several options:

- shoot, if she's open and in her range
- drive the rest of the way
- pass to 5 for an easy jump shot

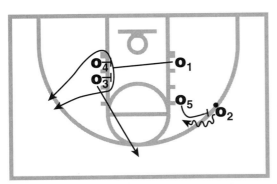

B. Pick-and-roll and double screen in the UCLA-Cut Offense.

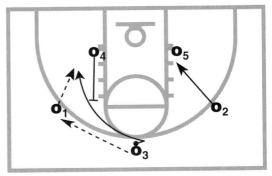

D. Continuity in the UCLA-Cut Offense.

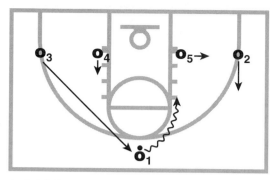

A. Initial movement in the 1-4 Low Play.

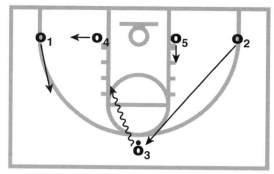

C. Continuity in the 1-4 Low Play.

- pass to 4 for an easy jump shot
- pass to 2 for a 3-point shot
- if she can't do any of these things, come to a jump stop, pivot, and pass out to 3

If 2 and 3 are also skilled 1-on-1 players, you can turn the 1-4 Low Play into a continuity offense by having 1 cut to 3's original corner and 5 and 2 relocate to where they started. Now 3 is the new 1-on-1 player.

Isolation Play

If you see a situation where one of your players is better than her defender, run an *isolation play* (or *iso*), a play designed to get your player the ball and to clear out the other players so she can play 1-on-1 without other defenders nearby. Isolation plays are also useful when one of the other team's players is in foul trouble. If you isolate her against one of your players, she won't be able to defend as aggressively as she might otherwise because she won't want to commit another foul.

Start the play with 1 at the top and the other players in a double stack formation as if about to run a continuity offense. If 3's defender is the player you want to isolate, 2 uses 5's screen to cut to the wing as usual, but 3 uses 4's screen to cut to the free throw line area.

When 1 passes 3 the ball, 4 and 5 step away from the block area to their respective short corners. This leaves 3 matched up 1-on-1 against her defender. If she drives by her defender, and if 4's or 5's defender comes over to prevent an easy basket, 3 passes to the open player. She can also pass to 2, who moves on the perimeter to get open.

Clear-Out Play

This play is more advanced but works well if you have a skilled 2 and 4 or 5 who play well together. Assuming that it's 4, the play starts out in a double low stack formation. Player 1 starts the play by dribbling to one side of the court. It doesn't matter which side she chooses, because the play can be run on either side. In

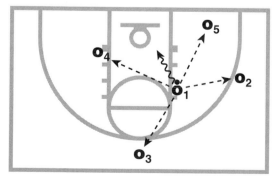

B. Options for 1 in the 1-4 Low Play.

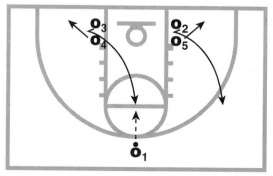

A. Initial movement in an isolation play.

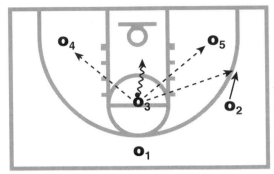

B. Options for 3 in an isolation play.

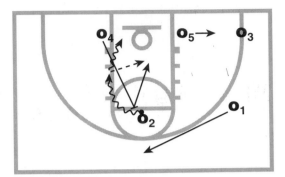

B. Pick-and-roll in the Clear-Out Play.

this example, 1 dribbles to the right, 3 cuts across the lane to the corner, and 2 comes *up the gut*—cuts up the lane to the top of the circle.

As 2 receives the ball, 4 comes to set a screen, creating a pick-and-roll situation. Since that side of the court has cleared out, if 4 sets a good screen, 2 can often dribble all the way to the basket. Some coaches want 4 to roll immediately to the basket, but I prefer to have her stay in the high post area for a second to give 2 more room to try to take the ball to the basket. If 2 can't drive all the way, then 4 can roll, looking for the pass from 2.

As 2 and 4 play a pick-and-roll, 5 steps to the short corner to draw her defender out of the way, and 1 goes back to the top of the circle to be the safety.

Box Play

This is an advanced play that begins in a *box formation*—four players form a square using the corners of the lane area. Our opponents have

run this play against my teams with some success. The play features two lob options off back screens that are hard to defend. If the defenders stay back to prevent the lob, a shooter is wide open on the perimeter. If the defenders switch on the screens, your posts will have an opportunity to post up against smaller defenders. This is an excellent play if your team has two good post players who can score.

The players set up with 2 and 3 on the blocks, facing the ball, and 4 and 5 at the 3-point line area off the elbows, their outside foot on the arc, ready to screen for 1. The play starts when 1 dribbles in between 4 and 5 and chooses a side. She should go as far toward the basket as possible before changing direction toward one of the posts.

After 1 uses 5's screen, 5 screens for 4, and 2 screens for 3. Player 1 looks first to see if 3 is open for the easy shot. If she isn't, 1 passes to 4. After 2 sets her cross screen, she continues in that direction until she's out of the lane (to avoid a 3-second lane violation), cuts up to the

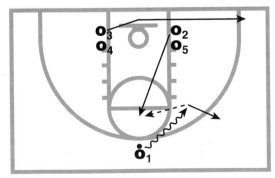

A. Initial movement in the Clear-Out Play.

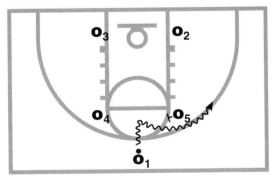

A. Initial movement in the Box Play.

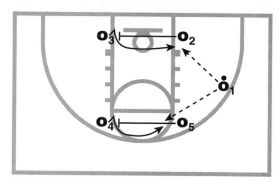

B. Cross screens in the Box Play.

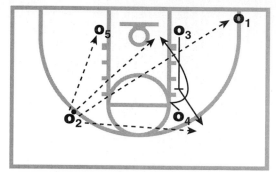

D. Options for 2 in the Box Play.

elbow, and sets a back screen for 5. After that, 2 steps out to a spot above the 3-point line. Player 4 makes a lob pass to 5 for a layup or passes to 2 for a jump shot.

After 4 passes to 2, 3 runs up the side of the lane, sets a back screen for 4, and moves into position for a possible 3-point shot. Player 2 has a number of good options—passing to 5 posting up, making a lob pass to 4, or passing to 3 or 1 for the jump shot.

The Box Play can be used as a continuity offense, with the ball going back and forth to the 3-point shooter until a lob pass is possible. After 1 starts the play and passes the ball, she can move to a spot between the circle and midcourt as a safety, or if 1 is a good shooter, she can move to the corner as another option.

Zone Offense

In man-to-man defense, each defender guards an opposing player (her *man*). In zone defense,

each defender guards a specific area (her *zone*). When any offensive player comes into that area, with or without the ball, the defender guards her.

Zone defenses are described by using numbers based on the initial alignment of the defenders as viewed from overhead. The most common zones are the 1-2-2, the 1-3-1, the 2-3, and the 2-1-2. Zones are also described by the number of players positioned at the *top of the zone* (the area closest to midcourt). Zones that have one player at the top (1-2-2 and 1-3-1 zones) have *one-guard fronts*. Zones that have two players at the top (2-3 and 2-1-2 zones) have *two-guard fronts*.

Every zone defense has inherent weaknesses— holes and seams without defenders. The offenses used to play against zones try to exploit these weaknesses. For that reason, it's essential to identify what kind of zone the other team is playing so you know how to attack it (see diagrams below and next page).

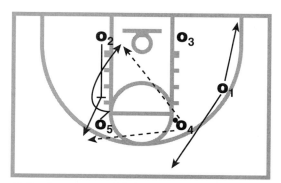

C. Back screen and lob in the Box Play.

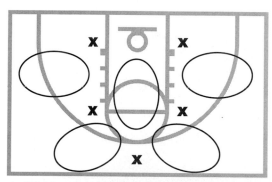

A. Weaknesses in the 1-2-2 zone.

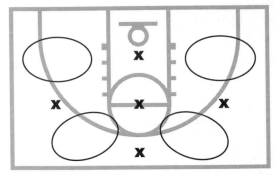

B. Weaknesses in the 1-3-1 zone.

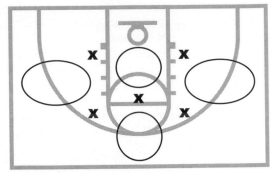

D. Weaknesses in the 2-1-2 zone.

Principles of Zone Offense

Regardless of which zone offense you decide to use, there are certain principles that apply to attacking any zone defense:

Beat the zone before it sets up. The best offense against any zone is to run a fast break before the defenders can set up in their designated areas. When your team gains possession of the ball, your players should push it up the court as fast as possible. There are often more opportunities to score in transition against a zone defense versus a man-to-man defense because the defenders in the zone don't have assigned players. This sometimes causes confusion and allows alert offensive players to cut into the lane for an easy score.

Make the zone move. Your players should be patient in attacking the zone. Zone defenders love nothing more than when the point guard makes one pass and the wing takes a long-distance shot. The defenders don't have

to move much, and they're in perfect rebounding position. Teach your players to make the zone defenders work. They should pass the ball around and make the defenders shift position again and again. Your players should take their time until a good shot opens up.

Reverse the ball. Your team should *swing* (pass) the ball from one wing to the other by passing it through the point, through the high post, or by using a *skip* pass (a pass from one wing to the other over the top of the zone). Ball reversal forces zone defenders to move rapidly to new positions. As they move back and forth, they tire and lose focus and intensity, which opens up gaps and seams for drives and passes.

Attack the seams of the zone with the dribble. This is called *dribble penetration.* Anytime one of your perimeter players sees an opening in the zone, she should dribble into it. This draws defenders to her, making it easy to pass to an open teammate.

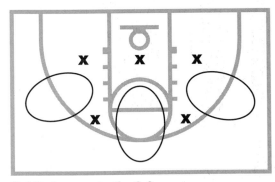

C. Weaknesses in the 2-3 zone.

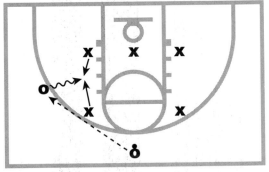

Dribble penetration.

Make two players guard the dribbler.
This is part of dribble penetration. Teach your players to dribble directly between two defenders. This draws both of them to the dribbler, which means that one of her teammates is wide open.

Use ball fakes. Zone defenders react to ball fakes, so offensive players should use them often to open up passing lanes and driving lanes. Don't just tell your players to use ball fakes. Practice them.

Attack the zone from behind. Zone defenders tend to face the player with the ball and not look behind them. The alert offensive player can take advantage of this by cutting along the baseline area looking for a chance to get open. By the time the defense realizes it, the ball zips by their noses, and the offensive player scores 2 points.

Flash from the help side. As a zone shifts to adjust to the movement of the ball, holes will appear in the zone. Offensive players on the help side should be alert for the chances to *flash* (cut) into these holes. Zone defenders often lose track of players outside of their area, particularly away from the ball.

Use the short corners. The short corners are a vulnerable area for all zones. The back defenders will usually be closer to the basket.

Attack the boards. Offensive rebounding is easier against zone defenses because, again, zone defenders don't have an assigned man to guard. When a shot is taken from one side of the basket, the offensive players on the help side should immediately cut to the basket for a possible rebound.

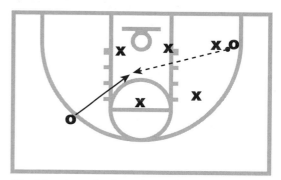

Flashing into the lane from the help side.

Two-Guard Offense

The most common zone defenses with a one-guard front are the 1-2-2 and the 1-3-1. Sometimes you'll see what's called a 3-2 zone, which starts out looking like the 1-2-2. The difference is that in the 1-2-2, the defender at the top stays out on the perimeter to pressure the point guard, whereas in the 3-2, the top player drops down to the free throw line when the ball is passed to the wing. Attack 1-2-2 and 3-2 zones with the same offense.

To play against a zone, place your players to take advantage of the gaps in the zone. Against one-guard fronts, position two guards at the top, each to one side of the top zone defender. It's impossible for the defender to cover both guards. Position your best passing forward (4 or 5) at the free throw line and 3 and the other forward each in a short corner.

The offense begins when 1 has the ball. She dribbles toward the gap between the top defender and the elbow defender. When they come to guard her, she has several options:

- pass to 2, who will be open
- pass to 3, who should be trying to sneak behind the defense
- pass to 4 in the middle
- pass to 5 posting up

The primary weakness of the 1-2-2 zone is in the middle, so the player with the ball should always look for chances to pass to 4. The primary weakness of the 1-3-1 is along the baseline, because there is only one defender assigned to

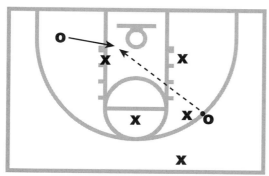

Attacking the zone from behind.

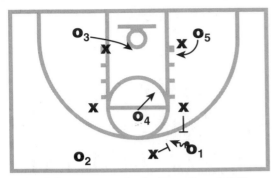

A. *Initial movement in the Two-Guard Offense.*

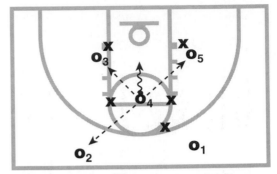

C. *Options for 4 in the Two-Guard Offense.*

the area. Against that zone, the player with the ball should look for chances to pass to the short corners.

When the ball goes to the middle, 4 has several options:

- shoot, if she's open
- pass to 3 or 5, if either is open
- drive to the basket, if no one is guarding her when she catches the ball
- pass to the opposite wing

Anytime the player in the middle catches the ball, she's dangerous. Your players should always look for chances to pass to the high post area.

When the ball goes to one of the short corners, 4 has several options:

- set a screen for the player with the ball
- set a screen for the player in the opposite short corner

- cut to the basket for a pass, if she has an open lane
- call for the ball, if she's wide open

One of the most effective passes in the Two-Guard Offense is the diagonal pass, either from an outside player to a short corner player, or vice versa. This pass is often available, particularly when playing against the 1-3-1, for the reason mentioned above—zone defenders are often so focused on the ball that they lose track of who is on the help side and who is behind them.

One-Guard Offense

Use the One-Guard Offense when your team plays against two-guard fronts (2-3 and 2-1-2 zones).

In this offense, because these zones have two defenders at the top, 1 positions herself at the top between the defenders. Players 2 and 3

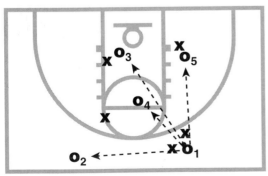

B. *Options for 1 in the Two-Guard Offense.*

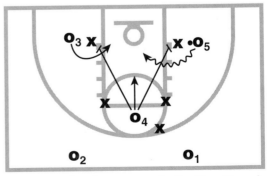

D. *Ball in the short corner in the Two-Guard Offense.*

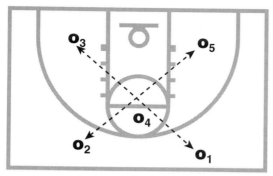

E. Diagonal passes in the Two-Guard Offense.

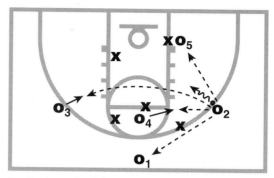

B. Options for 2 in the One-Guard Offense.

are at the wings. They're not on the same line with the two top defenders, but closer to the baseline so they split the gaps between the top defenders and the bottom defenders. Again, your best post passer starts in the middle, just above the free throw line. The other post starts on one side of the lane in the block area. It doesn't matter which side she starts on.

The offense begins when 1 dribbles at a spot in between the two top defenders. When they close in to stop her, 1 has two options:

- pass to a wing who is open (2 and 3 should adjust their position as 1 dribbles to create an open passing lane)
- pass to 4, if she's open

When 1 passes to 2, 5 posts up, 4 tries to get open in the ball-side elbow area, and 3 finds an open space on the help side for the skip pass. After 1 passes to 2, she relocates back to the top of the circle to be ready for a ball reversal pass from 2. At this point, 2 has several options:

- shoot, if she's open and in her range (she shouldn't shoot on the first pass)
- drive, if she has an opening
- pass to 5 posting up
- pass to 4, if she's open
- make a skip pass to 3
- pass back to 1

When the ball reverses, either through 1 or 4, or from a skip pass to 3, 5 cuts diagonally to the opposite elbow, and 4 cuts diagonally to the opposite block. When 3 catches the ball, she has these options:

- shoot, if she's open and in her range
- drive, if there's an opening
- pass to 4 posting up
- pass to 5 at the elbow
- make a skip pass to 2
- pass back to 1

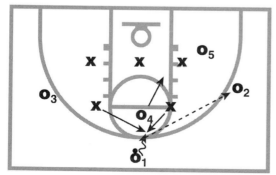

A. Initial movement in the One-Guard Offense.

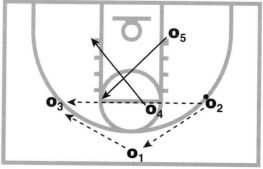

C. Ball reversal in the One-Guard Offense.

Question: My post players are never open after they make their diagonal cuts in the One-Guard Offense. Any suggestions?

Answer: They might be cutting too fast. They should wait for a count of one after the wing catches the ball to give the defenders time to shift to their new positions. The defense will react to ball reversal immediately. By waiting for a second, your post players will see where the new gaps are and can cut to the gaps, instead of fighting for space occupied by the defenders.

Every time the ball swings to the other side, 4 and 5 cut diagonally. Whoever is on the block cuts to the opposite elbow, and whoever is at the elbow cuts to the opposite block.

The One-Guard Offense, like all good offenses, will eventually yield good shots, as long as the offensive team is patient.

Overload Offense

The Overload Offense works well against all zones. The principle is to have more offensive players in an area than there are defenders (one side of the zone is *overloaded* with offensive players). This results in having 3-on-2 and 2-on-1 situations, which give the offensive team an excellent chance for a good shot.

In the Overload Offense, the players set up in the same formation used in the One-Guard Offense. Play begins when 1 passes to either wing. After 1 passes to 2, she cuts down the center of the lane and goes to the ball-side corner. As she does this, 3 comes up to the open area halfway between the top of the circle and where she started on the wing. The

zone is now overloaded. Four offensive players are on the ball side, guarded by only three defenders.

At this point, 2 has several options:

- shoot, if she's open (again, not on the first pass)
- drive, if she can
- pass to 1 in the corner (1 will usually be wide open)
- pass to 5 posting up
- pass to 4 in the high post area
- pass to 3

If 2 passes to 1, 1 has several options:

- shoot (only if she's in her range)
- pass to 5 posting up
- pass to 4, who is also posting up or cutting to the basket
- pass back to 2, who has the same options listed above
- make a skip pass to 3

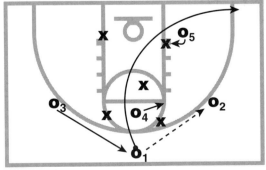

A. Initial movement in the Overload Offense.

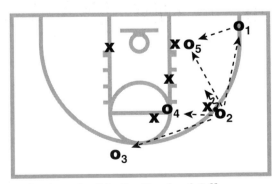

B. Options for 2 in the Overload Offense.

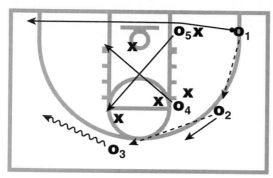

C. Ball reversal in the Overload Offense.

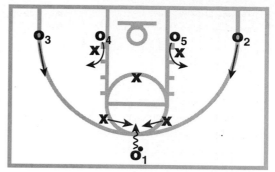

A. Initial movement in the Baseline Offense.

If the ball reverses, either from 1 to 2 or 3, 1 cuts to the opposite corner, 4 and 5 cut diagonally as in the One-Guard Offense, and 2 comes up to a spot on the perimeter midway between the wing and the top of the circle. The zone is now overloaded on the other side, and play continues as it did before. If the defense covers the options, and no good shot is available, the ball reverses again.

With patience and ball reversal, the offensive players will eventually have a numerical advantage.

Baseline Offense

The Baseline Offense is suited to attack all zones and is an excellent option if you have good wing shooters. The setup is the same as the one used in the 1-4 Low Play. Having players in the corners forces any zone to flatten out into a 2-3 formation.

The play begins when 1 dribbles between the two players at the top of the zone. As the

defenders close in on 1, 2 and 3 come up the sideline slightly to be open for a pass, and 4 and 5 post up. Player 1 has the following options:

- pass to 2
- pass to 3
- pass to 4 posting up
- pass to 5 posting up
- if no one is open, dribble back out to try again

If 1 passes to 2, these are 2's options:

- shoot
- pass to 5 posting up
- pass to 1 for ball reversal
- make a skip pass to 3

When 2 receives the ball, this creates a dilemma for the player guarding 5. If she stays with 5, 2 has an open shot. If she goes out to guard 2, 5 will be open for post feed. This is a

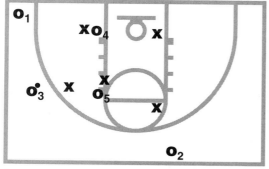

D. New overload in the Overload Offense.

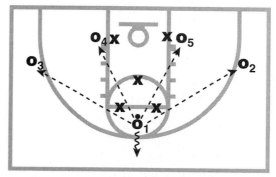

B. Options for 1 in the Baseline Offense.

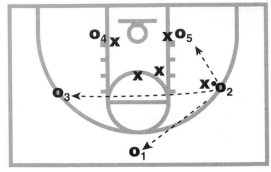

C. Options for 2 in the Baseline Offense.

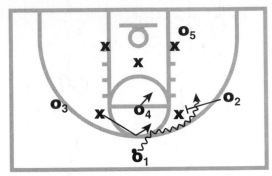

Elbow screen in the One-Guard Offense.

good 2-on-1 opportunity. If the defender at the top of the zone nearest to 2 drops to cover her, 1 should cut into the open space for the pass.

Screening the Zone

Many coaches think that screens are effective when playing against man-to-man defenses, but they are just as valuable when attacking zones.

In the Two-Guard Offense, I explained how the player in the middle (4) screens for the short corner players. You can also have 4 set a back screen for 1 or 2. This creates a pick-and-roll situation. After her teammate uses the screen, 4 rolls to the basket for a possible pass.

In the One-Guard Offense, as 1 dribbles to draw in the top defender, 2 sets a screen on the defender at the nearest elbow. As she comes to screen, 1 sets up the defender by dribbling with her left hand. Once the screen is set, she crosses the ball to her right hand and drives by the

screen. If the defender in the middle comes over to guard her, 4 will be open for a pass.

Another option is for 4 to screen the elbow defender. If 1 can't drive or shoot off the screen, 2 will be wide open for the pass.

A third screening option is to have 5 *stay at home*—stay on the low block when the ball reverses (part 1). When 2 sees that 5 isn't cutting to the opposite elbow, she slides down toward the corner. When 3 catches the ball, she quickly passes to 2. As the ball is in the air, 5 posts up on her player. Player 2 should be open for a shot or a post feed to 5 (part 2).

Fast-Break Offense

Fast-break offense (also called *transition* offense) occurs when your players push the ball up the court as fast as they can after gaining possession of it. The goal is to take a good shot before the other team has all their players back on

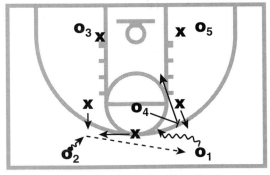

Back screen and pick-and-roll in the Two-Guard Offense.

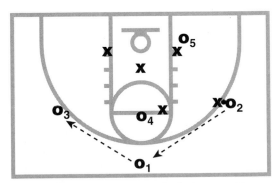

Stay-at-home screen, part 1: 5 stays on the block during ball reversal.

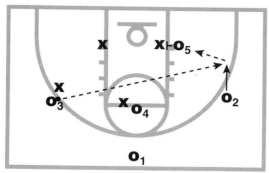

Stay-at-home screen, part 2: as 3 passes to 2, 5 posts up.

defense. A fast break can begin from a steal, a defensive rebound, a deflected pass, a made or missed free throw, or a made or missed field goal.

Transition offense is a different game than half-court offense. It's played at maximum speed with minimal structure. It thrives off defensive confusion and tries to wear the other team down. A team that's unprepared to defend the fast break will find itself quickly outscored and out of breath. Fans like to watch fast-break basketball, players like to play it, and if your team is good at it, you'll like it, too.

A successful fast break results in a *numbers advantage*—when your team has more players near the other team's basket than the other team does. This can be a 1-on-0 situation (one player driving to the basket with no defender in her way), a 2-on-1 situation (two players against one defender), a 3-on-2 (three players against two defenders), a 4-on-3 situation (four against three defenders), and a 5-on-4 (all your players are attacking the basket, but only four defenders are back).

When the fast break involves only a few players from each team (a 1-on-0, 2-on-1, or 3-on-2 situation), it's called a *primary break*. When more players are back on defense, but the offense still has a numbers advantage (a 4-on-3 or 5-on-4 situation), it's called a *secondary break*. Unless your players are experienced in running fast breaks, teach them only how to run the primary break. If your players don't understand how to run a primary break, they won't understand the secondary break. If your players are

experienced, teach them how to run the secondary break. If your team is blessed with fast post players, you'll find that you can score some easy points on secondary break action.

In order to know where to run on the fast break, teach your players how to *run the lanes*. Imagine that the court is divided into three lengthwise *lanes*. As the fast break develops, each player runs in a specific lane, based on where she is at the start of the break and what position she plays. There is a left lane, a middle lane, and a right lane, as viewed from the team's own basket.

Following are the principles of running a successful fast break:

1. **Sprint up the court.** Much of the success of being able to score on a fast break is simply outrunning the defenders.

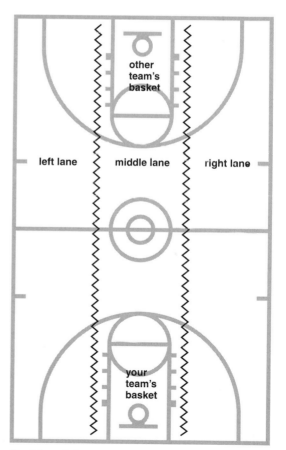

Fast-break lanes.

2. **Run the lanes.** This makes it hard for the defense to stop a fast break.

3. **Get a shot off before the defense gets back.** If your players have a numbers advantage, they shouldn't wait for the numbers to even out. You don't want your players to take bad shots, but as long as they take a good shot, even if it misses, your team will have a good chance for an offensive rebound.

4. **Pass to an open player who is farther down the court.** The ball moves up the court faster through the air than when someone dribbles it.

5. **If passing ahead won't work, dribble the ball to the center of the court.** This gives the dribbler more options than if she dribbles along one side of the court.

6. **If there's no one guarding a player, she should take the ball all the way.** Is there any more exciting way to score than on a *coast-to-coast* (length-of-the-court) fast break?

Responsibilities on the Fast Break

When running a primary fast break, every player on offense has a specific job. The post who gets the defensive rebound immediately chins the ball, pivots away from the defense, and throws an outlet pass to the point guard. The point guard finds an open area somewhere between the top of the circle and the sideline, where the post can throw an accurate pass. The point guard stands with her back to the sideline so she can see the court and yells "Outlet!" so the rebounder will know where she is.

As this happens, the other post sprints up the court in the middle lane, on a straight line to the basket. The other two perimeter players *fill the lanes*—run up the two empty side lanes. Designate which lane 2 should use and which lane 3 should use. With my teams, 2 fills the right lane and 3 fills the left lane. They run close to the sideline. Once they're at the free throw

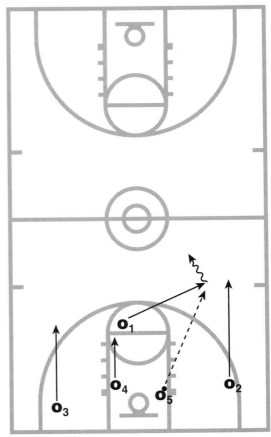

A. The primary break begins after 5 gets the rebound.

line extended, they make a 45-degree-angle cut to the basket. If they don't receive the ball, once they reach the block area, they go to their respective short corners.

Once 1 has the ball, she looks up the court to see if either 2 or 3 is open ahead of her. If so, she passes the ball. If not, she speed dribbles in a straight line to the top of the opposite circle. If a defender comes out to guard her, 1 comes to a jump stop and passes to 2 or 3 cutting to the basket.

Once 4 arrives in the lane, if 1 passes to 3, 4 cuts to the ball-side block. If she beats her defender down the court, she'll be open for a pass and a layup. If a defender guards her, she posts up. Player 3 passes her the ball before the rest of the defense comes down. After throwing

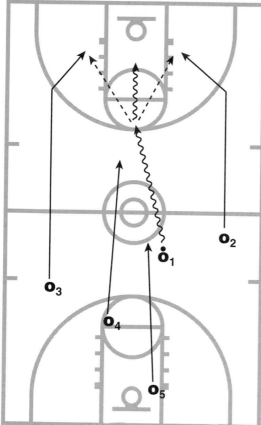

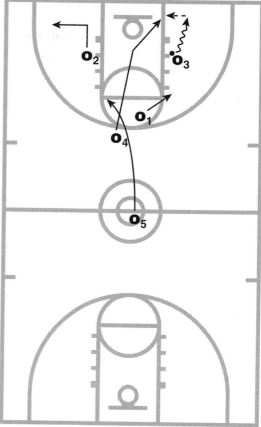

B. The primary break ends in a 2-on-1 or a 3-on-2 situation.

C. The secondary break begins when the primary break doesn't produce an easy shot.

the outlet pass, 5 sprints down the middle lane as the *trailer* (the last player on the fast break). She heads for the elbow opposite to where the ball goes and stops there to be ready for a pass from the wing. At this point—when the defense has three or more players back in position—the primary break ends and the secondary break begins.

If 3 can't pass to 4, she passes to 1, who passes to 5, who has several options:

- take the ball to the basket, if no one is guarding her
- pass to 2 (completing the ball reversal)
- pass to 4 posting up
- shoot from the elbow (only if this is a good shot for her)

If those options aren't available, 5 passes to 2 and cuts to the basket for a return pass. If 2 doesn't pass back to 5, 5 and 4 set a double screen for 3 cutting across the lane.

The secondary break is over when all five defenders are back in position. If a shot hasn't been taken, the ball should go back to 1 so she can initiate the half-court offense.

It will take time and playing experience for your players to learn how to read the defense and make good decisions when running the fast break. The more you practice transition offense, the better your team will be at using it in games.

Teach fast-break offense in stages. Begin with a few players involved and work up to having more players as the team improves. See Fast-Break Drills in Chapter 7, Drills 67–75.

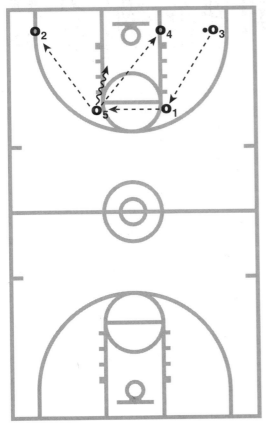

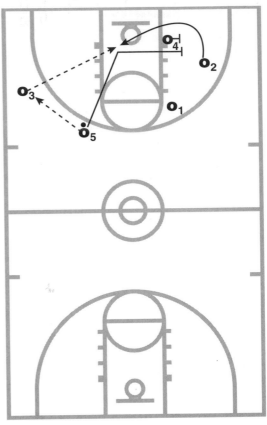

D. The secondary break continues with quick ball reversal.

E. The last option in the secondary break is to set a double screen for the help-side wing.

Question: No matter what I say, I can't get my eighth-grade girls to yell "Outlet!" They just giggle like it's funny. Is there something going on I don't know about?

Answer: In general, girls don't like to yell as much as boys do. They have to learn that it's not only expected, but it's fine to yell. At the next practice, line your players up and tell them to shout "Outlet!" as loud as they can, one by one. Tell them that the team will run a ladder every time someone doesn't shout at the top of her lungs. Once the quieter girls hear all their teammates yelling, they'll start to yell, too.

Question: My players insist on dribbling the ball up the court instead of passing it. We miss out on some good fast breaks. How can I change this habit?

Answer: In your next practice, illustrate the point by having a race. Set up five passers in a line from one end of the court to the other. The first player is behind the baseline with a ball and the last player in line is on the block at the far basket. Have a player who insists on dribbling the ball up the court line up behind the baseline with a ball, next to the other player with the ball. At your signal, the passers pass the ball up the court and the dribbler dribbles up the court. It will be obvious which method advances the ball faster.

Out-of-Bounds Plays

In every game, there are situations when the referee stops play, and your team has to inbound the ball:

- when a player from the other team commits a nonshooting foul

- when a player from the other team commits a moving violation

- when a player from the other team is the last player to touch the ball before it goes out-of-bounds

- when the alternating arrow awards a held ball to your team

In these instances, the referee hands the ball to your inbounder at the spot where the ball went out-of-bounds or the spot closest to the foul or violation. Your team then runs an *out-of-bounds play*, which is designed to inbound the ball successfully and provide your team with a good shot opportunity.

One of the first considerations in running these plays is having a good passer as the inbounder. Choose players for this role who see the court well, have good arm strength, don't panic under pressure, and make good decisions.

Sideline Plays

If the ball is inbounded along either sideline, your team runs a *sideline play*. For all your inbounds plays, designate an inbounder. In the following plays, I assume that 3 is the inbounder, because most 3s are good passers and taller than the other perimeter players. The most important quality of your inbounder is that she's a smart passer under pressure.

Sideline Screen Play. In the Sideline Screen Play, 1 and 2 line up facing 3. Player 1 is first, and 2 is right behind her so no defender can stand in between them. Player 5 is at the top of the circle (at the other team's basket), and 4 is on the ball-side block. When ready, 3 slaps the ball as a signal to the other players to begin the play. Remind your players that the inbounder has only 5 seconds to pass the ball. The 5-second count begins when the referee

hands the ball to the inbounder, not when the inbounder slaps the ball.

When the play begins, 2 sets a screen for 1. How she sets it depends on where 1's defender is. Most of the time, the defender is next to 1 between her and the basket. In that case, 2 stays where she is to set the screen. Player 1 spins, cuts by 2's shoulder, and heads toward to the basket. If 1's defender plays off of 1, anticipating the cut, 1 uses 2's screen and cuts toward the other sideline. If 1's defender plays her by standing between her and the ball, at the ball slap, 2 takes a step toward the basket to set the screen, and 1 spins and cuts by her. This is another example of a team *taking what the defense gives them*.

After 2 sets the screen, she comes to the ball as a second option. If 1 can't get open for the pass, 3 passes to 2.

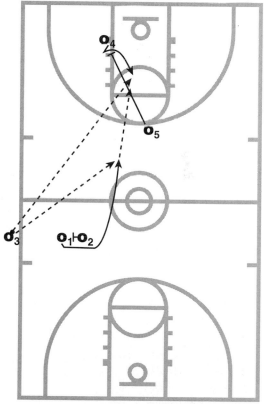

Sideline Screen Play.

As 1 and 2 make their moves, 5 sets a down screen for 4. This frees 4 to cut to the free throw line area as the third option. If 3 is close enough, she passes to 4. If the spot of the inbounds is too far from 4, 1 or 2 can pass to 4.

Sideline Stack Play. In the Sideline Stack Play, the other four players *stack up*—form a *stack* (line) with the first player about 6 feet from the inbounder. The players face the inbounder and stand close together so no defender can squeeze in between them. The first player in line is 1, followed by 2, 4, and 5. When they're ready, 3 slaps the ball.

The first option is to pass to 2. After the slap, 2 spins away from 3, uses 4 and 5 as screens, and sprints toward the basket. If the other team is playing tight man-to-man defense, this often results in a layup. If the other team leaves a post defender to protect the basket, 2 should take advantage of her superior quickness and look to drive on the defender.

The second option is to pass to 1. As 2 makes her cut, 1 takes four steps toward her team's basket, plants her foot as in a V-cut, and sprints back to where she was, looking for the short pass. As she cuts by where the inbounder is standing, 5 sets a screen for her. If 1's defender is delayed by the screen, 1 has a chance for a drive to the basket or a 2-on-1 play with 2.

The third option is to pass to 4. While 1 and 2 are making their cuts, 4 turns away from 3, uses 5 as a screen, and heads away from the inbounder. This draws her defender with her, leaving the scoring area more open for 1 and 2. If 3 passes to 4, 4 looks to pass to 2 or 1.

In the Sideline Stack Play, 5's role is to set screens. However, she's also the last option. After she screens for 2, then 4, she steps toward the inbounder and screens for 1. If 3 can't pass to anyone else, she passes to 5, who then waits for 1 to come back and take the ball.

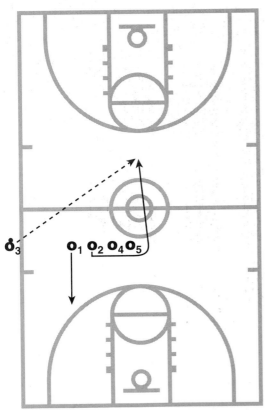

A. First option in the Sideline Stack Play.

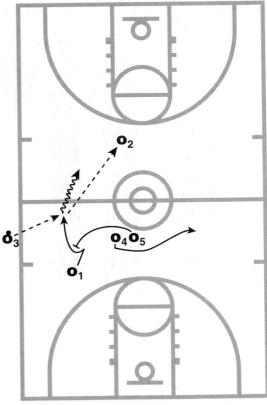

B. Second option in the Sideline Stack Play.

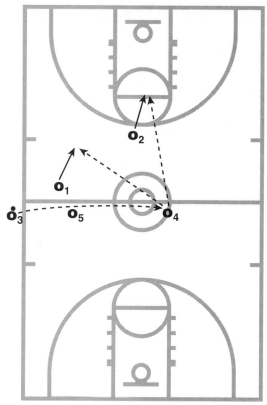

C. Third option in the Sideline Stack Play.

Remind your inbounders that if they can't make a good pass, they should call a time-out before the 5 seconds are up. It's far better to use a time-out than turn the ball over to the other team. Of course, if your team has no more time-outs left, remind your inbounders that they can't call a time-out, no matter what. In that case, a turnover is preferable to a technical foul.

Baseline Out-of-Bounds Plays

When the ball goes out-of-bounds along the baseline behind the other team's basket, your team will run a *baseline out-of-bounds play*. This is an excellent opportunity to get a high-percentage shot, because the ball is inbounded so close to the basket.

As with your sideline plays, designate an inbounder. Again, choose someone who passes well, who is a smart player, and who won't panic. I again assume 3 is the inbounder (if your 3 isn't a good passer, choose someone else).

When the ball goes out-of-bounds along the baseline, the referee will give it to the inbounder on one side of the basket or the other. The inbounder should stand 3 feet outside the baseline, at the extension of the lane line on that side. She shouldn't stand behind the basket because the bottom part of the backboard restricts how high she can throw the pass. As with sideline plays, the inbounder signals the start of the play by slapping the ball.

You should have one baseline out-of-bounds play for when the other team plays man-to-man defense and a second play for when they play zone defense. Teams that play zone in this situation usually use a 2-3 zone because the other zones don't have enough players near the baseline and are too easy to exploit.

I've included two plays for each defense: one that uses a box formation, and one that uses a stack formation. I've labeled them for the defenses for which they're suited. Change the names of any of these plays to make them recognizable to your players.

Against Man-to-Man Defense. Against man-to-man defense, run the Box Man Play or the Stack Man Play. In the *Box Man Play*, the other four players set up in a box formation. Player 1 is at the ball-side elbow, 2 is at the help-side elbow, 4 is at the ball-side block, and 5 is at the help-side block.

On the ball slap, 1 sets a cross screen for 2, and 4 sets a cross screen for 5. The first option is to pass to 5 for a short jump shot. If 5 is taller than her defender, this will be an easy pass and

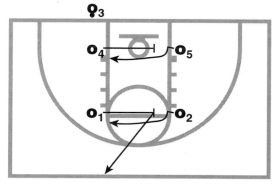

A. Initial movement in the Box Man Play.

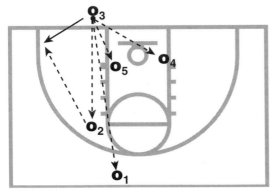

B. Options in the Box Man Play.

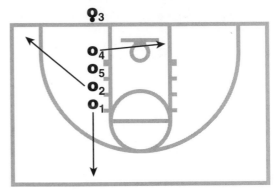

B. Second ball slap in the Stack Man Play.

an easy shot. The second option is to pass to 2, who either shoots an open jump shot, passes to 5 posting up, or passes to 3, who comes in from out-of-bounds to the ball-side corner.

After 4 sets her screen, she seals the defender and tries to post up in the lane. If she doesn't get the ball right away, she goes to the block that 5 vacated to avoid a 3-second lane violation.

After 1 sets her screen, she goes to the top of the circle to be the safety and the last option for 3. If 3 can't pass to anyone else, she should not panic, because 1 will be there. If 1's defender is guarding her closely, 3 should pass the ball over 1's head so 1 can race to it before her defender can. This isn't a backcourt violation. As long as the ball is entered from out-of-bounds, the rules allow a player to retrieve the ball in the backcourt.

The *Stack Man Play* starts out looking like the Box Man Play but has two ball slaps. At the first one, the four other players line up in a

stack formation as in the Sideline Stack Play, except the order is reversed. This time, 4 is first in line at the block, followed by 5, 2, and 1.

At the second ball slap, 1 drops back as a safety and last-resort pass, 2 cuts to the ball-side corner, 4 cuts to the opposite block, and 5 posts up where she is. Player 5 is the first option, because the area will be clear of everyone except for her and her defender. Depending on how her defender plays her, 5 either posts up for the bounce pass or for a lob pass.

The second option is to pass to 4. If 4 can post up in the lane with her defender on her back, she'll be open for an easy shot. The third option is to pass to 2, and the last option is to pass to 1. If this happens, 3 steps in to screen 5's defender, and 1 passes to 2 for a jump shot.

Against Zone Defense. Against zone defense, run the Box Zone Play or the Stack Zone Play. In the *Box Zone Play*, the players start in the box formation as they did in the Box

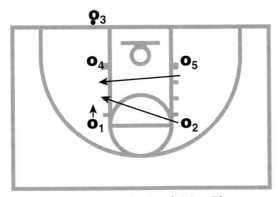

A. First ball slap in the Stack Man Play.

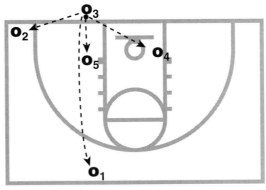

C. Options in the Stack Man Play.

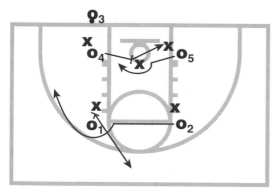

A. *Screens in the Box Zone Play.*

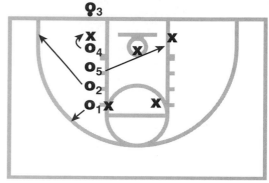

A. *Second ball slap in the Stack Zone Play.*

Man Play. At the ball slap, 4 screens the middle defender (usually their tallest player), 5 uses the screen to get open for a short jump shot, 1 sets a screen on the nearest zone defender, and 2 uses 1's screen to cut to the wing. If 3 passes to 1, 2 drops back to be the safety. If 3 doesn't pass to 1, 1 goes to be the safety.

The first option is the lob pass to 5. Again, if your 5 is tall, she'll often be open. The second option is to pass to 4, if 4 can post up. If 4 and 5 don't get the ball, they must remember to leave the lane to avoid the 3-second lane violation. The third option is to pass to 2 for a jump shot or post feed to 5. A long pass to 1 over the top of the zone is always available as a last resort.

The *Stack Zone Play* is another two-slap play. The formation starts out looking like the Box Zone Play, but after the first ball slap, the players form a stack, as in the Stack Man Play.

On the second slap, 5 posts up on the farthest baseline defender, usually positioned

inside the opposite block. If 5 is good at posting up, she'll be open for a layup. At the same time, 4 posts up on the block in front of the inbounder, 2 cuts to the ball-side corner, and 1 cuts to the 3-point line halfway between the corner and the top of the circle.

The inbounder should first look for 5, then for 4. If they aren't open, she passes to 1. As the ball is in the air, 2 sets a screen on the closest baseline defender, who is usually in the block area guarding 4. After 3 passes to 1, she goes to the corner that 2 vacated. With 2's screen, 3 will have an open jump shot almost every time. After passing to 3, 1 stays back as the safety.

Press Offense

When a team guards the offensive players in the backcourt, they are *pressing* them. The formations used to do this are called *presses*. Just

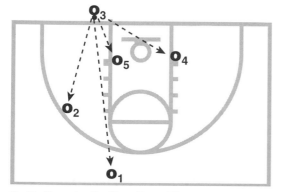

B. *Options in the Box Zone Play.*

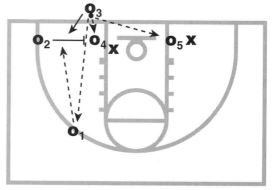

B. *Options in the Stack Zone Play.*

like half-court defenses, presses can be either man-to-man or zone. In *full-court presses*, the defenders guard the offensive players from baseline to baseline. In *three-quarter-court presses*, the defenders don't start guarding until the ball reaches the free throw line extended.

Most pressing teams press after they score a basket. It takes a second or two for a player from the team that was scored on to take the ball out of the basket and set up behind the baseline, which gives the defenders time to set up in the press formation. Some teams also press after a missed field goal or a missed free throw. When playing a team that doesn't start out pressing, expect them to press when the game is close, especially when time is running out and your team is ahead.

Different presses have different purposes, but in general, they all are designed to accomplish the following:

1. **Cause turnovers.** Presses create confusion and bad decisions that lead to bad passes and steals. Steals off the press, because they're so close to the basket, often result in easy scores.

2. **Speed up the offense.** Particularly against a team that doesn't play fast, the press forces them to play at an uncomfortable pace.

3. **Get the other team rattled.** When the press causes turnovers, the offensive players start to panic and lose confidence. This hurts the way they play at both ends of the court.

4. **Wear down the other team's ball handlers.** Most teams use their guards to advance the ball against the press. If the press is on all game long, the guards will have expended a lot of energy by the end of the game. This makes them more likely to make bad decisions and mistakes as the second half goes on.

For these reasons, your team needs to know how to play against the press—how to *break the press*. You need to teach a good *press offense* (also called a *press break*). Regardless of which one you choose (or if you choose another press break from another source), there are several principles that apply when breaking any press:

1. **Get the ball in the middle.** When the offense gets the ball in the middle, away from the trapping areas, the press is broken. The two press breaks explained below have players cutting to the middle for that purpose.

2. **Reverse the ball.** Attacking a full-court defense is no different than attacking a half-court defense. Ball reversal forces the defenders to change position rapidly. This presents opportunities for the offense to advance the ball.

3. **Hit the open man.** Every time an offensive player catches the ball, she should first look up the court to see if someone is open. If she spots someone open within her passing range, she should immediately get that player the ball.

4. **Pass before dribbling.** The ball moves faster through the air than on the floor. Your players should think of passing as the first option and dribbling as the second.

5. **Avoid traps.** Players who catch the ball against the press are likely to face traps. They should be alert and not dribble into the obvious trapping areas.

6. **Try to score.** Don't settle only for advancing the ball up the court. If possible, attack the other team's basket. Many presses trap. These are opportunities to have a numbers advantage at the other end of the court. Once the press is broken, run the fast break. If your team can score two or three easy baskets, the other team will likely *pull off* (stop) the press.

Types of Press Breaks

The *V Press Break* is best suited for man-to-man presses, but it also works for zone presses.

As 3 takes the ball out of the basket, 1 and 2 set up at the free throw line, facing 3. Player 1 stands behind 2, her hands on 2's shoulders. Players 4 and 5 set up in the half-court corners, facing 3. They form the top of the V, and 1 and 2 form the bottom point.

On the ball slap, 1 pushes 2's shoulders to the left or to the right and cuts in the other direction on a diagonal line to the corner. Player 2 cuts to the corner indicated by 1's push. They shouldn't go all the way to the corner, or they'll put themselves in an ideal spot for a trap. To make it harder for the defenders to stay with them every time, 1 varies which way she goes. As 1 and 2 make their cuts, 4 also cuts diagonally, sprinting hard toward the free throw line. Player 5 takes a few steps toward the inbounder, then heads back to the mid-court line.

Player 3 waits to see who gets open. The first option is to pass to 4, because the press will be broken at that point. When 4 receives the pass, the other players sprint toward the other basket, looking for the fast break. If 4 isn't open, the second option is to pass to the player cutting toward the ball-side corner. The third option is to pass to the player heading toward the other corner. If 5's defender is more than a few steps in front of 5 and 3 has a good arm, 3 throws a baseball pass for a *home run ball* over 5's head. It should be easy for 5 to outrace her defender and shoot a layup.

After 3 passes, she steps onto the court, staying near the basket in case 1 or 2 is in trouble. Player 3 is the means for ball reversal. If 1 is trapped and can't dribble or pass up the court,

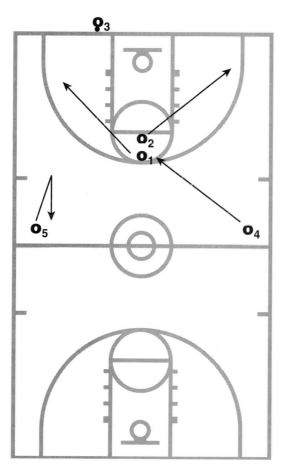

A. Initial movement in the V Press Break.

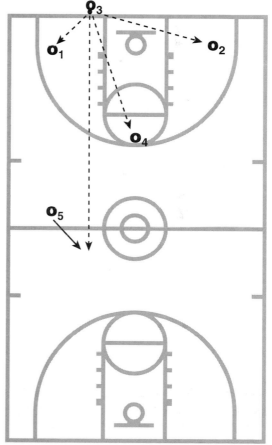

B. Options in the V Press Break.

she passes back to 3, who immediately passes to 2. When this happens, 4 cuts back to her original position, and 5 now cuts to the middle. When 2 catches the ball, she first looks up the court for 4 or 5. If neither are open and she's guarded, she passes back to 3, again reversing the ball. As long as the team crosses the mid-court line within 10 seconds, there's no limit as to how many times the players can reverse the ball. Usually, it takes only one or two ball reversals before the press is broken.

The *4-Across Press Break* is suited for both man-to-man or zone presses. The four players on the court set up on the free throw line extended, evenly spaced, facing the inbounder. As viewed from the baseline, 4 is at the far left, 1 is on the help-side elbow, 2 is on the ball-side elbow, and 5 is at the far right.

When 3 slaps the ball, 2 takes two steps toward 1 and screens for her. Player 1 uses the screen and cuts to the ball-side corner. After 1 makes her cut off 2's shoulder, 2 cuts toward the help-side corner. Just as in the V Press Break, neither player should go too deep into the corner because of the danger of an easy trap. While 1 and 2 make their cuts, 4 cuts almost to the mid-court line, plants her outside foot, and makes a V-cut, sprinting to the free throw area. Meanwhile, 5 takes three steps toward 3, as if to receive the pass, and then cuts hard toward the midcourt line.

At this point, 3 has several options:

- pass to 4 (the best option because the ball is in the middle)

- pass to 1 or 2

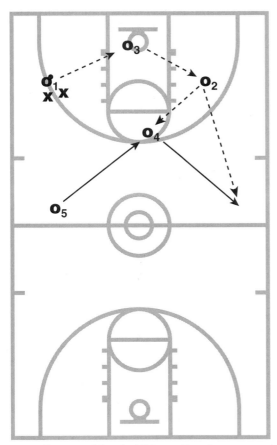

C. Ball reversal in the V Press Break.

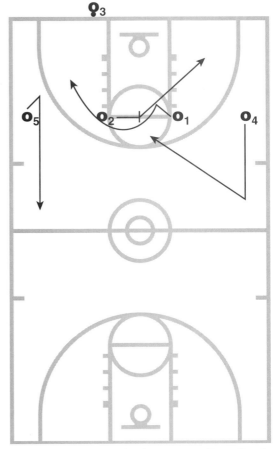

A. Initial movement in the 4-Across Press Break.

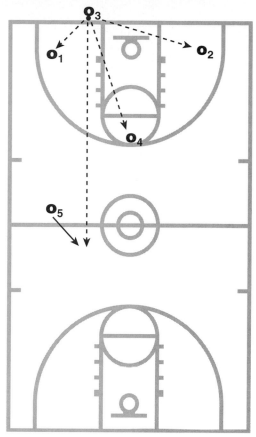

B. Options in the 4-Across Press Break.

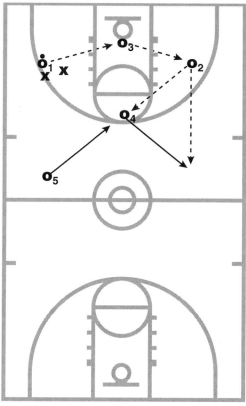

C. Ball reversal in the 4-Across Press Break.

- pass to 5 (3 must have a good arm to complete this pass)

After 3 inbounds the ball, she stays back for ball reversal, if needed. If 1 catches the ball and can't pass up the court or dribble, she passes to 3, who immediately passes to 2.

A key to the 4-Across Press Break is for 4 to wait until 1 and 2 have cleared out of the middle. If 4 rushes her cut, the middle won't be

Question: How do I get my kids to make good cuts in our press break? They cut like they're in slow motion.

Answer: First, making cuts is a skill that needs to be learned and practiced (beginners won't have any idea what a cut is, much less how to make one properly). Making sharp, hard cuts is a vital part of good offense. Before you teach any team offense, teach your players how to make good cuts.

Second, when you practice the press break (or any other offense), make the drills competitive with winners and losers. Losers should have a penalty such as running or push-ups. This makes your drills more intense and encourages maximum effort for everything, including making good cuts.

Third, even if your players are a bit on the slow side, they can still learn to be good cutters. Speed is only one part of the skill. Timing the cut and setting up the defender to get her off balance are just as important.

open, the defenders will be close together, and the press will be harder to break.

Delay Offense

There are times when you want your team to hold on to the ball and not shoot right away. Maybe there's 1 minute left in the half, and you don't want to give the other team a chance to rebound and score. Maybe your team is ahead in the waning minutes of the game, and your strategy is to force the other team to foul your players and put them on the free throw line. In these situations, you can run one of your regular offenses or, with the right personnel, you can run a *delay offense*.

The sole purpose of a delay offense is to run time off the clock while your team maintains possession of the ball. If you coach middle school players, there's no need (or time) to teach a delay offense. When you want to run time off the clock, use one of your basic offenses. Tell your players to take no shots other than layups. If you coach AAU or high school and you have good ball handlers, a delay offense might be right for your team.

One of the most popular delay offenses was an innovation Coach Dean Smith made famous—the Four Corners. This offense depends on having a great point guard (Coach Smith had Phil Ford, one of the best college point guards ever).

The Four Corners Offense has 1 in the middle of the floor, 2 and 3 near the midcourt corners, and 4 and 5 near the baseline corners. Player 1 dribbles in the center area. If she has trouble protecting the ball against her defender, 4 and 5 cut up the sideline to receive a pass. Whoever receives the pass immediately passes back to 1, who resumes dribbling. Player 1 can also pass to 2 or 3. If she passes to 2, and if 2 can also handle the ball, 2 dribbles to the center area, and 1 replaces 2 near the midcourt corner. If at any time 1 sees an opening, she drives to the basket. If either 4 or 5's defender comes over to help, 1 passes to her open teammate, who passes back right away.

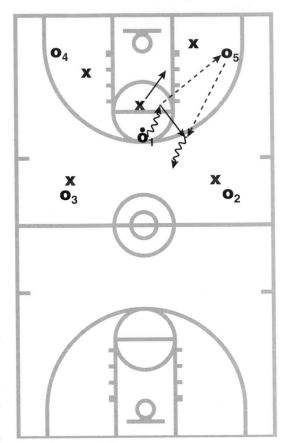

Four Corners Offense.

The Four Corners Offense is a high-pressure game of keep-away. It won many a game for Coach Smith. Maybe it can help your team, too.

Last-Second Plays

In close games, sometimes who wins comes down to whether a team can run a last-second play successfully. At the end of the game, defenses toughen up. The defenders see the finish line. They realize that if they make one more defensive stop, they win the game. A team that's behind with time running out is forced to play fast to catch up. It can't afford to run its regular offense. There's no time to pass the ball around, waiting for the defense to provide an opening. Instead, the team has to run a *last-second play*, a play designed to get a good shot within seconds of inbounding the ball. The odds the play will succeed are based on how well the players execute the play. The only way to execute plays well is (no surprise!) to practice them over and over so the players can run them in their sleep.

You don't need to teach more than one or two last-second plays. The same one can be used when you have to go the length of the court or when you inbound the ball near mid-court. Last-second plays can also be used as time is running out in the first half.

In the *Zoom Play*, 3 is the inbounder (again, this assumes she's a good passer who doesn't get rattled). If the other team has just scored, under the rules, 3 can *run the baseline*—run anywhere outside the baseline, as long as she inbounds

the ball within 5 seconds. She should be careful not to throw the ball from behind the basket, or she might hit the backboard.

While 3 takes the ball out of the basket, 1 and 2 set up at the closest free throw line, facing her. Player 1 stands behind 2. Player 5 sets up at the top of the circle at the other basket and 4 sets up in front of the basket (until someone touches the ball, there's no danger of getting a 3-second lane violation). It's critical that the players run to their spots while 3 takes the ball out of the basket, because the clock keeps running after a score. If your team is setting up to run the Zoom Play after a time-out, the players don't have to worry about the clock running until the ball comes into play.

After a made basket, the inbounder can run the baseline.

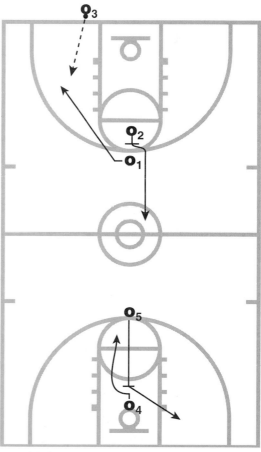

A. Initial movement in the Zoom Play.

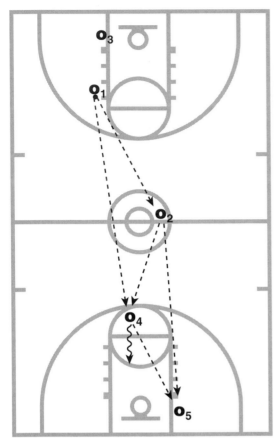

B. Options in the Zoom Play.

To start the play, 2 turns away from 3 and sets a screen on 1's defender. Player 1 cuts off the screen toward the ball-side corner to get the pass. After 2 screens, she runs up the court, looking over her shoulder to make sure 1 isn't being trapped. If 2 sees that the other team intends to trap 1, she runs to a spot where 1 can pass to her.

As this happens, 5 sets a screen on 4's defender, and 4 cuts toward the ball.

The goal is to get the ball to 4 at the free throw line so she can drive, shoot, or pass to 5 posting up. It depends on how much time is left. If 10 seconds are left, that's enough time for 3 to pass to 1, for 1 to pass to 2, and for 2 to pass to 4. If there are 5 seconds or less, there will be time for two passes at the most before the quick shot. In that case, 1 must throw the long baseball pass to 4.

If you coach high school or older AAU girls, you may have a player who can throw a long full-court pass with accuracy. If so, use her as the inbounder. If you coach younger girls, you'll have no choice but to get the ball up the court with two or three passes.

The *Two-Screen Play* is designed for when there's no time for any dribbling, only time for two rapid-fire passes and a shot. If 3 is your best inbounder, 4 is your best long passer, and 2 is your most reliable shooter, set your players in a box formation as follows: 4 and 5 are at mid-court, facing 3, each 4 to 5 feet off the center circle. Player 4 is on the ball side, and 5 is on the help side. Players 2 and 1 stand 10 to 12 feet in front of 4 and 5, respectively, also facing 3. On the ball slap, 2 and 1 take a hard step toward 3, as if trying to get open for a pass, reverse direction, cut to 4's and 5's defenders, respectively, and set screens. Players 4 and 5 use their screens and cut hard to the ball. If all goes well, 3 passes to 4 (or 5).

After setting their screens, 2 and 1 cut to the opposite basket. After receiving the pass, 4 turns (there's no time for even one dribble) and

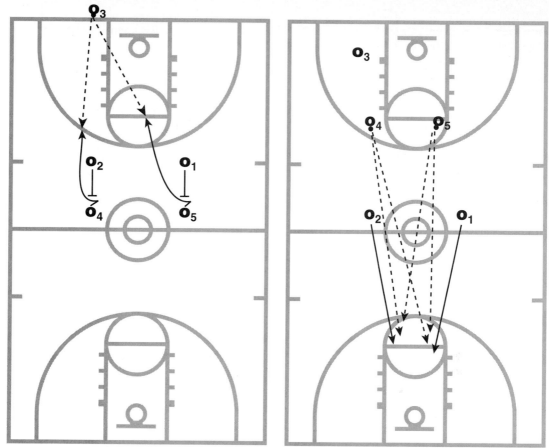

A. Initial movement in the Two-Screen Play.   *B. Options in the Two-Screen Play.*

ASK THE COACH

Question: In our last game, after a time-out, we set up to run the Two-Screen Play. Before the ref handed the ball to our player, the other coach called a time-out. When they came out after the time-out was over, the other team switched from man-to-man to a 2-3 zone. What should we have done?

Answer: The Zoom Play and the Two-Screen Play are intended for man-to-man defense. If only a few seconds are left in the game, and your team has to go the full length of the court against a team playing zone, you'll have trouble getting the ball inside the zone with the dribble or a pass. The best strategy is to put your three best shooters along the perimeter and have the inbounder roll the ball to the point guard (if the other coach is smart, he or she will have one player stay back to avoid this). If there are more than 3 seconds left, she can dribble hard into the offensive half of the court and try to find an open player. If there's less time, the best she can do is to heave a long pass to one of the shooters. The odds are that your team won't get a good shot in this situation, but you never know until you try. That's why people refer to last-second desperation shots as "Hail Marys."

passes to 2. If there's time, 2 drives for the layup. If not, she catches the ball, turns, and shoots. A second option for 4 is to pass to 1. Or, if 3 passes to 5 initially, 5 can pass to 2 or 1.

It's better to get a shot off from farther out than to try to get the layup and run out of time. As your team practices this play, practice both situations. When practicing the plays your team will use, practice all the options, not just the most desirable option.

Time and Score Situations

Besides last-second plays, it's important to practice other *time and score situations*—special situations your team may face in the last few minutes in games. Here are some examples of these situations:

- your team is down 3 points and has the ball at midcourt, 1 minute is left, and the other team is in the bonus
- your team is down 3 points, the other team has the ball along the baseline, 3 minutes are left, and both teams are in the bonus
- your team is up 5 points, the other team has the ball under its own basket, and 3 minutes are left
- your team has the ball under its own basket with 20 seconds left, and the score is tied
- your team is up by 4 points with 1 minute left, but the other team is inbounding the ball under your basket
- your team is up by 1 point, there are 30 seconds left, both teams are in the bonus, and the other team is inbounding the ball at midcourt

The number of possible time and score situations you can create is limited only by your imagination. The point is to practice end-game situations routinely so your team will be poised and confident when they happen. A

great time to practice them is at the end of practice. Players love to practice them, and it's always good to end practice on an upbeat note.

Opening Jump Ball

The game of basketball begins with a *jump ball* at the center circle. One player from each team stands inside the circle in the half nearest her team's basket. The players face each other. The other eight players line up outside the circle. When the referee is ready to start the game, he or she tosses the ball up underhanded between the two players, who jump and try to tip it to a teammate. The game is on.

Controlling the opening tip is a great way to start the game. Most teams use their tallest

It's time to play hoops. Let's tip it up!

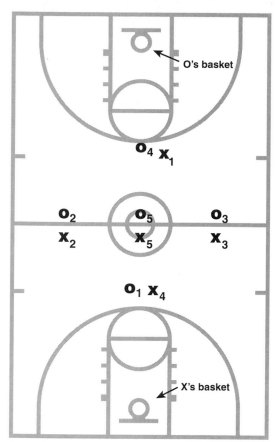

Jump ball setup.

player for that purpose, on the assumption she's the best choice for a jump ball. Before you decide who will be your jump ball player, run a little test. Have your most likely candidates line up by a wall. Hand the first player a blackboard eraser with chalk dust on it. Tell her to take it in her strong hand and prepare to jump. On your signal, she jumps as high as she can and makes a mark on the wall with the eraser. After all the candidates jump, choose the player who made the highest mark. If there's a tie between two players, have them jump again.

After you've chosen your jump ball player, align the other four players. Unless your jump ball player is certain to control the tip, assume the other team will get the tip. Set up in a defensive alignment, where 4 or 5 is back defending the basket, 2 and 3 are on the midcourt line, and 1 is on the other side of the circle. Player 1 will be the primary target for the tip, but the jump ball player should learn how to tip it to other players if 1 is covered.

Like every other part of team offense, practice the jump ball.

Chapter 4

TEAM DEFENSE

Half-Court Defense

There are three kinds of half-court defenses: man-to-man defenses, zone defenses, and combination defenses (part man-to-man and part zone; also called *junk defenses*). Combination defenses have limited value; though I'll cover them, I suggest you choose either a man-to-man or a zone as your team's primary defense.

Here are the principles of all team defenses:

1. **Prevent easy baskets.** That's the first priority of any defense. Even if a player's man is left wide open, if that player is the one defender who can stop a drive to the basket, she should leave her man and stop the ball.

2. **Keep the ball out of the lane.** This includes the high post area. It's preferable to let a team shoot from outside than let them shoot close to the basket.

3. **Force the ball to one side of the court.** The defender guarding the point guard at the top of the circle should force her to dribble to one side. This establishes a ball side and a help side, clarifying the responsibility of each defender. Everyone knows who should help on drives to the basket. If the point guard can keep the ball in the middle of the half court, she has many more options. When a player with the ball is close to the sideline, her options are limited.

4. **Keep the ball on one side of the court.** Once the ball is on one side of the court, defenders should try to keep it there. Ball reversal distorts the defense and causes holes and seams. Defenders have to cover a lot of ground to adjust their positions. When defenders can keep the ball on one side, they have much less to worry about.

5. **Drop to the level of the ball.** The closer the ball comes to the baseline, the closer the defenders are to the basket. If the ball gets to the low post, five defenders should be nearby, trying to force the post player to pass it back out. The farther the ball is from the basket, the less it can hurt the defense.

On page 86, I talked about the importance of teaching man-to-man principles and techniques even if your team will play a zone.

Before reading further, I suggest you reread that section.

Man-to-Man Versus Zone Defense

In deciding whether to play man-to-man or zone as your team's primary defense, consider:

- the experience, talent, and skill levels of your players
- the competition your team is facing
- the relative strengths and weaknesses of each defense

Man-to-man defenses and zone defenses have different strengths and weaknesses.

Advantages of man-to-man over zone:

- **More aggressive play.** The defenders guard a man as opposed to an area of the court, so they tend to play with more aggression and intensity. They take it as a personal challenge to stop their man.

- **Better matchups.** In man-to-man, you can put your best defenders on the other team's most dangerous players. In a zone, the other team can move its best players to the areas guarded by your weakest defenders.

- **More pressure on the ball.** In man-to-man, every dribble, every pass, and every shot can be contested. In a zone, the offense can easily pass the ball around the perimeter by moving to spots outside of the zone.

- **Better chances for creating turnovers.** This is a corollary of the first three points. Aggressive play, better matchups, and more pressure on the ball mean more forced turnovers.

- **Faster pace.** Man-to-man defense causes the offense to play faster. It forces the offensive players to rush their decisions and make more mistakes.

- **More transition opportunities.** Constant pressure on the ball and a faster pace give the defensive team more chances to run the fast break.

- **Better rebounding.** Because man-to-man defenders have specific players to guard, they know exactly whom to block out when a shot is taken. In a zone, the defenders often are unsure of whom they should block out. Any hesitation by a zone defender means that an offensive player can get the rebound and go up for an easy shot.

- **More pressure on outside shooters.** If a team has good shooters, man-to-man defenders can come out and guard them closely. This makes it harder for the offense to take uncontested shots.

After reading about the advantages of man-to-man over zone, you might wonder why any team ever plays zone. Read on . . .

Advantages of zone over man:

- **Easier to learn.** This is a major plus when you coach inexperienced players. It takes longer to learn how to play man-to-man defense than it does to learn how to play zone defense. The concepts of zone defense are simpler: "Here, Eileen. This is your area. Guard anyone who comes into it."

- **Easier to play.** Zone defenders have less square footage to defend. They have to worry about fewer offensive players. Because zone offenses use screens less than man-to-man offenses, zone defenders don't have to be as good at defending screens.

- **Better basket coverage.** Dribble penetration is harder against the zone. Wherever a dribbler tries to drive, there's a defender ready to stop her. Zone defenders never stray far from the basket.

- **Better post coverage.** In a man-to-man defense, the offensive team can take a tall post defender away from the basket by moving her player out of the lane. In a zone, the post defenders stay near the basket. This makes it harder to get the ball inside and for the posts to shoot a good shot.

- **Less chance of fouling.** As man-to-man defenders follow their players all over the court, they are often out of position. Zone defenders are less likely to be out of position. This means they are less likely to commit the most common fouls that result from being out of position—reaching and blocking.

- **Better defense against poor shooting teams.** Zone defenses allow lots of chances for outside shots. If a team doesn't shoot well from the perimeter and the zone defenders keep the ball out of the lane, the offense won't score much.

- **Forces a slower tempo.** Offenses become more deliberate when playing against a zone. There are fewer opportunities to get the ball in the lane, so it takes longer to find ways to get good shots. This favors teams that like to play at a slower pace. Fast-paced teams often are frustrated when playing a zone and become impatient. They start forcing bad shots and passes. Zone defenses get fast-paced offenses out of their rhythm.

- **Not as tiring to play.** Playing man-to-man takes more effort than playing zone because the players have more ground to cover.

My teams play man-to-man defense, though every now and then, for a change of pace, we'll play a zone. The aggressive nature of man-to-man and its ability to force turnovers fits the style of basketball I like. This doesn't mean you should play man-to-man. After reading the rest of this section, you'll have a good idea of which defense suits your personality and your players. Of course, if your players are experienced, you don't have to choose one or the other. You can teach them how to play both kinds of defense.

Man-to-Man Defense

There are two kinds of man-to-man defense: sagging man-to-man and pressure man-to-man. In the sagging version, the defenders stay between their man and the basket. In the pressure version, the defenders stay between their man and the ball.

Sagging man-to-man is the more conservative of the two defenses. It allows the offensive players more room to catch the ball, but

---

ASK THE COACH

Question: My preference is to play man-to-man, but few of my JV girls have played it before. I'm concerned that we'll lose too many games while learning how to be good at it. If we play zone, I figure we'll win at least a few games. What should I do?

Answer: Everyone who coaches inexperienced players faces this question. Do you put in the defense that's easier to teach or the defense that takes longer to teach but creates more turnovers? Many middle school teams play zone, but many high schools play man-to-man defense. Players who come to high school without knowing how to play man-to-man will initially be at a disadvantage. My strong advice is to teach man-to-man principles. You might find that your players love the aggressive mental approach. The defense takes longer to learn, but once the players learn it, your defense will be tougher than if it were a zone. Even if you decide to play zone, you can't play good zone defense without learning man-to-man principles.

If there's a big gap between the athleticism and experience level of your players versus the teams they'll play, teach man-to-man principles and play zone. It's not worth suffering through blowout after blowout against better teams. Pack in the zone and force the other team to shoot outside shots. Even if your team doesn't win any games, at least the games won't be so one-sided.

Some coaches swear by man-to-man, and some swear by zone. There's no right or wrong approach. Choose what fits your team and your personality best.

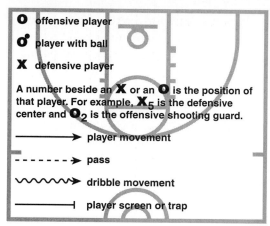

- **O** offensive player
- **O⃗** player with ball
- **X** defensive player

A number beside an **X** or an **O** is the position of that player. For example, **X₅** is the defensive center and **O₂** is the offensive shooting guard.

——————▶ player movement

- - - - - - ▶ pass

〰〰〰▶ dribble movement

———————┤ player screen or trap

Diagram key.

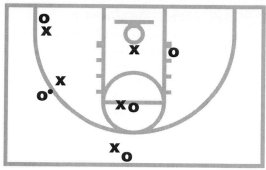

Pressure man-to-man defense.

the defender is in good on-ball position. The offense finds it easier to complete passes against this defense, but harder to drive to the basket.

Pressure man-to-man uses the concepts described on pages 86–94—on-ball defense, denial defense, and help-side defense. The four defenders guarding the players without the ball are either in the denial stance, with a hand and foot in the passing lane, or in the help-side stance, with a hand pointing to the ball and a hand pointing to the man. The goal of pressure man-to-man is to make it hard for the offensive players to do what they want to do. Every pass, dribble, shot, and cut is defended.

My teams play pressure man-to-man. The rest of this section will explain how to teach this defense. Here are the principles:

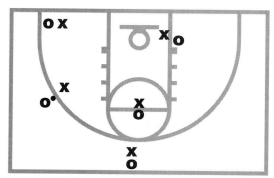

Sagging man-to-man defense.

1. When a pass is made, defenders should *jump to the ball*—change to a denial position so their man can't cut between them and the ball. They should get to their new position before the ball gets to the receiver.

2. When the ball is above the free throw line extended, and the defender's man is on the help side, the defender should have one foot in the lane.

3. When the ball is below the free throw line extended, and the defender's man is on the help side, the defender should be in the middle of the lane.

4. Each defender should know where the ball is at all times.

5. Each defender should know where her man is at all times.

6. When the ball is below the free throw line and the defender's man is in the ball-side low post area, the defender should front her.

7. Defenders should never front the high post. The player defending the high post isn't involved in help defense.

8. Defenders should remember that they can't help too early, but they can help too late. The goal of help defense is to stop the ball from coming into the lane.

9. Defenders should constantly talk. They should tell their teammates what they need to know.

Practicing Man-to-Man Defense

The best drills for teaching team defense are *shell drills*, which can be done with anywhere from two to five offensive players and defenders. (See Drills 58–61 in Chapter 7.) In shell drills, the offensive players set up in a particular alignment. They pass the ball around, and the defenders adjust their positions and stances accordingly. The defenders can't deflect or steal the ball—they must let the receivers catch it. Their focus is to react properly to every pass. Their goal is to arrive at their new spots, in their new stances, before the receiver catches the ball. This may not be possible when a defender has to cover a lot of distance (e.g., when moving from a help-side position to an on-ball position). However, if the defender concentrates on that goal, she'll get there in plenty of time to close out and prevent a drive.

When running a shell drill, follow a progression:

1. At first, the passers hold the ball until you're satisfied the defenders are in their proper positions and stances.

2. As the defenders improve, the offensive players hold the ball for only 2 seconds before passing.

3. Add the drive. When you call an offensive player's name, she drives by her defender (her defender stands still and lets her). This is how to practice defensive rotations.

4. Add the basket cut. When you call an offensive player's name, after she passes, she cuts to the basket. The other offensive players rotate to fill her spot. This is how to practice jumping to the ball when a defender's man passes.

5. Add the help-side cut. When you call an offensive player's name, she cuts into the lane from the help side. This is how to practice bumping the cutters.

6. Add the screen. Tell your players to screen away and to set down screens, ball screens, and cross screens. This is a critical element. As discussed later (see pages 154–57), defending screens is the hardest aspect to learn in playing team defense.

7. Lastly, add the shot. When you call an offensive player's name, she shoots. This practices defensive block outs.

Once you get to the Five-Man Shell (Drill 61), your team will be practicing its man-to-man pressure defense. Note that during any shell drill, the defenders should communicate on every pass. They should call out their new defensive assignment: "Ball!" or "Deny!" or "Help!" They should let their teammates know about cutters, shooters, and screeners. Your team won't play good defense until your players learn to communicate.

Practice shell drills every practice. Other good drills that work on individual defensive skills and team defense are to play 1-on-1, 2-on-2, and 3-on-3, without structured plays. If you have more than two baskets, this is an excellent way of having your whole team working at the same time. If you have only two baskets, you can still split into two groups, each at a basket.

An excellent drill that practices individual and team defense, along with offensive skills and decision making, is 3-on-3-on-3 (Drill 72). This drill can be run in the half court or full court and is one of the best conditioning drills.

Zone Defense

In zone defense, each defender has a specific area on the floor she's responsible for. It's her job to guard the offensive players that come into her area, whether they have the ball or not.

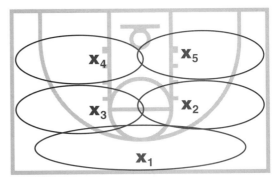

A. Coverage areas in the 1-2-2 zone.

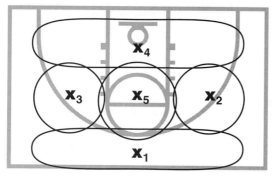

B. Coverage areas in the 1-3-1 zone.

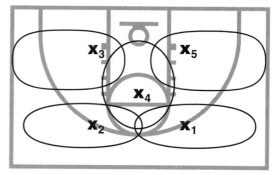

D. Coverage areas in the 2-1-2 zone.

The coverage areas for the most common zone defenses are shown opposite and this page.

The decision to play man-to-man or zone is more important than deciding which zone to play. If you plan to play zone, I suggest you teach a one-guard front zone and a two-guard front zone. The first type is better suited against outside shooting teams, and the second type is better suited against inside-oriented teams. That way, you'll have a zone for any team you face. Also, if the other team is beating your first defense, you'll have a second one to try as an option.

1-2-2 Zone. The 1-2-2 zone puts good pressure on the perimeter shooters and is a good choice when the other team shoots well. It also covers the block areas well. Its weakness is that it leaves a hole in the middle of the lane that can be exploited. The high post area is also vulnerable when the top player in the zone is

guarding the ball at the top of the circle. When the ball is on one side of the court, the help-side guard must move over to prevent the pass to the high post. Good offensive teams will flash players into the middle of the 1-2-2 from the help side, so your players must be alert at all times and must communicate well. When the ball is in the corner, if the offensive player is a good shooter, the ball-side post defender must come out to guard her, and the help-side post defender and help-side wing defender must rotate to protect the basket area.

The 1-2-2 offers trapping opportunities when the ball crosses the midcourt line. Have the top defender force the point guard to dribble to one side. As the point guard approaches the sideline, the top defender and the wing defender trap her in the corner. After she picks up her dribble, the other three defenders look for chances to steal the pass.

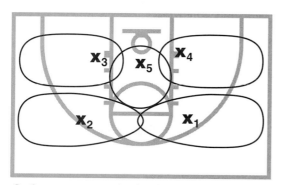

C. Coverage areas in the 2-3 zone.

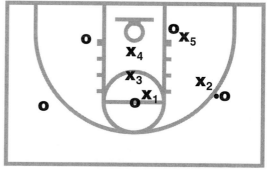

A. Ball on the wing in the 1-2-2 zone.

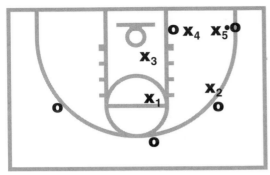

B. Ball in the corner in the 1-2-2 zone.

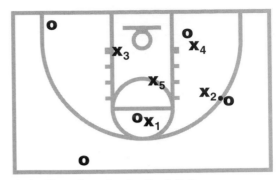

A. Ball on the wing in the 1-3-1 zone.

1-3-1 Zone. The 1-3-1 zone also covers the perimeter shooters well and provides excellent coverage of the middle of the lane. Its weakness is the lack of coverage along the baseline. The back defender is responsible for a lot of square footage, so put one of your best and quickest defenders there (some teams put their point guard back there). Good offensive teams will try to exploit the low post weakness, so the middle defender and the ball-side wing defenders must be ready to drop down to help. When the ball is in the corner, the defense must rotate to protect the basket area.

The 1-3-1 offers trapping opportunities in four corners, which is one reason this is a popular zone. If you have quick defenders, they should look for chances to trap, particularly if the other team has shaky ball handlers.

2-3 Zone. The 2-3 zone is a very popular zone defense. It provides excellent coverage near the basket and the strongest rebounding coverage of any zone, because three defenders are near the basket. Its weakness is in defending the high post area and the perimeter. When the ball is on the wing, the help-side guard must guard the high post. When the ball is in the corner, if the ball-side post goes out to guard the shooter, the middle defender drops to guard the low post. The 2-3 gives up lots of outside shots because two defenders must cover a large area against three offensive players. If the other team has a good inside game, this defense is a good choice, but if the other team has good shooters, the 1-2-2 or 1-3-1 zone would be a better choice.

The 2-3 zone offers two trapping opportunities: one when the dribbler brings the ball over the midcourt line, the other when the wing player receives the pass. For the latter to work, the ball-side posts must start out a few more steps away from the baseline. Otherwise, they won't have time to race out and set the trap.

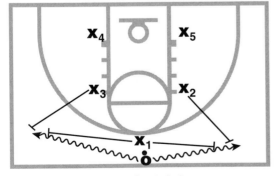

C. Trapping areas in the 1-2-2 zone.

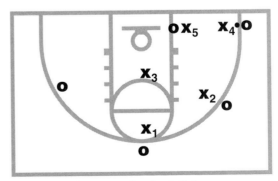

B. Ball in the corner in the 1-3-1 zone.

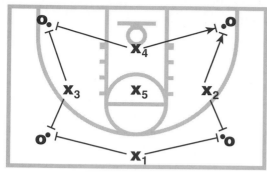

C. Trapping areas in the 1-3-1 zone.

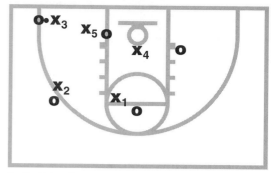

B. Ball in the corner in the 2-3 zone.

2-1-2 Zone. The 2-1-2 zone is a 2-3 zone with one difference—the middle player guards the high post area. However, when the ball drops toward the baseline, the middle player also drops down, as if she's in a 2-3. The 2-1-2 gives up some basket coverage but is strong in defending the high post. Other than that, everything about the 2-1-2 zone is the same as in the 2-3 zone, including the trapping areas.

Practicing Zone Defense

To practice zone defense, use shell drills. (Even if you plan to play zone, read the explanation there so you'll understand how to run a shell drill when practicing zone defense.)

Start with just the players at the top of the zone and place offensive players in the gaps. Have the offensive players pass the ball as the defenders change their positions as fast as they can. Work up to the point where the offensive players pass after a count of one.

Then, add the rest of the offense and the other defenders. Make sure every offensive player receives and passes the ball. Have them reverse the ball through the point and the high post and by a skip pass. Add bumping the cutter. Make sure the defenders call "Cutter!" as soon as a player starts to flash into the lane. Make sure a defender bumps her. Add the drive element. Teach the players to rotate properly. As with man-to-man, when a post defender leaves to help, two players must rotate from their positions, the help-side post defender and the help-side wing defender.

Combination Defense

When the other team has one standout offensive player, a defensive strategy is to play a *combination* (or *junk*) defense—a box-and-one or a diamond-and-one.

In a *box-and-one*, the four defenders set up in a box with two posts on the blocks and two

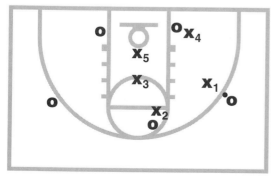

A. Ball on the wing in the 2-3 zone.

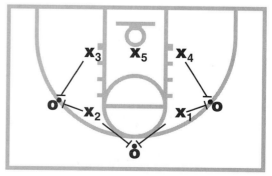

C. Trapping areas in the 2-3 zone.

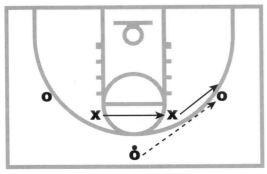

A. Top of 2-3 zone in the shell drill.

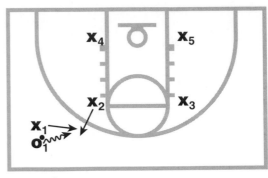

Box-and-one.

guards at the elbows. They play a zone, no different than if it were a regular five-player zone. The fifth defender plays man-to-man on the star and tries to keep her from touching the ball. Obviously, your best defender should be assigned to guard the star (assuming she isn't in foul trouble). Anytime the star gets the ball, the nearest zone defender comes over to double-team the star. The goals are to prevent the star from scoring a decisive number of points and to force her teammates to play bigger scoring roles than they're used to. When this happens, the star often becomes frustrated and makes bad decisions, and the other offensive players struggle to take up the slack.

In a *diamond-and-one*, the four zone players set up in a diamond shape with a post in front of the basket, two defenders on the wing (not all the way to the 3-point line), and the quickest defender at the top of the circle. The fifth defender plays man-to-man on the star.

In both defenses, the defender guarding the star has no responsibility to help. Even if her man is on the help side far from the ball, she sticks with her, trying to keep her from getting open. She should play physically, bumping the star every time she tries to cut to the ball. The defender must be good at defending screens because the other team will likely set screens to try to get the star open.

Choose which defense to use in defending a star player based on the strengths of the four other offensive players. If they're good outside shooters, the diamond-and-one gives better coverage on the perimeter. If they have good post players, the box-and-one gives better protection in the low post areas.

When the other team has two offensive stars, a possible defensive strategy is to play a *triangle-and-two*. In this defense, three defenders play zone, and the other two defenders guard the stars man-to-man. The zone defenders form

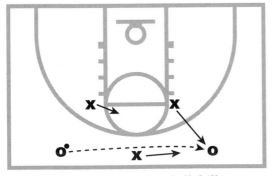

B. Top of 1-2-2 zone in the shell drill.

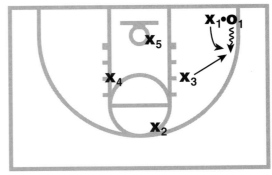

Diamond-and-one.

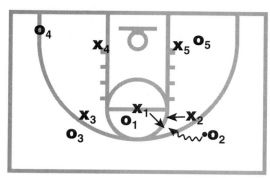

Triangle-and-two.

a triangle—one defender is at the free throw line and two defenders are on the blocks. As in other combination defenses, the man-to-man defenders have no help duties. They stick with their men wherever they go.

If you coach middle school, don't spend any time on junk defenses. If you coach high school and want to have one in your back pocket, don't make a junk defense your primary defense. They're limited in use because good coaches will devise effective strategies to counter them. Although you might want to practice one and pull it out as a surprise tactic now and then, concentrate the bulk of your practice time allocated to team defense to learning how to play man-to-man or zone.

Full-Court Defense

Teach your team how to *press*—guard the other players in the backcourt before they bring the ball past midcourt. Without the ability to attack the ball full court, it will be hard for your team to catch up if you're behind late in the game. If you have aggressive, quick players, a full-court press is a powerful defensive tool. A good pressing team dictates the pace of the game, scores easy points off steals, wears the other players down, and forces them into repeated mistakes. A good pressing team playing a team with suspect ball handlers causes chaos and confusion.

Man-to-Man Press

If your team plays man-to-man half court, it makes sense to play man-to-man full court as well. After your team scores, as a player from the other team takes the ball out of the basket and runs off the court to inbound it, each of your players runs to guard her man. The defender assumes the defensive stance and position based on man-to-man ball-side or help-side half-court principles (see page 143). If the player is one pass away from the ball, the defender guards her in the denial stance. If the defender is on the help side, the defender guards her in a help-side stance. The primary role of the player guarding

---

ASK THE COACH

Question: I coach a very good high school team with talented players, and I'm thinking of making either the triangle-and-two or the box-and-one a major part of our defense. I hear what you say about the limitations of these defenses, but I've talked to several coaches who say they don't spend time practicing offense against these defenses. Doesn't it make sense to use a defense that few teams prepare for?

Answer: Yes and no. You might get a few defensive stops from switching to a junk defense during a game, but the offense will learn how to get good shots after a while. Coaches with star players will be prepared with strategies to counter these defenses. Their teams will have practiced taking advantage of the weaknesses of these defenses. Smart coaches will have the star set screens, effectively occupying two defenders. This will leave an offensive player wide open. Smart coaches will have that wide-open player set up in the gaps of the zones. These players will have uncontested shots not far from the basket. You might say, "Well, not all the coaches we face are that smart, so they won't know how to adjust for the box-and-one." True, but if they're not that smart, your primary defense should be too much for them anyway.

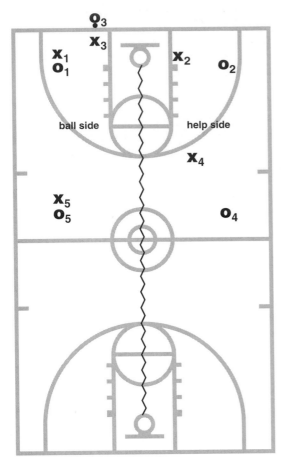

Full-court man-to-man press.

In Rover Middle, the rover lines up near the top of the circle. This defends the pass thrown over the top of the initial defenders in the press.

In Rover Back, the rover lines up at midcourt to prevent the home run pass. As the game goes on, mix up where the rover is to keep the offense off balance. Put one of your best defenders at rover. Ideally, the rover will be quick, smart, and have great anticipation.

Since most presses try to force the ball to the sideline, most presses are broken when the ball is passed to the middle of the court. At that point, the player with the ball can dribble up the court or pass to another player ahead. When the ball goes to the middle, the defenders should immediately stop pressing and sprint

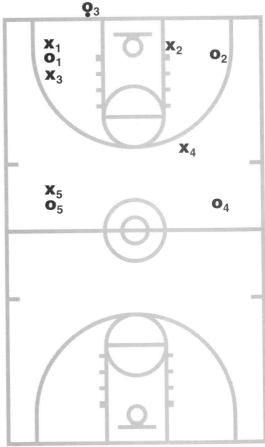

A. Rover Up.

the inbounder is to prevent the long pass. The defender stands upright, waving her hands high, yelling, "Ball, ball, ball!" trying to distract the inbounder and impair her vision.

A variation of the full-court man-to-man press you can call from the bench is called Rover. The *rover* is the defender assigned to guard the inbounder. Instead of lining up directly on the inbounder, the rover lines up somewhere else, depending on how the offensive team likes to inbound the ball. If they like to pass to the point guard, the rover and the point guard's defender double-team the point guard. The rover plays behind her, preventing the lob pass, and the other defender plays between the point guard and the passer, preventing the cut to the ball. I call this setup Rover Up.

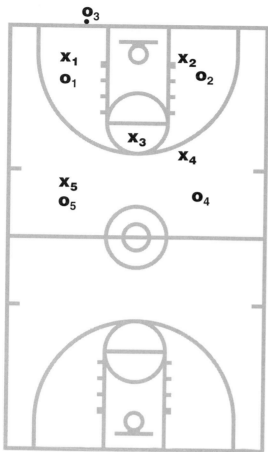

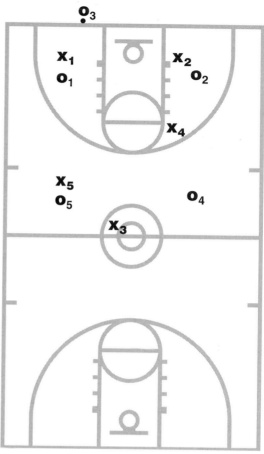

B. Rover Middle.   *C. Rover Back.*

toward their basket so the other team can't run a fast break. They sprint on a straight line to the middle of the lane, looking over their shoulder every few steps to see where the ball is.

This is a key part of *defensive transition*—when an offense no longer has the ball and converts to playing defense. Emphasize that in transition, your defenders have three goals, in this order of importance:

1. **Protect the basket.** This means preventing a layup or a short jump shot. This is the job of the first player back on defense. She should sprint to a spot 5 feet in front of the basket to make sure the other team can't get an easy shot.

2. **Stop the ball.** The second player back on defense, seeing that the basket is protected, has the job of stopping the ball—guarding the player with the ball so she can't continue to dribble to the basket. This allows the rest of the defenders to get back in time to assume their defensive responsibilities.

3. **Guard your man or zone.** Once the basket is protected and the forward movement of the ball is stopped, the rest of the defenders can sprint to their positions, whether this means guarding their assigned man or positioning themselves properly in their assigned area in the zone.

Zone Press

There are several kinds of full-court zone presses. They operate like half-court zones—the defenders guard specific areas, not specific players.

1-2-1-1 Press. One of the most popular and effective full-court zones is the 1-2-1-1 Press (also called a Diamond Press because the four defenders nearest the ball form a diamond shape). The defenders line up as follows:

- the quickest post player (4) guards the inbounder
- two perimeter players (1 and 2) are at the elbow
- the quickest perimeter player (3) is at midcourt

- the biggest post (5) is at the top of the opposite circle to guard against the fast break

The goal of the Diamond Press is to force a pass to one of the players cutting toward the corners. The job of 4 is to keep her hands active and up to discourage a long pass over the front defenders. When the inbounder passes to the player heading for the near corner, as the ball is in the air, 4 runs to set a trap with 1. Simultaneously, 2 comes over to guard the middle, 3 slides over to the ball-side sideline to guard the pass up the court, and 5 slides over to prevent the home run pass.

If the player with the ball reverses it through the inbounder, the zone shifts to set a trap on the other side. Player 4 follows the ball and sets a trap with 2, 1 goes diagonally to

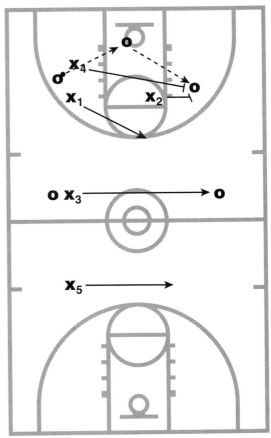

A. *Covering the pass to the near corner in the Diamond Press.*

B. *Defending ball reversal in the Diamond Press.*

guard the middle, 3 covers the next pass up the court, and 5 shifts to cover the long pass.

Once the ball goes to the middle of the court or over the heads of 1 and 2, the press is broken. At that point, the defenders sprint back to the lane to protect against the fast break.

2-2-1 Press. In the 2-2-1 Press, four players (1, 2, 3, and 4) set up in a box formation, and 5 stays back to protect the basket. This press allows the ball to be inbounded but tries to trap along the sideline or in the middle. When the pass goes to a player in the near corner, 1 positions herself so the player can't dribble to the middle and can't pass back to the inbounder. As soon as the player makes her first dribble along the sideline, the defense rotates. Player 2 covers the middle, 3 comes up

to set a trap with 1, 4 covers a diagonal pass, and 5 slides over to prevent a pass ahead of the dribbler.

If 1 can't force the player to the sideline and the player dribbles to the middle, 2 comes to trap with 1 while 3 and 4 guard against the forward pass. Player 5 stays back to protect the basket.

The 2-2-1 Press is a conservative press in that it allows the inbounds pass, and only four players are involved in pressuring the ball. Its weakness is in protecting a pass to the middle, so the defenders must be ready to sprint back if that happens. Its strengths are that it slows down the offensive players and makes them take time to advance the ball into the front-court. This is a good press to use against teams

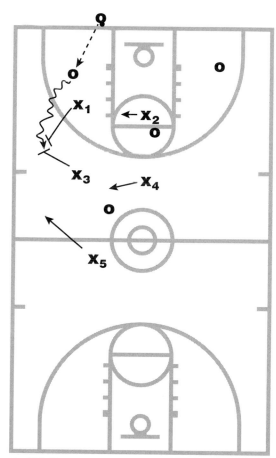

A. Sideline trap in the 2-2-1 Press.

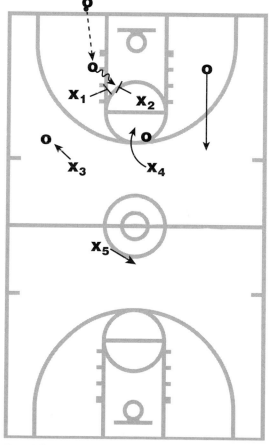

B. Middle trap in the 2-2-1 Press.

that like to make a fast break. The basket is always protected, and the fast break is stymied.

2-1-2 Press. In a 2-1-2 Press, the defenders set up with 1 and 2 at the elbows, 3 in the middle, and 4 and 5 around midcourt. Players 1 and 2 try to deny the inbounds pass but make sure the players they're trying to guard don't get open behind them. If the ball is passed to a player near the basket, 1 and 2 trap her. If the ball is passed to a player near the sideline, 1 forces her to dribble along the sideline, 2 rotates to defend the middle, 3 comes over to trap, 4 guards against a pass up the court, and 5 rotates over to protect the basket.

In this press, 3 plays the same role as the rover in the man-to-man press, so she should be one of your fastest and best defenders.

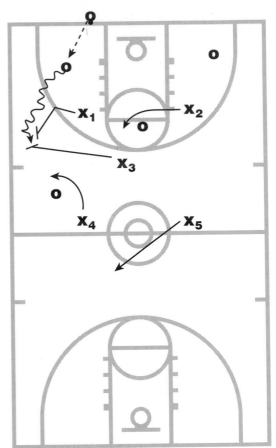

B. Sideline trap in the 2-1-2 Press.

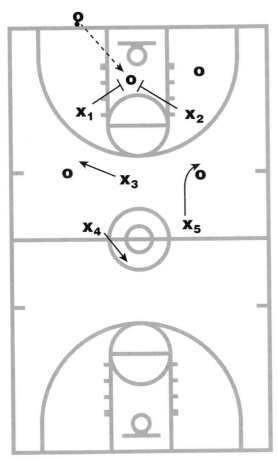

A. Middle trap in the 2-1-2 Press.

Defending Screens

Defending screens is one of the hardest things to do when playing defense. If you coach middle school, you might play some teams that don't screen, but you should teach your players how to defend screens for the teams that do. In high school, every team uses screens as a staple of their offense. Teach defending screens early and often.

The first key to defending any screen is good communication. The instant a defender sees that her man intends to set a screen on a teammate, she shouts, "Screen right!" or "Screen left!" Given adequate warning, her teammate will have enough time to take the appropriate action so the screen won't succeed.

There are three ways to defend a *player screen* (a screen set to get an offensive player open for a pass):

1. **Go over the top of the screen.** The defender being screened fights over the top of the screener—she stays with her man as she tries to use the screen. If the cutter is doing her job right, this will not be easy because there will be little or no room between the screener and her man. However, if her teammate communicates early that a screener is headed her way, the defender can *jam the cutter* (get right on her, denial arm out, so she's ready to bump her on the cut) before the screener arrives, impeding the cutter's progress. Without this vital communication, the defender will be hung up on the screen, and the cutter will get open.

2. **Go under the screen.** The defender steps toward the basket and slides behind the screener, picking up her man again on the other side. This is easier to do than going over, because the defender avoids trying to squeeze through a tight space, and it works well against a cutter who isn't a threat to shoot the outside shot. However, if the cutter is a good shooter, going under allows her to step back for a fade cut for an easy pass and an uncontested shot. For that reason, I recommend teaching your players to fight over the top of screens.

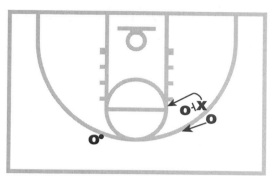

Going under the screen.

3. **Switch.** In this approach, when the screener arrives to set the screen, the defenders switch the players they're guarding. This has the advantage of not allowing the cutter to drive around the screen or fade for an easy pass. The disadvantages are that a savvy screener, seeing the defenders switch, can pivot from her screening position and seal the defender on her back before the defender can get on the other side of her to be in good denial position. The result is an easy pass to the screener. The second disadvantage is that switching on down screens or up screens results in mismatches. If the screener is a post and her teammate is a guard, after the switch the guard will be guarding a bigger player, and the post will be guarding a quicker player. Good teams recognize mismatches and take advantage of

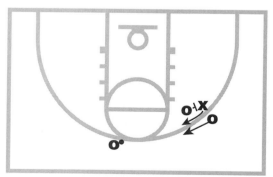

Going over the top of the screen.

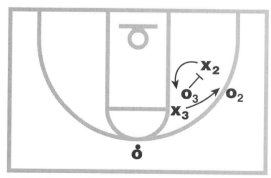

Switching on the screen.

them—the offensive post will easily post up the smaller player, and the offensive guard will drive on her slower defender. For these reasons, I prefer going over the top of screens as compared to switching as a defensive tactic.

When defending a *ball screen* (a screen set to get the player with the ball open), things are more complicated. The same defensive options explained above are available, as well as two additional options:

1. **Hedging.** As the defender being screened fights over the top, the screener's defender *hedges* on the dribbler—she momentarily leaves her man and steps out in the path of the dribbler. The goal is to prevent the dribbler from driving around the screen. If the defender hedges soon enough, the dribbler will have to hesitate or dribble away from the basket. Either way, she can't drive around the screen. This allows the dribbler's defender time to fight over the top and resume guarding her. As the defender picks up her man again, the defender who hedged recovers to her man. Note that the player must not hedge too far from the screener (an arm's length from the screener's near shoulder

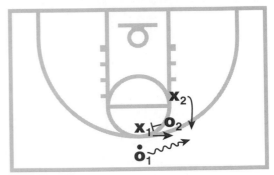

Hedging on the screen. The screener's defender (X_2) will recover to guard her man after her teammate gets around the screen.

is the best distance), or the dribbler can suddenly drive in the gap between her and her teammate. Hedging is a key tactic used in stopping a pick-and-roll.

2. **Trapping.** If the player with the ball is a threat to drive to the basket or a threat to step back and hit the outside shot, the defenders can trap her. As the screener arrives to set the screen, her defender steps out to hedge but does not go back to guard her man. She and her teammate trap the dribbler. This is a good surprise tactic if the defenders haven't trapped before. However, this leaves the screener

The screener's defender steps out to hedge.

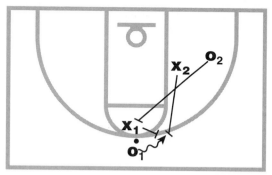

Trapping the dribbler in the pick-and-roll.

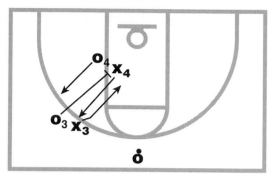

B. Defending the down screen.

open for a roll to the basket, so a third defender must be alert and ready to help.

Defending cross screens near the basket presents a problem for defenses. Many offenses have their posts run cross screens from block to block. A successful cross screen in this area results in an easy basket. The rule to teach your defenders is that the ball-side player guards the low cut, and the help-side player guards the high cut. As the screener goes across the lane, the ball-side defender drops down under the basket, facing the other basket so she can still see the ball. This allows her to stop a drive to the basket. The help-side defender steps up to guard against the high cut. If the cutter tries to cut low, the ball-side defender steps in her way to impede her progress, and she and her teammate switch players. If the

cutter tries to cut high, after the cut the defenders keep guarding the same players. Unless the screen involves an offensive guard and an offensive post, the switch will be fine. Post defenders will still be guarding posts.

Where switching can be a problem is on down screens, up screens, and back screens. In these types of screens, one perimeter player and one post player are involved. If the defenders switch, this leaves a post player guarding a quicker player and a perimeter player guarding a taller player. Good offensive teams will exploit these size and speed mismatches. On these screens, have the defender screened go under the screen, which will keep her between her man and the ball. Her teammate must leave enough space for her to slide under, or they'll get in each other's way.

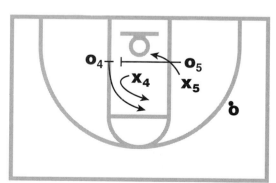

A. Defending the cross screen.

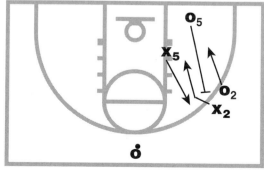

C. Defending the back screen.

Chapter 5

TEAM MANAGEMENT

Handling Players

Handling your players so the team has a good chance of reaching its goals requires skill, smarts, and patience. Back in the Introduction (see page xi), I talked about the importance of being consistent and not playing favorites. These points cannot be overemphasized. If you're not consistent in the way you treat your players or if you show favoritism to certain players, you'll damage team trust and unity, which are so critical to having a successful season.

Chemistry 101

Coaches in team sports talk about *team chemistry*. It's a vague term that means how well the players and the coaches all get along with each other. Do they root for each other at all times? Do they support each other through the tough times? When a team has good chemistry, it means that the players are *team players*—each player puts the team's best interests above her own interests (e.g., wanting to be a starter, wanting more playing time, etc.). When you have twelve to fifteen players on a team, each with her unique personality, goals, and agenda,

this is no easy feat. As the team leader, your goal is to create an environment where every player is motivated to give her best for the sake of the team, not for her own sake. One of my favorite sayings is "It's amazing what can be accomplished when no one cares who gets the credit."

Chemistry is like a strong wind. You can't see it, but you sure can see the results of it. If your team has good chemistry, it has a good chance of reaching its potential. If your team doesn't, it will have problems.

How does a coach foster good team chemistry? This is easy to answer and hard to do. You need a combination of things:

Good ingredients. Other than choosing players at tryouts, you have no control over the players on your roster (if you're a JV coach, you have no control over who the Varsity coach picks and who is left over). The best you can do is choose players at tryouts who seem to have positive, team-oriented attitudes. This is a hit-or-miss proposition, because everyone trying out is on her best behavior (if you see someone who exhibits a poor attitude at tryouts, eliminate her from your list of possibilities). Selfish traits and difficult personalities probably won't be visible. If you've coached some of the players trying out, this gives you an advantage. You already know if they're team players. However, for the players who are new to you, it's guesswork on your part. If you know a coach who has coached a player you're considering, he or she can often be a good source of information.

The team is number one. From the start, emphasize "team first." You've no doubt heard the saying "There's no 'I' in team." Coaches use corny clichés, but kids respond to them. Encourage and praise team play. At North Carolina, Coach Dean Smith was the first coach to have his players acknowledge assists. After scoring, his players pointed to the player who passed them the ball that led to the scoring opportunity. This habit has become commonplace across the country. Everyone notices and talks about players who score points, but few people talk about other individual accomplishments. Emphasize the unselfish things that are just as important to a team, such as making assists, setting screens, diving on the floor for loose balls, and taking charges.

Everyone has an important role. A key part of having a unified team is having players accept their roles. For your team to succeed, you must have players who can do various things well. You need capable starters, capable middle-game players, and capable end-game players. You need shooters, rebounders, defenders, and ball handlers, as well as press specialists, zone specialists, and so on. Your best players may have several roles, but most of your players will have only one or two roles. Every year in preseason, I have my players write out what they think their roles are going to be. I also write out how I see each of their roles. I never give anyone more than three roles. Then I sit down with each player and talk about it. Be honest. Don't tell someone they'll play a lot if they won't. Most of the time, my players and I are on the same page.

Your challenge is to have each player accept her role. She'll only do this if she believes her role is as important as any other role. Coach Smith also developed the Blue Team concept when he coached. The Blue Team consisted of five players who were not as skilled as the starters, but they knew their roles and were proud of them. When Coach Smith put them in games so the starters could rest, they gave several minutes of all-out effort. Their goal was to play great defense and protect the ball on offense. When they came out of the game, the home crowd always gave them a standing ovation. The Blue Team was an excellent example of players with limited skills accepting their limited roles.

ASK THE COACH

Question: I have some good players on my JV team, but I have four girls new to basketball who aren't good players. I'm having a hard time making them feel positive about their contributions. Any suggestions?

Answer: Keeping every player on the team happy is a challenge every coach faces. With only so many minutes of playing time available, the kids who play the least can become discouraged and lose confidence.

Part of how you avoid that is when choosing your team in tryouts. Sure, you want to have some stars. But every team needs role players, kids who know they're not as skilled but are glad to be on the team, knowing their time will come—maybe next year. When you choose your team, pick a few players whom you think will be happy in a limited role.

Another part is how you treat those players in practice. If you cater to the best players and give them most of the attention and scrimmage time, you'll lose the other players. On the other hand, if you go out of your way to make those players feel as important as the best players, they're much more likely to accept their role. What you do is more important than what you say.

Motivating Players

The number of books written on how to motivate people to do their best would fill a small library. I don't claim to know a fail-safe method for inspiring a group of basketball players to do their best in every practice and every game. However, I've learned there are certain approaches that can help inspire and motivate your team.

Provide positive reinforcement. Most people respond to praise, and girls are no exception. When a player does something that deserves praise, be sure to let her know verbally. Be specific. "Good job" is fine—coaches often say this—but "Good rebound" is better. Particularly when a player learns a new skill, praise her for her accomplishment. However, don't overdo praise. If you give nonstop praise to your players, though you might mean it every time, your words soon become less meaningful. For praise to be effective, you must dole it out selectively.

Avoid negative reinforcement. Part of coaching is providing feedback so players know when they're performing well and when they're not. It's your job to point out mistakes and the areas that need improvement so your players can learn. The trick is pointing things out the right way, not the wrong way.

First, the way you give feedback is important. You want to be clear, matter-of-fact, and not angry. Saying "Remember to use your inside foot as your pivot foot" calmly and with a smile is a lot different than saying it with a glare or a sigh of exasperation.

Second, never make criticism personal. You should never say "Jennifer, what's wrong with you? Didn't you hear me?" or "Everyone else understands what we're doing. Why don't you?" Comments like that destroy a player's trust in you. There's no need to embarrass a player in front of the team. It's much better to say "Let's review the play again" or "Try it again, this time bringing your shooting hand up like this."

Third, when you criticize, include a positive comment. Saying "I liked the way you posted up, Melissa, but next time show a good target with your hands" tells the player you also appreciate what she has learned.

Fourth, don't criticize any player repeatedly. If you continue to find fault with a particular player, she'll feel singled out. What's the right amount of criticism? It varies from player to player, but if you see a player looking uncomfortable or embarrassed, you should stop. You'll have players who will make the same mistake over and over and players who won't grasp what to other players are simple concepts, but refrain from excessive criticism. There's no need to keep telling a player what she already knows—that she's doing it wrong. Dip into your bag of patience, smile, and move on to another drill.

Building Team Unity

A big part of good team chemistry is for your players to know and trust each other. You can't dictate that everyone likes each other, nor can you force it, but you can do things that encourage closeness and trust. I tell my players, "You don't have to like each other, but you have to learn how to work with each other." I also tell them to treat each other like they want to be treated themselves.

Team activities. Every now and then, get your team together for nonbasketball social activities, like going out to eat pizza or bowling. I sometimes take my players to the movies (I pick the movie). If I think they need a break from practice—maybe it's a tough part of the season and they're mentally and physically tired—I'll rent a good sports movie that we'll watch together (*Hoosiers* is a classic). Depending on where you live, you could take your kids to an amusement park or for an overnight camping trip (along with a few other responsible adults, of course).

Away basketball trips. If your team can go away for a night or two to another town to play in a tournament, this an excellent way for the girls to spend time together and become closer as a team.

Team-Building Exercises

There are a number of team-building exercises you can do to help your players know each other better and trust each other more. These range from the simple to the elaborate. Every year, my players go to a "ropes" course, where they face a difficult physical challenge together and learn how to communicate and work together.

Here are some other team-building exercises:

Blindfolded Partners. You'll need blindfolds for this exercise (bandanas, napkins, and even practice pinnies will do). Split your team into pairs, pairing up girls who don't know each other well or who don't ever talk together. Have one player in each pair blindfold her partner. Instruct the seeing players to guide their blindfolded teammates to a specific spot without using their hands. In other words, they have to guide them with words alone, with communication. Pick a spot that is familiar, easily accessible, and safe. Obviously, you don't want the blindfolded players to navigate up or down long flights of stairs, next to drop-offs, or through places cluttered with such objects as ladders and shovels. Every pair must finish before the exercise is over. Give a token reward to the winning pair, such as not having to do the end-of-practice conditioning drill. After every pair finishes, have the blindfolded players put the blindfolds on their partners and do the exercise again.

I Like You. Every now and then, before a practice starts, before the players' hands are sweaty, we do this exercise. I print out a piece of paper that says at the top: "I Like You . . ." I put each player's name on a sheet and put the sheets in a box. The players pull out one sheet, go to a spot where they can have some privacy, write something to complete the sentence, stick it back in the box, and go to practice. The next day, I'll have each sheet in each player's locker so she can read what her teammate said about her. Girls love that kind of feedback.

Circle Drawing. I do this exercise with my players every year, early in the season. It might sound childish, but the kids love it. We spend an afternoon in the locker room. I give each player a sheet of poster board (2 feet by 3 feet), and on the floor are crayons, markers, and colored pencils. I ask players to draw a big circle, representing a basketball. Then I say, "Any way you want to, divide the basketball into four

parts. You're going to draw pictures. No words allowed. First, draw a picture of what you want to be doing five years from now. Next, draw your personal goals for this year—not just for basketball, but for school or whatever. Then, draw the team goals for this year. Last, draw your favorite toy as a child." The players spend a lot of time on this. Once they're finished, they display their drawings on an easel and explain them. After everyone has taken a turn, we tape each girl's drawing to the back of her locker with two-sided tape. Our lockers are open, so every time the players walk into the locker room, they see their posters. The players enjoy this exercise, and everyone on the team learns a lot from it. I find that after we do this activity, the players start forming relationships. The team starts developing chemistry. The players begin to think of the team as more of a family.

Injuries

You don't need medical training to be a coach—that would eliminate most of the coaches around—but you should know the difference between when a player is injured and when she's hurt. Injuries are serious matters like sprained ankles, concussions, torn cartilage or ligaments, pulled muscles, and broken bones. Hurts are temporary pains from bumps and bruises. Given the physical nature of basketball, bumps and bruises happen often. Most players who are hurt can play with some pain, but some kids have a low pain threshold. Never make someone play if she says she's in too much pain or discomfort.

Pay attention to injuries. The last thing you want is to play an injured player and risk making her injury worse. If a player is injured, she shouldn't play basketball until her family doctor and parent/guardian give their approval. You'll find that injured players want to rush back into playing well before they're ready. Don't be swayed by their enthusiasm ("I'm fine, Coach, I really am!") or the need to get their scoring ability back on the court. Unless you write "M.D." after your name, don't try to be a doctor. The risks to the player's health are too great. Insist that your injured player follow her doctor's orders.

FOR ANY INJURY THAT IS NOT A FRACTURE (LIKE STRAINS AND SPRAINS), THINK RICE:

Rest the area to avoid further injury, but continue to move the injured area gently. Early gentle movement promotes healing.

Ice the area to reduce swelling. Apply ice to the affected area for 20 minutes and then leave it off for half an hour. *Note:* Don't use ice on a player who has circulatory problems.

Compress the area with an elastic wrap (when icing, secure the ice bag under the wrap). Compression reduces swelling and promotes healing. If a player has an ankle injury, leave her shoe on with the laces tied.

Elevate the injured area above the level of the heart. Elevation is especially effective when used in conjunction with compression. Continue to elevate intermittently until swelling is gone.

When an injury happens to one of my players, after our trainer checks to see what's wrong, we move the player to the other end of the floor right away. There's no need to have her situation distract and alarm the other players. Keep the rest of the team focused on the game or the practice session.

I have a rule that if a player misses practice the day before a game, she can't play in the game. Even if she's sick, I want her to attend

---

ASK THE COACH

Question: I have a player who complains a lot in practice about not feeling well. She looks fine to me, but I let her sit out when she says she feels "bad." This never happens in games, though. She's always ready to go. My assistant and I are starting to wonder if she's faking it. What should we do?

Answer: Anytime a player complains about not feeling well, take it seriously until proven wrong. Whenever a younger player says she feels bad and wants to sit out, mention it to the parent who picks her up. You may learn about a medical condition the player has that you should know about (parents sometimes leave out important information on the medical release). Maybe the parent isn't aware that his or her daughter is feeling sick. Maybe the player has something serious going on, like a virus or a parasite that hasn't been checked out yet. Or, the player could be faking.

Some kids will do anything to get attention. If they don't get it positively because they're not doing what they're supposed to be doing, they'll get it by pretending to be hurt. Maybe they'll use "I don't feel well" as an excuse to get out of working hard. I had a player like that a few years ago. I could predict when she was going to be "injured" or "hurt" because she needed attention. After a big game, she wanted to sit out because she felt she deserved not to practice hard the next day. As we coaches prepared for practice, one of us would say, "Watch. She won't be able to practice today. Something will be wrong." Most of the time, we were right. I finally called the player's bluff. The next time it happened, I told her if she didn't practice that afternoon, it would hurt her preparation for the next game, and I wouldn't be able to start her. Magically, the problem went away.

Question: I have a player who sprained her ankle and is on crutches. Should I make her attend practice?

Answer: Yes. Unless she has physical therapy sessions that conflict with practice time, she's still part of the team and should be there to support her teammates. When we have someone hurt or injured, we put them on the sidelines and have them do something physical, like riding a stationary bike, doing push-ups or sit-ups (obviously, this player can't do that). Our thinking is that if a player has something wrong, we'll find another part of her body where there's nothing wrong, and we'll condition it. We find that our hurt and injured players want to be back in action as soon as possible.

---

practice, because the next day she might feel fine and be ready to play. If a player is so sick that she can't attend practice, obviously she's too sick to play the next day.

This approach may or may not work with players who depend on others to transport them to and from practice. You may find that a parent who has a hard time leaving work early to drive his or her daughter to the gym may be reluctant to take the time to bring her there just to sit and watch. You'll have to judge it on a case-by-case basis. Also, you don't want someone with a contagious illness hacking and sneezing on the sidelines, possibly infecting the rest of your team.

Dealing with Parents

Most parents are a positive part of your season. Unfortunately, it only takes one or two difficult parents to taint what is otherwise a successful, fun season. You can count on it—sooner or later, you'll run into a parent problem. Though you can't avoid unreasonable parents, you can do some things to reduce the likelihood that parents will be upset:

Be accessible. Encourage parents to let you know when they have questions or concerns. Tell them you want to solve small problems before they become big problems. Give them your phone numbers and e-mail address in the handout you pass out at the player/parent meeting at the beginning of the season.

Communicate, communicate. Parents don't like surprises in the schedule. If you forgot to tell them that practice was canceled but they drove their daughter over in the snow anyway, expect some complaints.

Explain team rules and expectations up front. Be specific. If the consequence for missing practice is no playing time in the next game, tell players and parents before it happens. The parents of a player who misses practice might still grumble, but they can't say you didn't warn them. Also tell them that you expect them to be supportive and positive no matter what happens on the court.

Get used to reality. In coaching, it's a given that you can't please everyone involved.

Even on the most harmonious teams, a player can be upset about not playing more or about playing behind another player whom she perceives as less skilled. If one of your players is upset, it's likely her parents will be, too. And if her parents are upset, you can expect to hear about it. Do your best to listen to unhappy players and parents, fix what you think needs fixing (if anything), and move on. Just like sneakers and layups, the occasional unhappy parent is part of coaching basketball.

Be calm under fire. When you find yourself face-to-face with an unhappy parent, take him or her aside for a private conversation. It's no one else's business, and you don't want to upset your players or another parent. When you're sure you're out of anyone else's earshot, handle the matter as you would handle any other personal disagreement. Listen carefully to what the parent is saying. Wait until he or she is finished airing out all the grievances before you respond.

If you're angry and emotional, tell the parent you need to think about it overnight and that you'll respond tomorrow. If the problem was your fault, admit it and apologize. If your assistant or another player did something to upset the parent, you may have to talk to the individual involved. Depending on the circumstances, you may need to be a peacemaker. Above all, be calm and professional, even if the parent isn't. If the conversation turns heated, tell the parent you'll be glad to continue it when he or she has calmed down. Just because you're the coach doesn't mean a parent has the right to speak to you rudely or abusively. If you and the parent can't resolve the matter, take it to a higher authority like the athletic director of your school or the director of your league.

Set boundaries. The prime issue unhappy parents bring up is playing time. Most parents aren't objective about their daughter's skills, nor are they basketball experts. Most parents think their daughter is a better player than she is. Some coaches have a policy of not discussing playing time with parents. Some will talk about playing time. I tell parents that I'll talk to them about anything they want to talk about, but I won't discuss how I coach the team, and I won't discuss other players. We have a player on our team whose dad coached her in high school. On his team, she was a star, but on our team, she's not. That's been difficult for him. I've reminded him that he isn't at the practices and doesn't see what we coaches see.

While playing time is the grievance voiced most often by parents, it's not the only issue. The list of possible parental dissatisfactions includes playing the daughter in the "wrong" position ("She's a shooting guard, not a point"), not recognizing her obvious talents ("She's the best shooter on her AAU team"), not spending enough individual time working with the daughter ("Last year's coach used to work with her a lot more"), tampering with the daughter's shooting form ("She didn't used to miss like she

ASK THE COACH

Question: Should I let parents watch practice?

Answer: I don't allow parents at my practices, because their presence distracts their daughters. It's a different situation with middle school and JV practices. Parents are necessarily part of the landscape because they drop off and pick up their daughters. In my view, if a parent gets there 5 minutes early and watches the end of practice, I'd have no problem with that. However, if a parent starts to watch practices with regularity, I would have a problem with that. Somewhere between those examples, there's a line. You have to decide where to draw that line.

Question: A dad of one of my players is a former college player. During the games, he sits right behind our bench and yells at his daughter to do this and do that. He has a booming voice, so everyone in the stands can hear him, as can his daughter, who looks at him when she runs up the court. She sometimes doesn't do what I want her to do because it's not what he told her to do. This is becoming a big problem. What do I do?

Answer: Welcome to the "frustrated coach" syndrome, exhibited by the parent who was a player, or maybe is a coach, or maybe is just an overeager fan. Regardless, that parent thinks he or she knows everything there is to know about basketball. As you've discovered, this turns into a problem when he coaches his daughter (and other players) from the stands. What the parent doesn't realize is that his shouting instructions to her as she runs up the court puts her in a difficult situation—do I listen to Dad, who is telling me to shoot, or do I listen to Coach, who is telling me to pass? Make it a priority to talk to the dad before the next game. Tell him you appreciate his support and enthusiasm, but he can't coach his daughter during games, because she already has a coach.

Question: The mother of a player called me up last night, demanding to know what I have against her daughter. She said her daughter is very upset and thinking about quitting the team. She said the girl who started in front of her daughter played 22 minutes in the last game, while her daughter only played 6. She can't understand why that happened because her daughter is "obviously the better player." I was caught unaware and didn't know what to say. I told her I would call her back after thinking about it. What should I tell her?

Answer: Let her know you care about her daughter and will do your best to have her improve her skills, but you discuss playing time only with players, not parents. Remind her that a big part of playing time is based on what goes on in practice, and that it's impossible for someone who hasn't been at practice to make an informed judgment on who should start and who should play how much. Remind her that you don't think it's fair to discuss another player with the parents of a different player. As you talk to the parent, keep thinking: calm and professional, calm and professional. If you don't placate her, don't worry about it. You've done all you can.

Question: One of the fathers volunteered to run the clock at our games. He seems like a nice guy, but after hearing stories about hostile parents, I don't know whether to say yes to the guy or not.

Answer: Although we coaches all have to deal with an unhappy parent now and then, they are very much in the minority. Most parents are reasonable, nice, supportive folks. By all means, say yes.

does now"), and so on. When discussing these or other issues with parents, be open-minded and calm. Ask the parents not to voice their complaints to their daughter because that will only harm her attitude. Then do what you think is best and move on.

Over my career, I've had good relationships with parents. I've had only a few unpleasant situations. One season I had a father who came into my office and carried on about his daughter—playing time and other issues. He tried to intimidate me with a gruff, hostile manner. I told him calmly that he couldn't talk to me like that. I walked over to the door and opened it for him to leave. He stood and said, "Coach, you're right. I'm sorry. I was wrong." We talked for a few more minutes, and he left. He never spoke to me again about his daughter. He came to all our games and supported us and was never a problem again.

Chapter 6

GAME MANAGEMENT

You're in the third week of the season. You've done your best to prepare your players. You've emphasized fundamentals and drilled them on zone offense, man-to-man defense, out-of-bounds plays, and too many other things to count. Now it's time for the first test, a game against your first opponent of the season.

Are the girls ready? Will they remember everything you taught them? Will they take good shots? Will they get rattled under pressure? Will they protect the ball or make silly passes? How will the starters fare against players who might be more talented? You're about to find out. It's game time!

Mind-Set and Expectations

Naturally, you're excited and maybe even jittery. You've looked forward to this day for weeks. You've put a lot into it. But step back for a moment. It's important to put yourself into the right mind-set. It's important to have realistic expectations.

Be cool and calm. Hide your jitters. You might be nervous, but if you act uptight, your players will see it, and that will make them uptight. They'll be anxious enough as it is. Don't make it worse. If they're nervous, joke around a bit. Loosen them up. Be positive. Be calm. One of your jobs at game time is to be the stabilizing, calming influence.

Expect mistakes. Basketball is a game of continuous mistakes. Have you ever seen a game with no turnovers and no missed shots? I haven't and don't expect I ever will. The more inexperienced your team is, the more mistakes you'll see. You'll see players do boneheaded things, like dribble into trouble, pass to the second row in the stands, and heave up wild shots that have no chance of going in the basket. You'll see some players confused about what to do on offense, where to be, and where to go. At times, it might look like they've never practiced anything but putting on their uniforms. You might see more than one player with the "deer in the headlights" look, or worse, you might see chaos and panic. The best you can hope for is that your team makes fewer mistakes than the other team does. The team that makes fewer mistakes often is the winner, but no team plays without mistakes.

Expect ugly losses. Coaches at all levels experience games when the other team looks like the Los Angeles Lakers, and it's obvious after 5 minutes that they will crush your team. There will be moments when your players look like they don't know the first thing about basketball and when you look like you can't coach a lick. This is all part of coaching. If you coach long enough, you'll have your share of terrific wins and your share of ugly losses. If you expect the latter, you'll be better able to handle those games and keep them in perspective when they occur.

Ignore the fans. Focus on what's happening on the court every second of the game. Don't be distracted by the fan behind you who moans things like, "What a stupid pass! Did you see the stupid pass by number 33?" and "Put Mary in the game! Why doesn't the coach put Mary in the game? What's he doing?" You have enough details to think about besides what people are saying in the stands. Block out the fans. Believe me, you don't want to hear what some of them say anyway.

Ignore the refs. This is easy advice to give but sometimes hard to follow. The referees have a very difficult job. Every call they make (or don't make) automatically goes against the best interests of one of the teams on the court. In one-sided games, this isn't a problem. When it's clear that one team will win with ease, nobody on the benches or in the stands pays much attention to what the referees do. However, in a close, hotly contested game, every call is a meaningful part of the action. In these games, what the refs do or don't do is under intense scrutiny. In these games, it's a given that some fans will think every call against their team is flat-out wrong and unfair. Extreme fans will consider the calls part of a grand plot hatched by the referees to skew the game in the other team's favor. The reality is that there are good refs and there are not-so-good refs. If you coach a middle school or JV team, many of the refs at your games will be inexperienced, which increases the chances that they'll make mistakes. Expect inconsistent refereeing as the norm and even some bad refereeing now and then. The best approach is to ignore the refs, just as you ignore the fans. If you must protest a call, do so

with great respect. While you won't change the ref's mind, at least you won't make him or her mad, and your behavior will serve as an excellent example for your players.

Show good sportsmanship. Before the first game, talk to the team about sportsmanship. Define it. Give examples of good sportsmanship and bad sportsmanship. Make it clear that you view any display of the latter as unacceptable, and that it will result in taking a seat on the bench and/or a loss of playing time in the next game. Your words will only go so far. Your actions will be more important. At all times, no matter what you think about the other team, even if you think they're terrible sports, stick to the principles of good sportsmanship—don't criticize or insult their players or coaches. Shake their hands after the game and tell them they played a good game.

Win with grace. It's easy to be a good sport when you win. After pummeling the other team by 45 points, what player or coach can't smile and say "Good game" in the shake-hands line? Teach your players that winning demands good sportsmanship too. Never laugh at the other team or gloat in victory. You may have scored more points, but you shouldn't disrespect their heart and effort. The other team played just as hard as your team did. Maybe their skills and experience didn't match up, but the effort and energy they played with should be respected and acknowledged.

Lose with grace. It's more fun to win than it is to lose. Nothing you tell your players will change that fact. Yes, a few teams go through a season undefeated, but 99 percent of all teams at all levels lose games, and many teams lose a majority of their games. Teach your players to view losing as an opportunity to improve. As long as they learn from the loss, they'll benefit and improve. Again, your behavior will set the tone more than your words. Hold your head up during and after a tough loss. Stay positive and enthusiastic. If your players see you react angrily or as if the loss is the end of civilization, they'll think that's how they should react. Life is full of disappointments. Learning how to lose with grace can be one of the most lasting skills you teach your players all season long.

Pregame Routine

I'm surprised at how unstructured some teams are in their pregame routines. The players seem to do what they feel like. They might shoot for a while, they might stretch for a while, and they chitchat about things that have nothing to do with basketball. Even if they run the standard Two-Line Layups (Drill 46), they do it at half-speed.

Maybe this approach works for those teams, but I don't recommend it. Your pregame routine should be structured with two goals in mind: to warm up the players' bodies, and to warm up the players' minds.

Many players think warming up means running around to get their hearts pumping and their muscles working. That's only half of it. It's just as important to prepare mentally and emotionally for competition as it is to prepare physically. We've all seen teams that come out *flat* at the start of the game. They move at three-quarters speed, while the other team moves at full throttle. They don't match the intensity, toughness, and energy of the other team. They seem a bit dazed by the action, always a step slow. The result? The other team out-hustles them for loose balls, outrebounds them, and scores easy transition baskets. After 4 minutes, the flat team is down 13-2. The other team has all the momentum and enthusiasm. Even if the flat team finally wakes up, it has to play the rest of the game in catch-up mode, a difficult task at best. Nine times out of ten, even with a valiant effort, the flat team loses in the end.

An inadequate pregame routine dooms your team to a bad start. That's not to say that if your players warm up their bodies and minds properly you won't quickly fall behind— sometimes the other team has much better players—but you'll have better odds of getting off to a good start with the other team. Here are the principles for having a sound pregame routine:

1. Establish a specific time and event sequence. For example:
   - 1 hour before the game, the players are in the gym, dressed, ready to shoot informally.
   - 30 minutes before the game, the players and coaches meet in the locker room, where you go over the game plan.
   - 20 minutes before the game, the players run out on the court and begin a sequence of predetermined warm-up drills.
   - 30 seconds before the game, the players gather at the center circle for a few moments of team unity.
   - 20 seconds before the game, the players come to the bench, and the starters sit down to receive your last-minute instructions (nothing new, just reminders of the main things you went over in the locker room).

2. Game warm-up drills should include ball handling, shooting, defense, and rebounding.

3. Game warm-up drills should be designed so the players break into a sweat (note that some girls, no matter how hard they work, never sweat). With 2 minutes to go, have the players sprint up and back two times in their half of the court. If your team doesn't sprint during warm-ups, you can't expect them to be ready to sprint right away in the game.

4. Throughout warm-ups, the players should be serious and focused. There's plenty of time after the game to socialize.

You'll see a wide variety of warm-up drills used by different teams. As long as your drills cover the key areas outlined in #2 above, choose the drills you think work best. The drills should be ones you run in practice. Warming up before a game is not the time to introduce new material to your players.

You'll also see a wide variety in what teams do to pump themselves up right before tip-off.

Question: I realize each team warms up in only one half of the court, but does it matter which half?

Answer: Before the game starts, each team always warms up at the far basket—the basket they'll be attacking in the first half. Before the second half starts, since the teams switch baskets at halftime, each team now warms up at the near basket.

Some teams cluster in a circle, lock arms, and sway from side to side in unison. Some teams drape arms over each other's shoulders. Some teams hold their fists together, pointed to the ceiling. Some teams sing a short verse, some teams yell something (like "Intensity!" or "Team!"), and some teams say a brief prayer. It doesn't matter what your players do, as long as they're focused and together. Don't dictate what they do, even if you think it's silly or too "girly." If they're unsure of what to do, throw out some suggestions, but let them figure it out for themselves. It should be their special ritual, not yours. If it's something they create, it will be more meaningful to them.

Choosing a Starting Five

The players who start the game are responsible for getting the team off to a good start. As a general rule, the players you choose for this role should be the five best players on the team. However, there are times when you have no choice, when a starter is injured or ill, or has missed practice. And there are many times when prudent strategy dictates that you change your starting lineup:

Your team isn't balanced offensively. For example, if your two best post players are slow, bulky low post types, you might start a quicker high post type over one of them so you have a scoring threat from the free throw line area. What you give up in back-to-the-basket skills you gain in spreading out the defense.

One of your five best players isn't a good starter. Some kids are good at starting. They have confidence in themselves, the limelight doesn't bother them, and they begin games with high intensity and energy. Other players are better at coming off the bench. They feel too much pressure at tip-off. They need time to settle their nerves. Maybe they lack confidence. This isn't a bad thing. One of the most important roles on your team is the first player off the bench, a player who provides instant energy on defense, offense, or both. Many teams consider that first off-the-bench player to be their *sixth starter*.

You need to counter the other team's strengths. If you play a tall, inside-oriented team, consider starting "your big team," which may include one or two players who aren't part of your top five. If you play a quick team that plays man-to-man and likes to pressure the ball, consider starting "your ball-handling team." If you play a team that plays zone defense, you'll want your better outside shooters in the game, so consider starting "your zone-busting team."

You want to send a message. If one of your starters isn't working as hard as you think she should, or isn't displaying a team-first attitude, consider keeping her out of the starting lineup. When she brings herself up to the standards you expect, you can put her back as a starter.

You want to reward a player. As motivation, you might tell the team that one spot will be reserved in the next game for the Practice Player of the Week or for the player who shows the most hustle.

You aren't happy with the starting five. You may not be pleased with the effort or attitudes of your starters. They may be too cocky, too complacent, and may have stopped working as hard as they used to. Not starting them in the next game will change their outlook fast.

Question: I'm having trouble choosing my starting five. My team is full of beginners, and no one stands out. How do I pick the starters?

Answer: Start by identifying your best team players. From that group, decide who is best at the key skills. Don't get hung up on positions or size. Put your best ball handler at 1, your best shooter at 2, and your best rebounder at 5 (she may or may not be your biggest player). From the remaining players, pick the two best defenders and put them at 3 and 4.

Some coaches play the same starters in every game, and some change their starting lineups often. You have to find what works for you, given the players you have and the competition you face.

Unfortunately, players (and parents) focus way too much on who starts and who doesn't. From the first game on, deemphasize who starts. Explain that the team needs players who contribute in many ways—players who get the team off to a strong start, players who keep the momentum going until the end of the half, players who get the team off to a strong start in the second half, and players who help the team finish strong. A few of your players—the stars—might participate in all those roles, but most of the players will participate in only one or two of the roles. Coaches often say, "I'm not concerned about who starts. I'm concerned about who plays at crunch time."

If you can, give each player on your team a chance to start a game. For some of them, this will be the highlight of their season. Presumably, you have more games on your schedule than players on the team, so you can pick and choose when to do this. Of course, if you coach a Varsity high school team, you'll have a Senior Night the last home game of the season when you start all your seniors. Make sure they're in near the end of the game, so the fans can give each player an ovation as you take them out one by one.

Substitutions

If you coach a middle school team that must comply with a policy of equal playing time, you'll play everyone based on arithmetic—24 minutes of game time divided by twelve players means everyone plays about two quarters. Your only decisions are who should play in which quarters. There are two ways to do this. You can play your best players in quarters 1 and 3, hoping that your other players can hang on in the other quarters. Or you can split the team into two balanced groups. The trade-off is you won't have a powerhouse group playing at any one time, but you won't have a unit in the game that can lose ground quickly. My choice would be to have the balanced groups, but a case can be made for either approach.

If you coach an AAU or high school team, you don't have to consider playing everyone equally. The decisions on substitutions are based on other factors, like who is hot, who is tired, what the matchups are, and so on. A fresh player who hits three jump shots in a row can rejuvenate your offense and trigger a comeback. A fresh trio of quick players that forces back-to-back turnovers can change the momentum of the game.

It will take the first few games of the season to develop a good feel for how to rotate your players in and out of games. Here are a few rules of thumb:

Take out tired players. When you see a player gasping for air, bending over, holding the front of her shorts, it's time to give her a rest. Instruct your players to let you know when they're tired (such as by a raised fist), but players don't always do this because they want to stay in the game. Be alert during games for who is tired and who is not.

Take out players who aren't hustling. A player who doesn't sprint back on defense must be physically or mentally tired. Either way, your team can't afford to have her in the game.

Take out players who make repeated mistakes. This is tricky. Every player deserves to be in the game long enough to get into the flow of the action. If you yank someone out after 1 minute because she threw a bad pass, you haven't given her enough time to adjust from sitting cold on the bench to playing at full capacity. However, if a player has been in for 5 minutes and continues to make the same mistakes, it's time to take her out.

Put in players who don't play much. It's not right to keep your less-skilled players on the bench game after game. How are they going to learn how to play in games if they don't play in games? Put them in as often as you can. And not just for 37 seconds. That amount of time doesn't do anyone any good, least of all the player and her confidence.

Put in less-skilled players with better players. When you want to give playing time to your end-of-the-bench players, don't put them in all at the same time. This doesn't give them much chance for success. Mix them in with two or three of your best players so they can be a part of a good combination.

Put in specialists when needed. This was covered earlier. When you need to adjust to the other team, put in "your big team" or "your quick team," etc. Put in combinations of players that work well together.

Put in the bench when it's a blowout. If you find yourself behind or ahead by an insurmountable lead in the last quarter, this is an excellent time to put in everyone who hasn't played much. If the other team *clears its bench*—takes out its starters—clear your bench too. If the other team leaves its best players in the game (some coaches won't ease up even if their team is ahead by 40 points), then you'll have to mix less-skilled and more-skilled players as described above.

Substitution Procedure

Remind your players about the proper way to substitute. The player going in the game walks to the front of the scorers' table, checks in, kneels, and waits for the referee to stop play and motion for her to come in. As she runs in, she calls out the name of the player she's replacing. As they pass each other, the player coming out tells the substitute who she's guarding ("I've got 22") and runs off the court. This bit of communication is critical. Otherwise, the new player won't be where she should be on defense. To make sure my players talk to each other during the substitution procedure, I have the player who is coming in carry a towel and

---

ASK THE COACH

Question: I have a player who double dribbles or travels every time I put her in the game. I take her out right away, which makes her feel bad. We work on dribbling every practice, and she does fine, but in games she falls apart. What can I do besides grin and bear it?

Answer: Try a different approach. You and the player are in a bad cycle. If you keep taking her out right away, her confidence will keep going down, which will mean she'll be more tentative the next time she plays and will keep making mistakes. Change the dynamics. The next game, find a time when you can keep her in for at least 3 minutes, maybe at the end of the first half. Tell her before she goes in that you have confidence in her and she's going to play for the rest of the half.

I sometimes let my players play through mistakes. It depends on the situation and the player. If some players make one mistake, they'll then make two or three more because they can't let go of the prior mistake. With these players, I take them out and tell them to settle down and get in control before I put them back in. Once they get back in, they're fine. Each player reacts differently to mistakes. As you watch your players on the court, learn to recognize their differences and adjust accordingly.

hand it to the player coming out. That way, the communication is more likely to happen.

We reserve an empty chair at the coach's end of the bench for a player who is just come out of the game. I may speak to her for a moment, but usually I'll say nothing to her. In my view, coaching is done in practice, not in games.

Time-Outs

In high school games, each team is allowed five time-outs during regulation play—three 1-minute time-outs, called *full time-outs*, and two 30-second time-outs (plus an additional time-out during each overtime period). If you don't coach a high school team, check the rules of your league so you know how many time-outs you have. Most coaches try not to use their allotment before the end of the game, in case they need to call time-outs during the critical last minutes.

Calling a time-out when you have none left is an automatic technical foul. A famous instance of this was in the 1993 NCAA Men's National Championship game, when Chris Webber of Michigan called a time-out near the end of the game. This gave North Carolina three free throws and the ball. Many people think this was the difference that allowed North Carolina to win the game. The lessons are clear: always know how many time-outs you have left, and don't call one if you don't have one to avoid a technical foul.

When to call a time-out is a matter of instinct and strategy. I call one when I think my team is out of control, when we're going backward instead of forward, or when we have to do something to stop the other team's momentum. A time-out can change the flow of the game. Sometimes, when we have a lead and the other team is catching up, I'll call one to pause the action and regroup. I don't call time-outs to change the offense or defense because I can do that from the bench. Younger players aren't as able to change on the fly, so you might have to call a time-out if they're in an offense or defense that isn't working.

Here are the key points about managing time-outs:

1. Know how many time-outs you have before the game starts.

2. Give an assistant the job of keeping track of your team's time-outs, so at any time you can find out how many you have left.

3. Save one or two time-outs for the end of the game, if possible. If you use them up too early, you may regret it at crunch time.

4. Try not to call a time-out near the end of a quarter. If there are less than a couple of minutes remaining, hold off. Hopefully your team won't lose much more ground. However, if the other team is scoring points in rapid succession, don't hesitate to call a time-out to stop the bleeding.

Time-Out Procedure

Given the shortness of time-outs, it's important not to waste a second. Organization is the key. Practice having your players run on and off the court during time-outs, so they're ready to listen to you in no more than 10 seconds.

In a *full time-out* (1 minute), have your players run to the bench and immediately sit down. The rest of the players should stand to make room for them. Someone should hand each seated player her water bottle, so the player doesn't have to wander along the bench, looking for it. While the players are getting settled and drinking water (insist that they drink, even if they think they're not thirsty), take 10 seconds to confer with your assistants and plan what you're going to say.

Most coaches don't plan where the players sit in a full time-out, but I do. The point guard always sits to my right (as I face the bench), the wing players sit next to her, and the post players sit to my left. That way, if I have something to say about breaking the press, I know exactly where to find my point guard. If we're getting outrebounded, I know exactly where to find my post players. I have the players not in the game stand behind me in the same order as the players seated. The 1s stand to my right, followed by the 2s, then the 3s, and so on. That way, if any of them has to come in the game, she'll know what the instructions are for her position.

In a *30-second time-out*, there isn't enough time for the players to sit. They should run to you and huddle on the court as you talk to them. The rest of the players should gather around so they can hear what you're saying. They should bring water bottles so the players in the game can have a drink.

Make sure the players not in the game are attentive during time-outs. They might be going in the game at any moment and should know what the strategy is. When a time-out is called, have your bench players stand and clap as the players run off the floor. This lets the players know that their teammates acknowledge and appreciate their efforts.

In a time-out, be clear and brief. If you overload your players with more information than they can absorb, the time-out will be wasted or, worse, you may cause confusion that will cause problems on the court. In a full time-out, give them no more than two things to think about. In a 30-second time-out, give them only one. It's fine to tell one player something specific in addition, but for most of them, you'll find that with the excitement of the game, that's all the information they can handle.

Following are some good things to communicate during time-outs:

- **A change in defensive strategy.** "We're changing to our 1-3-1 zone," or "Number 32 is killing us. Let's double-team her every time she gets the ball."

- **A change in offensive strategy.** "Motion isn't working. Let's switch to our 1-4 High," or "Molly can score against her defender, so let's get the ball to her in the high post and clear out."

- **A likely change in the opponent's strategy** (this often happens when the other coach calls the time-out). "They're probably going to press, so be ready for it.

After we score, set up in our 4-Across, OK?" or "They're probably going to start fouling us now, so we want the ball in Betsy's hands or Joelle's hands. No one else. Got it?"

- **A change in intensity or effort.** "We're not playing like we can out there. They're beating us to all the loose balls. Come on. Let's start playing like the good team we are!"

- **A change in tempo.** "We're playing too fast and making too many mistakes. Slow it down. Take your time. There's no shot clock. Play at our pace, not theirs."

- **Praise.** If the team is playing well and there's no need to make an adjustment in strategy, tell them how well they're playing. "You're doing great out there. Keep it up!"

Full time-outs are also useful for giving your team a rest. If the players look tired and lack zip, call a time-out to give them a much-needed break. Don't feel like you always have to say something meaningful during a time-out. If all is going well, and they just need a rest, there's no need for you to talk. Let them drink water and rest.

Halftime

When the buzzer ending the first half goes off, your players should run off the court to the locker room (or wherever they will rest during halftime). If they take their time leaving the bench and walk off slowly, valuable time will be wasted. Running off the court shows the other team that no matter what the score is, your team is still full of energy and hustle.

Give your players the first 2 minutes of halftime to talk among themselves, use the bathroom, and drink water. During that time, talk to your assistants, look at the stat sheet, and plan what to say. When you talk to your players, be brief and to the point. If you want them to change something, be clear. Draw what you want to do on the whiteboard on the wall (or on your own portable whiteboard). Some kids understand well without visual aids, but other

Question: I called a time-out the other day so we could change from man-to-man to a 2-3 zone. I was stunned to see that half the girls stayed in man-to-man. I thought I was crystal clear. What can I do differently to get my point across?

Answer: All coaches experience times when it seems that your players didn't hear a word you said in the huddle. Maybe the gym noise was too loud, maybe you weren't as clear as you thought you were, or maybe some of your players were too caught up in the moment to focus. To many players, the game is a blur. The action and pace of the game are so fast, it's hard for them to listen well. It's no surprise that they don't understand what you said. Their minds are going a million miles a minute.

Don't assume that a player understands when she nods her head. You might think you're clear as a bell, but to her, your words are a jumble. Don't say, "OK, girls, we're switching to a 2-3 zone," and leave it at that. Go overboard in making your point. Repeat the instruction, looking at each player in the eye. Then, ask, "So, what defense are we playing now?" If they answer, "2-3 zone," there's no guarantee, but maybe, just maybe, the information registered. You'll find out in the next minute.

kids need to see something before they understand it. Tell them who will start in the second half. Remind them that the team that starts out strongest in the first 3 or 4 minutes of the second half often controls the rest of the game.

At halftime, I often ask my players, "What do you see out there? Is there a problem or an opportunity we aren't seeing from the bench?" Now and then, they respond with some good information.

Have your players come back to the court with at least 4 minutes left before the second half. Have an assistant or manager keep track of the time and tell you when it's time. A few fancy locker rooms have a clock synched with the game clock, but most locker rooms don't. It's easy to forget the time as you talk to your players. You don't want to stay in there so long your players have to scramble to the bench to make it in time for the buzzer.

Whether you have your players shoot or run a drill before the second half starts is a matter of personal preference. Whoever played in the first half is obviously warmed up, but if you plan to put in other players, it's a good idea to have them warm up. Also, if your team shot poorly in the first half, you might want them to do a shooting drill. If your team is playing well, however, let the players do what they want, whether it's shoot, stretch, or rest on the bench. Sometimes a player uses that time to talk to me privately, because they don't want to talk in front of the group. Make yourself available if that happens.

With 30 seconds to go, call them over and huddle them up. Repeat the key instructions you gave them in the locker room (as with time-outs, this should be a maximum of three things), and send them out to play.

Pep Talks

Every coach has his or her repertoire of *pep talks*, speeches designed to fire up the team. My view is that the coach can inspire the team

Question: I'm a guy coaching girls for the first time. Should I go into the locker room at halftime? What if someone is changing or using the bathroom?

Answer: It's perfectly fine to go into the locker room, but only after you knock loudly, and the players tell you it's fine to come in. Common courtesy avoids embarrassing situations.

only so much. True motivation and passion have to come from within. If a player doesn't have an intense competitive drive, there's probably not much you can say or do to change that.

Most of the time, my halftime comments are about X's and O's and execution. Every now and then, however, if I think we're playing poorly, or if we're playing way below our capabilities, I'll let my players have it. That can mean different things to different coaches. It's fine to be honest, opinionated, and loud, but it's not OK to make personal attacks, use bad language, or be abusive (see Ask the Coach sidebar below).

One of the times I let my team have it made it into the Women's Basketball Hall of Fame in Knoxville, Tennessee. In a room called the Locker Room, there's a big screen set up where you can choose to see halftime speeches made by different coaches. One of the choices is a speech I made to my players during a game against North Carolina State a few years ago. We were playing an absolutely awful game, so I made the players put their hands on their hearts to check if their hearts were beating. As it happened, the game turned around, and we won it. The Hall of Fame employee told me my speech is the most watched of all. I don't know whether to be proud or embarrassed.

ASK THE COACH

Question: We played a terrible first half the other day. The starters had no energy. They made lazy passes and didn't move their feet on defense. At halftime, I thought about starting five different players, but I didn't because I was afraid of hurting their confidence (they've started every game for us), and because there's a big drop-off from the first group to the next. The starters played better in the second half, but the scoring gap was too big, and we still lost by a lot. In hindsight, should I have started the other players?

Answer: Don't hesitate to change the lineup when a starter isn't playing the way she should, especially if she's not working hard, like not moving her feet on defense. Not starting sends a strong message that the team can't afford to have her out there if she doesn't do her best. In the locker room, you could say something like, "I don't think we hustled in the first half like we can, so I'm going to start a different group of players to see what they can do."

Question: We played so lousy in the first half the other day that by the end of it, I was hopping mad. At halftime we went into the locker room and I let them have it. I've seen plenty of college coaches rip into their players on the bench, so I figured it was fine to let my emotions out. It's not like I hit anyone. Now that I've calmed down, I feel bad about getting on them like I did. Was it wrong to let them have it?

Answer: It depends on how you did it and what you communicated. First, don't model your behavior after what you see other coaches doing. Most coaches handle themselves well, but unfortunately, some coaches behave poorly and unprofessionally when things don't go their way. The result is they embarrass themselves, hurt their players' confidence, and damage the trust their players have in them.

Second, don't ever lose sight of the all-important goal of treating your players with respect and dignity. When times are toughest is when you must adhere to this principle the most. Your kids are counting on you to be an anchor, not a loose cannon.

Third, there are certain actions that go far beyond the realm of good coaching—profanity, screaming, throwing things, kicking things, putting your hands on a player, and berating a player. If you did any of the above, your behavior was out of line and unacceptable (and you probably have heard from a parent, your athletic director, or the head of the league by now). Apologize to your players and their parents, and don't do it again. If you have a habit of repeatedly doing any of the above, get out of coaching. It's not in your best interests or in the best interests of your players. You might have good intentions, but you're not emotionally ready to handle the responsibility.

Statistics

Coaches differ on how they view the importance of basketball statistics. Some coaches think stats have little value, and make no effort to track them. Some coaches consider stats as a major factor in their decision making.

I lean toward the second approach. In practice, my assistants chart information like shooting percentages so I can see how each player progresses as the season goes along. At halftime in games, I always check certain key stats before talking to the team. I look at *points in the paint* (baskets scored in the lane area) and *outside points* (baskets scored outside the lane area) for both teams. I want to know how each of our defensive strategies has done, how many times the other team scored off our man-to-man defense, and so on. If the other team shot 2 for 16, we don't need to adjust our defense. If they shot 12 for 16, we need to change something. Maybe it's the formation, maybe it's the intensity—but something needs to change.

Review your game stats after each game. If you've never used stats before, this might seem like a waste of time. After all, you saw what happened out there. You don't need a sheet of paper to tell you that their number 50 scored a ton of points in the low post. Stats don't have much value in that sense. Their value is in clarifying the subtleties, in pointing out little things that were obscured by the big things. It's seeing that your shooting guard played a fine all-around game, though she scored only 3 points. You didn't notice at the time, but she also had 5 assists, 4 rebounds, 3 steals, and not a single turnover. Now that's a good player.

Stats are valuable in evaluating player progress. As the season advances, look for trends. The numbers will tell you who is doing a better job on the boards since the beginning of the season and who is not. Hey, look at this—when the season began, your backup 3 didn't contribute much during the few minutes she played in each game, but now you see that she averages 5 points and 3 rebounds per game, and she's still only playing 3 to 4 minutes. It's time to get her more playing time, isn't it? Imagine what she might do if she played 10 to 15 minutes a game.

Stats don't tell you everything you need to know, but what they tell you can't be learned from another source. The more you use and consider stats, the more you'll come to appreciate them.

Stat Keepers

Assign an assistant, a manager, or a parent to be a stat keeper during games. This should be a different person than the person who keeps the scorebook at the scorers' table. Don't assume the person you assign knows how to keep stats correctly, even if the person says he or she does. Keeping stats correctly involves understanding several gray areas, such as turnovers and assists, which are subject to interpretation. Go over the stat sheet with the stat keeper. Have him or her keep stats for a scrimmage or two before the first game, so the kinks will be worked out.

Keeping game stats isn't easy. Events happen rapid-fire, and even an experienced stat keeper can't keep up with every event. Assign another volunteer to be a spotter to help the stat keeper.

The stat sheet your stat keeper uses doesn't have to be fancy. A sample stat sheet is included in the Appendix (the sample sheet doesn't include shooting stats because those are kept by the person who keeps the scorebook).

Assistants

In addition to helping you run more effective practices, your assistants can help you do a better job of bench coaching, too.

Assign an assistant to keep track of fouls and time-outs for both teams. He or she should be able to tell you at any moment how many fouls each player on both teams has, how many team fouls each teams has, and how many time-outs each team has left in the game. These pieces of information are crucial. You can't make good decisions without them. If, after a nonshooting foul, the referee is about to hand the ball to your player for an inbounds play, your assistant should immediately tell you that it's the seventh team foul and that your player should go to the free throw line, so you can let the referee know. Before you call a time-out in the closing minutes, the assistant should tell you what the time-out situation is, so you can tell the players (remember—calling a time-out when you have none left is a technical foul).

Assistants can be excellent sources of information. Encourage them to give you their opinions during the game, even when not asked. They might notice that a player is hurt or tired before you do. They might pick up that when the other coach yells "Blue," that means an isolation play for their shooter on the right side. They might suggest that the other team's help-side guard always doubles down on your post player, so your post player should look to kick the ball out to the help-side wing. A keen assistant with a good basketball mind is a major plus for a team.

Assistants are there to help you and the team. It's foolish not to ask for and consider their opinions. Doing so also has another benefit—you'll make them feel more a part of the team. They'll realize that you value their contributions, and next year, when you ask, they'll be eager to help.

Scouting

Scouting an opponent—watching the other team play in person to learn as much as you can about how they play basketball—is overkill for a middle school team, but important for a high school team.

If you coach a high school team, scout your opponents as often as you can. Find out their schedule and go to a game, preferably a few days before your team plays them. Take a notepad, a couple of pencils, and a scouting sheet (see the sample in the Appendix). Sit in the middle of the stands, high up, where you have a bird's-eye view. Make notes throughout the game on anything you think is important. Some coaches focus on team aspects in the first half and evaluate individual players in the second half. It doesn't matter how you approach it. The goal is to learn as much as you can in order to prepare the best possible game plan. This includes understanding the coach's game plan, how they play offense and defense, who their best players are, what the team is good at, and what it's not good at.

ASK THE COACH

Question: The first game of the season is coming up. It will also be the other team's first game, so I can't scout them. How can I prepare my team well if I don't know anything about the other team?

Answer: If you prepare your team properly, you already have a sound game plan. Your players will know how to play against man-to-man defense or zone defense. They'll know how to break a press and how to attack with the fast break. If you've done your job well, though the opponent will be unfamiliar, your players won't face anything on the court they haven't seen in practice. Preparation creates confidence and poise, no matter what team you're playing.

As the first half progresses, learn about the other team. Be flexible. If necessary, change your strategies on the fly. As you see what they do well, how they like to score, how they play defense, and what their strengths and weaknesses are, adjust your game plan to fit the circumstances. By halftime, you'll know plenty about the other team. If things aren't going well, make more adjustments. That's what great coaching is all about!

Game Plans and Strategies

Let's say you've scouted your opponent. Now you're ready to create a *game plan*—a written list of strategies and tactics you'll use in the game. How do you go about this? Here are some general guidelines:

Play to your individual strengths. If you have a good low post scorer, design your offense to get her the ball as often as possible. If you have a good outside shooter, design some plays that set screens for her so she can get open. If you have a good 1-on-1 player who can drive to the basket, put in a couple of clear-out plays to isolate her on one side of the basket.

Play to your team strengths. If you have a quick, aggressive team, press. If you have a tall team, pack in your defense so your rebounders are in good position to get the ball after a shot.

Neutralize the opponent's strengths. If the other team has a good outside shooter, put your best perimeter defender on her and try to limit how often the shooter touches the ball. If they're good at running the fast break, designate two safeties whose assignment is to sprint back right away after a shot at the other team's basket.

Attack the opponent's weaknesses. If their point guard isn't a strong ball handler, trap her when she has the ball. If their post players are smaller than your post players, pass the ball around the perimeter until there's an opening to pass it to the low post. If one of their posts has a tendency to foul, get the ball to whomever she's guarding.

Take advantage of favorable match-ups. If they play man-to-man defense, and one of your players is better than her assigned defender, design an isolation play that gets the ball to your player so she can drive on the defender.

Part of your game plan is to decide:

- who the starters will be
- who the first subs will be
- what defense you'll play
- what offense you'll play if they come out in man-to-man
- what offense you'll play if they come out in zone
- how you'll handle the press, if it happens
- what you'll do if you're behind in the fourth quarter
- what you'll do if you're ahead in the fourth quarter

Of course, game plans only go so far. It will take game experience and trial and error to learn what strategies and tactics might be best for each game situation. Notice I say *might*. There are plenty of other variables, including how well your players carry out the game plan and what the other team does to counter them. And sometimes no game plan works. If the other team is flat-out better, you can change your game plan all game long, but the outcome isn't going to change. At those times, coach the best you can, and work hard to keep your team's spirits up.

Here are a few situations to consider:

When your game plan isn't working. If your team is behind by 18 points at halftime, should you scratch the game plan or stick with it? Before you can answer that, you have to analyze the situation. Why are you behind? Is it sloppy play on your team's part—poor execution of the game plan? How well is your team doing the things the game plan calls for?

If your players aren't playing as well as they can—if they're sluggish, throwing bad passes, committing silly fouls—this is a lack of intensity and focus, not a problem with the game plan. If your players aren't following the game plan—not running the plays, forgetting to double-team the post, not leaving a safety back on offense—again, these things aren't the result of a bad game plan, but are caused by lack of concentration and by confusion.

However, if your players are working hard but the other team has figured out how to get easy inside shots off your 1-2-2 zone, it's time to think about trying another defense. If one of their shooters suddenly gets hot from outside, it's time to extend the zone, switch to man-to-man, or maybe go to a box-and-one. Try something else for a few possessions; maybe something different will slow them down.

When your team is playing well but is outmatched. When your players are doing all they can against a superior team, the best strategy is to *shorten the game*—reduce the number of times the other team has the ball. Would you rather have the other team have 80 possessions or 40 possessions? Which alternative would likely result in a more lopsided game? To look at it in an extreme way, if you could choose that the game would be decided by each team having the ball only once, wouldn't you choose that? When the number of possessions is reduced, an underdog's chances of pulling off an upset increase.

In college games, coaches can shorten the game only so much, because of the 30-second shot clock. Middle school leagues, AAU tournaments, and many high school leagues don't use a shot clock. In theory, one team can pass the ball the whole half and try to get a good shot right at the end. In reality, maintaining possession for more than a minute is difficult for most teams. The more passes made, the more chances for error there are. Unless you have very good ball handlers, it's unwise to try to delay for too long. However, the more deliberate your team can play when it has the ball, the fewer possessions the other team will have. Therefore, you will have shortened the game.

When coaching in a game your team isn't likely to win, be realistic with your players. If the other team is a powerhouse that beat you before by 38 points, you won't have much credibility if you talk as if your team has an even chance. Deemphasize winning and losing. If all you talk about is winning, you're setting up your players (and yourself) for disappointment. Create some attainable goals for your team, like "Let's hold them to 10 points a quarter" or "Our goal is to have fewer than 20 turnovers" or "This time, let's see if we can outscore them in a quarter." Make the goals challenging, but achievable. If goals are too easy, reaching them won't mean anything to your players.

When I first started coaching at the University of North Carolina, the women's program wasn't strong. We're much better now, but we had to crawl before we could walk, and walk

ASK THE COACH

Question: What if my team is playing a much weaker team?

Answer: When your team is clearly the better team, don't *run up the score*—don't pile on the points unnecessarily. Show respect for the other team. Don't embarrass their players or their coaches. Nothing will anger the other coach and the players more than if it looks like you're trying to make a lopsided game worse.

If your team is ahead by more than 20 points, it's obvious which team will win. Don't turn the game into a humiliating rout. Call off the dogs: remove your first-string players, put in the end-of-the-bench subs, stop pressing, and switch to a zone defense. This is a good opportunity for your less-skilled players to get playing time. So what if the lead is down to 10 points by the end of the game? The goal is to win, not to set some kind of a scoring record, right?

Unfortunately, some coaches with dominating teams don't believe in this concept. In their mind, the goal is to score as many points as possible in the shortest amount of time. They keep their best players in until the very end. They press all game long and never switch to a more passive defense. My view is that "what goes around comes around," and that sooner or later, these coaches will find themselves on the bottom end of a mismatch, and they'll learn what it feels like.

My North Carolina teams sometimes play teams from "mid-major schools" (schools that don't play in one of the big national conferences). Though they're the underdog, the coaches of those teams are willing to play us at our gym because they know we won't run up the score. I've been in their shoes, and I want their players to feel like they played a good game. I want them to be able to say afterward, "Hey, we went to North Carolina and stayed within 20 points."

It's simple—not running up the score is a basic part of good sportsmanship.

Question: My team is winning by huge margins. I've followed your suggestions. In our last game, we stopped pressing after the first half, and I took out my starters in the middle of the third quarter. The other coach was still mad. What else can I do? I can't tell my players not to shoot, can I?

Answer: You can, but this is where it becomes a gray area. Some middle school leagues have a *mercy rule*, a rule that says when the scoring margin exceeds X points, regardless of how much time is left, the game is over.

Barring a mercy rule, you're faced with a legitimate question: how far should you go in calling off the dogs? You could go too far. For example, if you tell your players not to shoot, and there are 10 minutes left in the game, the other coach probably won't like that. Most coaches don't want their opponent to stop trying. It's as if you're saying "Coach, your team is so rotten, my players can play bad basketball and still kill you." Try to find a balance between running up the score and telling your players not to shoot anymore. Here are some ideas:

- Tell your players that only certain players (choose less-skilled players) can score. This makes them work to get the ball to the designated players and forces those players to work hard to get open.

- Tell your players to get the ball inside, that you want them to take only low post shots. This makes the perimeter players work on feeding the post.

- Tell your players that you want six passes or three ball reversals before a shot. This makes your players work on passing, moving without the ball, and making good decisions.

All these tactics slow down the rate of your team's scoring, while your players practice things you want them to work on, and the other team won't feel like your team is giving them anything for free.

You might find that even after making these adjustments, some coaches are still mad. At that point, you've done as much as you can reasonably do, so shake their hand and forget about it.

---

before we could run. We crawled, we walked, we ran, and, finally, we're sprinting. But it took a very long time. If your team is struggling, be patient and persistent. Be realistic about the competition, be honest with your players, set doable goals, teach them fundamentals, and your players will have a successful season.

When your team is playing against a great scorer. Coaches look at this situation in one of two ways. Some say, "Well, number 22 is going to score a lot no matter what we do, so our goal is to keep the other players from scoring. If we do that, there's no way she can score enough points to beat us single-handedly." If you choose this approach, the strategy is to play balanced defense. Put your best defender on the scorer, and don't worry too much when she scores. As long as one of the other players doesn't score much, your team will have a good chance to win.

Other coaches say, "The key to stopping their team is stopping number 22. No one else can hurt us. Since she averages 26 points a game, if we limit her to 15 or less, we should win the game." If you adhere to this approach, pay extra attention to defending the scorer. Here are some strategies:

- Keep a fresh defender on her. When one defender tires, replace her with another defender. Try to wear the scorer down.

- Tell the defenders who guard her that they don't have to play help defense. Their job is to keep the scorer from touching the ball and, whenever she does get the ball, to make her pass it instead of being able to take a shot.

- If the scorer likes to shoot outside jump shots, have the defenders guard her up close, so the player has no room to shoot and must dribble.

- If the scorer likes to dribble and drive, have the defenders play off her, so she'll have to think about shooting from outside instead.

- If the scorer is a post player, when the ball goes to the wing on her side of the lane, double-team her with one player in front of her and one behind.

- If the scorer scores a lot of transition baskets, have two or three players who sprint back on defense as soon as your team shoots the ball.

- Play a box-and-one or a diamond-and-one (see pages 147–49). Every time the scorer touches the ball, two defenders should guard her.

- Lastly, make the scorer work hard at the defensive end of the court. Try to get her in foul trouble by having the player she's guarding drive at her.

My personal preference is to attack the other team's star on defense and on offense. If someone is going to rack up 35 points on us, I want her to have to earn every single point.

When your team is behind, but there's still a lot of time left. Above all, don't panic. Make every possession count. Try to cut the margin down a basket at a time. Teams that are way behind tend to panic and play faster than they should. They rush their offensive possessions, force passes that aren't there, and take low-percentage shots. For your team to make up a big margin, as long as there's enough time, the players must be patient and poised. Set the example. If you're calm and focused, their confidence will grow. If you act like the world is falling apart, you can count on it—things will fall apart on the court.

When your team is only behind by a little, but time is running out. It depends on how much time is left and the difference in the score. If you're behind by 4 points with 3 minutes to go, you have plenty of time to catch up, but you need to increase your team's defensive pressure. If you have a quick team and aren't already in a full-court press, it's time to press. If your team has practiced trapping in a half-court set like a 1-2-2 or a 1-3-1, it's time to go to that set. At this point, you want to tighten the defense, but not play an all-out gambling defense. You don't want to give up easy baskets so they can extend the lead.

If you're down by 4 points with 1 minute to go, the situation is urgent. Coaches talk about *the clock being your enemy* now, more so than the other team. If your team has momentum and is forcing turnovers, and the other team is disorganized, even with a minute left, don't change anything. You can tie the game or win with two possessions. However, if the other team has good ball handlers and is able to take 20 to 30 seconds off the clock every possession, you'll have to go into an all-out aggressive mode. You can't let the other team run out the clock by dribbling and passing the ball around the court as the seconds tick away.

Call a time-out (be sure you have one left). Tell your players to foul the person with the ball right away. If you don't have a time-out, yell instructions from the bench (you should have practiced this exact situation). The goal is to stop the clock and put the other team on the free throw line in the hope that they'll miss one or both shots, and your team will get the rebound and the ball. At the offensive end, run the set play you've practiced. You don't have time to run your regular offense. If the other team is *in the bonus* (has seven or more team fouls this half), have your players drive to the basket, trying to draw a foul. When your team scores, have your players press and try to steal the ball. If they can't steal it, they should immediately foul the player who touches the ball.

Part of preparing your team to play games is practicing various end-game situations. That way, your team is less likely to be confused or surprised when those situations occur. Many a team has come back to win the game in the last minute because the players knew what to do.

Question: I'm confused about fouling at the end of the game. The rules say that an intentional foul results in two free throws. Yet I've seen games where the defender is obviously trying to foul the player with the ball, but the referee calls it a regular personal foul. Why isn't that an intentional foul?

Answer: It is, but this is a part of the game where referees, coaches, and players have an unspoken understanding. It's obvious to everyone watching that the defender is trying to foul to stop the clock. In that sense, fouls at the end of the game are all intentional. However, the unspoken understanding is that unless the foul is excessive, like a two-handed push in the back, the referees won't call it intentional.

This is why you should teach your players how to foul intentionally without committing an intentional foul. The key is to be sure the defender goes for the ball with her hand as if she's trying to steal it. If her hand, arm, or body hits the offensive player, then it's a foul. In other words, teach your players to go for the ball aggressively and try to steal it. If they can't get the steal, they should make contact with the offensive player so it's a foul.

Fouling intentionally is a skill that needs to be learned and practiced.

When your team is way ahead. Don't get too comfortable. Sometimes teams that have a big lead stop playing hard and lose intensity. When the other team scores a few easy baskets, their players start to believe they have a real chance. They become inspired, and what was an 18-point margin is suddenly down to 10 points, with plenty of time left in the game. Emphasize to your players that they can't ever afford to relax, because when they do, the other team will sneak up on them.

If the fast break is available, take advantage of it. If good shots are available, shoot them. Don't run up the score (it's bad sportsmanship), but keep the pressure on. Too many teams have learned the hard way that if they ease up too soon, they find they're in a dogfight at the end.

When your team is ahead 6 points with 2 minutes left. If your team is tired, call a full time-out (if you have one) so your team can rest up for what should be an energetic 2 minutes. Expect the other team to start pressing and fouling. Put your best free throw shooters and ball handlers into the game. Remind your players to set up your press break if the other team scores. Remind them that they don't have to score another field goal to win, that their primary goals are to run time off the clock, protect the ball, and make their free

---

Question: If we're ahead, but not by much, and they're scoring easily on our defense, would it be wise to switch to a triangle-and-two? We haven't practiced it, but I think it would throw them off balance.

Answer: First, analyze why the other team is scoring so easily. Are your players out of position? Are they tired? Is the other team scoring mainly in transition? Are they scoring mainly from the low post? You won't know what to fix if you don't know what the root of the problem is.

Second, it's generally a bad decision to suddenly play a defense or an offense you haven't practiced. The players may nod their heads during the time-out, and you might think what you've diagrammed is as clear as can be, but the odds are high that the players will go out on the floor confused. All it takes is for one player not to understand the unfamiliar concept, and the team execution will fail.

You'll be much more likely to slow down the other team if you try something you've practiced. If you want to have the triangle-and-two defense as an option to use in games, practice it beforehand.

---

throws. If they have practiced a delay offense, this is a good time to use it (if they haven't, don't try to improvise one now!). Emphasize the need to make good decisions with the ball (avoid traps, pass the ball quickly, stay calm) and that all they need to do to win is play with poise and sink their free throws.

When your team is in foul trouble. There are two kinds of foul trouble—*player foul trouble* and *team foul trouble*. When one of your players accumulates too many fouls too fast, this is player foul trouble. As a general guideline, once a player has more fouls than the number of the quarter, you should consider her in foul trouble. That is, a player who commits her second foul in the first quarter is in foul trouble, while a player who commits her second foul in the fourth quarter isn't. What you do about it depends on the player and the circumstance. If the player is a key player, take her out of the game right away. Keep her on the bench until you absolutely need her. If she's a smart player who knows how to play good defense without fouling, put her back in sooner. If she's a player who doesn't know how not to foul, keep her out longer. If the player in foul trouble is a bench player who isn't likely to play much the rest of the game, you might leave her in until she commits another foul.

A second strategy to protect a player in foul trouble is to switch her defensive assignment. She may not be capable of guarding a particular offensive player who is quicker or more skilled. Have her guard someone else.

A third strategy is to switch from man-to-man defense to zone. Zone defense is more passive. Because the players stay in one area, instead of following their man all over the court, there is less likelihood of fouling. If the other team has a player who likes to drive from the right wing, put the player in foul trouble on the left side of the court.

When the other team is in the bonus because your players committed seven or more fouls in a half, this is team foul trouble. The concern here isn't that one of your players will foul out, but that the other team will shoot at least one free throw every time your team commits another foul. Besides telling your players to play smart defense, switch to a zone defense for the reason mentioned above. If the other team doesn't shoot well from outside, pack in the defense and let them shoot away. Defensive rebounding is always important, but it's even more so in this situation because offensive rebounders are often fouled.

ASK THE COACH

Question: I heard a coach talk about his team making too many "silly fouls." What are those?

Answer: When coaches talk about silly fouls, they're referring to fouls players commit that don't make any sense, such as:

- **A foul 60 feet from the basket.** Why foul someone who is so far from the basket that she can't sink a shot from there?

- **A foul on a 3-point shot.** Unless your team is trying to stop the clock, this foul is a gift to the other team. Why give someone three shots from 15 feet when she's likely to miss one shot from 21 feet?

- **A lazy foul.** This occurs when the defender swipes at the dribbler, instead of moving her feet and getting in the proper on-ball defensive position.

- **A totally needless foul** that helps the other team, like reaching when the point guard has the ball or jumping on someone's back when rebounding.

Part of learning how to play good defense means learning how to be aggressive without fouling. It takes time, but anyone can learn to do it.

Postgame Routine

After a game ends, meet with your players for a few minutes. Keep your comments to a minimum because they will be distracted. If they won, they'll be too excited to listen. If they lost, they'll be too upset. Either way, be brief so they can go home.

If they won, congratulate them on a job well done. Unless a player has done something outstanding, like break a scoring record, don't talk about any one player. Remember—your focus should always be on the team, not on individuals.

If they lost, try not to make them more disappointed than they already are. Don't talk about what they did wrong (save that for the next practice), and again, this is not the time to single out a player. Remind them that they should never get too high or get too low after any game, that they played hard, and should hold their heads high when they walk out of the locker room.

When I'm upset about how my team played, I try not to say much about it until the next day. After watching the tape, I might feel differently about how the team played compared to how I felt during the game. If I were to let my emotions out right after the game, I might say something I'd later regret.

Before the team leaves the locker room, have them huddle up so they can end with their team ritual.

Learning from Games

Every game, win or lose, offers important lessons. A game is wasted if you and your team don't learn from it.

After the game, while your recollections are fresh, write down your observations. Use a blank notepad or fill out a game sheet (see the sample game sheet in the Appendix). Make notes about the other team—its tendencies on offense and defense, its best players, its strengths and weakness—and about your team—what worked well, what didn't. This has two useful purposes. It serves as an excellent scouting report for the next time you play the team, and it serves as a basis for deciding what your team needs to work on most as you prepare for the next game.

Don't throw out your notes at the end of the season. You might need them for next year!

After the Last Game

Right after the season ends, have a team party. Talk to the players to find out what they would enjoy. It should be casual, informal, and inexpensive. You can never go wrong with pizza as the entrée. Before the party, decide what awards you want to give. You can buy inexpensive plaques and trophies at some sporting goods outlets.

If you coach a middle school or AAU team, this is the time to recognize outstanding performances and attitudes. If you coach a high school team, the time for player recognition will be the Sports Banquet.

Be choosy about how many awards you give. If you go beyond a Most Valuable Player, a Most Improved Player, a Defensive Player of the Year, and a Spirit Award, you start to decrease the significance of those awards. Life doesn't hand out awards to everyone, and neither should you.

Give a little speech. Tell your players how much you enjoyed coaching them and how much they improved. Tell them to work on their game between now and next season (see below) so they don't forget most of what they learned.

Thank your assistants for all their contributions. Thank the parents for their support. Single out any parents who contributed to the season. Eat a slice of pizza and enjoy this time with the team. You've become attached to this group of girls. That's one of the joys of coaching.

Before too much time passes, sit down and make notes on the season. Ask your assistants for their input. What could you coaches have done better? What drills worked, and what drills didn't? Which offenses and defenses should you use next year, and which ones

Coach Hatchell with a happy group of players.

should you scrap? What are you going to do off-season to improve your coaching? Is there a good clinic coming up in your area? Good coaches never stop working to get better.

When you look back on the season, you realize that coaching girls' basketball has enriched your life. It's a lot of work and a big challenge, but it's also a joy.

Off-Season

Before the season ends, encourage your players to work on their game in the off-season. Remind them that playing basketball isn't like riding a bike. If they don't ride their bike for eight months, the first time they get on it, they might wobble for 10 seconds, but after that, they'll ride it as well as ever. If they don't play basketball for eight months, they won't pick up right where they left off. Over time, basketball skills erode. The timing and footwork they worked hard to develop aren't there any more. They forget how to do all the little things that made them good players. Their shooting touch will be gone.

There are plenty of ways for your players to work on their skills during the off-season: play on an AAU team, attend summer camps and clinics, attend a team camp, attend open gyms, play in pickup games in the park or at the Y, participate in fall conditioning and shooting workouts, and the old standby, shoot baskets in the driveway. It's not that important *how* your players work on their game off-season, but that they *do* work on it.

If you coach a Varsity high school team, off-season work for your players is essential if you want to keep up with your competition. You can be sure that the players on other teams are working on their game, so get your players to do the same. Provide each player with goals, things you want her to improve in the off-season. If the gym is available for your use in the summer and fall, schedule times for shooting workouts, conditioning, and open gyms.

Research the college and university team camps in your area and sign up your team for one or two. This is a great way to start focusing on next season. It's an excellent tool for you to evaluate your returning players and the new candidates for your team. Time spent at a team camp generates excitement about the upcoming season for everyone on the team.

Question: I coach a JV team, and I don't know if I want my players to be on an AAU team. I've heard some bad things about AAU ball: that the coaches only want the hotshot players, that there's a lot of politics involved, and that there's some under-the-table money. Is any of this true?

Answer: I've had many dealings with many AAU coaches from around the country and can tell you, in no uncertain terms, that 99 percent of them are good coaches and good people. Of course, it takes only a few bad apples to hurt the reputation of an AAU organization. If you're unsure about whether to have your players try out for an AAU team in your area, meet the AAU coaches, and decide for yourself. You'll find that in many instances, AAU coaches are also high school coaches. Also, talk to your Varsity coach and other high school coaches. They'll tell you about the AAU programs in town. If there's a problem, you'll hear about it.

Question: What can I do to make myself a better coach in the off-season?

Answer: It's just as important for you to work on your skills as it is for your players to work on theirs. There are plenty of ways to work on your game:

1. Attend some coaching clinics in your area. Ask other coaches and use the Internet to find dates and locations. Nike, for example, runs a number of clinics around the country every year.

2. Work at a summer basketball camp. You can hone your coaching skills and interact and network with other coaches.

3. Read books and watch tapes on coaching. There are lots of both out there.

4. Coach or help coach an AAU team. The more you coach, the better you'll coach.

5. Lastly, and this may sound a bit contradictory, take a break from coaching. Give yourself a chance to regroup, recharge, and renew. By the time the preseason rolls around, you'll be ready to roll!

Chapter 7

DRILLS

Footwork Drills

1. Pivoting and Jump Stop

The players start on the baseline, each with a ball. Spread them out so there's at least 3 feet between each player. If you have a big team and need more room, start the players along one of the sidelines.

On your signal, the players dribble up the court slowly with their right hand. When you blow the whistle, they come to a two-foot jump stop, the ball on their hip, in the triple threat position. On your signal, they resume dribbling. Every time they hear the whistle, they come to a jump stop. When they reach the other baseline, they come to a jump stop and make a 180-degree forward pivot using their

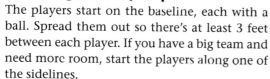

O	offensive player
O (with ball)	player with ball
X	defensive player

A number beside an **X** or an **O** is the position of that player. For example, **X₅** is the defensive center and **O₂** is the offensive shooting guard.

———————▶	player movement
– – – – –▶	pass
∿∿∿∿∿▶	dribble movement
————┤	player screen or trap

Diagram key.

right foot as the pivot foot. They dribble back down the court, this time with their left hand, stopping and starting when they hear the whistle. As they get better at this, have them dribble faster.

After they dribble up and back twice, tell them to switch their pivot foot.

Variation: Have the players pivot every time they stop, protecting the ball from an imaginary defender. On your signal, they continue in the same direction. You can also have

---

DEGREE-OF-DIFFICULTY KEY

beginner

intermediate

advanced

---

them pivot 180 degrees each time they stop and then continue in the new direction.

Emphasis: Encourage players not to lift or drag their pivot foot. Have them rip the ball across their body in a wide range of directions, from high to low and from side to side as they pivot.

2. Protect the Ball

Set up pairs of players, each pair with one ball. One player is the offensive player; the other is the defender. The player with the ball pivots while the defender moves around her, trying to pressure her. After 30 seconds, players change roles and go again.

Emphasis: Players should move the ball in a wide range of motion, not a limited arc. Remind them to keep their elbows out.

3. Machine Gun

Set up three lines of players across the court, facing you. The players are in a defensive stance. When you say "Go," they begin to *stutter step*, moving their feet up and down rapid-fire, lifting them only a few inches off the floor. When you point to one side, they swing step to face that direction for a moment, then swing step back to their original position. Players stutter step for 30 seconds, rest for 10 seconds, and go again. This drill is good for conditioning, agility, and improving foot speed.

Variation: After a swing step, the players do the machine gun facing the new direction.

Conditioning Drills

4. 5 in 65

Set up your players along the baseline. Have a stopwatch ready or use the second hand on your watch. At your signal, the players sprint as fast as they can to the opposite baseline and back five times. Time how long it takes them to finish. Most high school players can do this in less than 65 seconds.

Variation: Have players dribble a ball as they run, making jump stops and pivots at each

baseline. Adjust the time for them to beat to a reasonable standard.

5. Victory Sprints

Some coaches call these *ladders* or *suicides*. Line up your players along one baseline. They sprint up and down the court in this sequence: from the baseline to the near free throw line extended, back to the baseline, up to the mid-court line, back to the baseline, up to the far free throw line extended, back to the baseline, up to the far baseline, and back to the original baseline. This drill is good for conditioning and agility.

Variation: Have players touch the floor every time they plant their foot to reverse direction.

6. Victory Dribbles

The players follow the same sequence as in Victory Sprints, but they dribble a ball as they run. It's interesting to see that the players who run the sprints the fastest aren't always the players who dribble the fastest.

Variation: Have players touch the floor with their nondribbling hand every time they plant their foot to reverse direction.

Stationary Dribbling Drills

Players stand in a ring around the center circle, each holding a ball and with several feet between each player. Choose a player or a coach to lead the team through the following drills:

7. Ball Slaps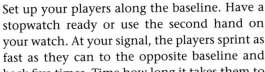

Each player holds the ball in her right hand and slaps it with her left hand for 15 seconds. She then holds the ball in her left hand and slaps it with her right hand for 15 seconds. This warms up the hands.

8. Pound Dribble

Each player dribbles a ball with her right hand while in a control dribble stance. The ball should bounce no higher than her knees and should hit the floor in hard bursts. After 30 seconds, the player switches the ball to her left hand and does the Pound Dribble for another 30 seconds.

Emphasis: Players should keep their head up and watch the leader in the middle of the center circle or look up at the ceiling. They should keep their back straight and not hunch over while dribbling.

9. Ball Wraps

Each player wraps the ball around her knees, her waist, and her head in one continuous motion. She then wraps the ball down to her knees, where she started. After 15 seconds, the players wrap the ball in the other direction for 15 seconds.

10. Crossover Dribble

Each player practices the crossover dribble, keeping her hands below her knees and switching the ball from one hand to the other for 30 seconds.

Emphasis: Players should look up, not at the ball. They should get into a rhythm, swaying slightly from side to side.

11. V Dribble

Each player dribbles with her right hand, dribbling the ball from side to side in front of her. The ball should make a small V as it bounces. After 30 seconds, she switches the ball to her left hand.

Variation: Have players dribble in a random pattern of crossovers and Vs. For example, they can do a crossover, then a V, then another crossover. Or, they can do a crossover, five Vs, then another crossover.

12. Ball Step-Throughs

This drill is an advanced version of Ball Wraps (Drill 9). Each player does four leg wraps as follows. She wraps the ball behind her knees (wrap 1). When the ball is back to her original hand, she steps with her right foot, passes the ball between her legs, and wraps it around her front leg (wrap 2). When the ball is back to her original hand, she brings her right foot back

and wraps the ball around both legs again (wrap 3). When the ball returns to her original hand, she steps with her left foot, passes the ball between her legs, and wraps it around her front leg (wrap 4). She repeats the sequence.

After 30 seconds, have the players wrap the ball in the opposite direction. Once the players get good at this, they'll be able to do dozens of wraps in a minute.

13. Figure-Eight Dribble

Each player spreads her feet wide and dribbles a ball between her legs in a figure-eight pattern. After 30 seconds, she dribbles in the opposite direction.

Variation: Have players dribble a ball for 30 seconds around their right leg, using only their right hand. Then they dribble a ball around their left leg, using only their left hand.

Emphasis: Players should keep their head up as they dribble.

Other Dribbling Drills

14. Line Dribbling Series

Have your players stand along one of the sidelines, facing the court, with 5 feet between each player. Each player has a ball. In this drill, players practice the following dribble moves (explained on pages 31–36) in any order you choose:

crossover dribble

hesitation dribble

inside-out move

between-the-legs dribble

behind-the-back dribble

spin dribble

pull-back dribble

On your signal, the players start dribbling across the court using their right hand. Call out one of the dribble moves ("Crossover!"). When they reach halfway (midcourt), they do the move and continue dribbling. They should dribble as fast as they can. When they reach the opposite sideline, they come to a jump stop, pivot, and begin dribbling back using their left hand. Before they reach midcourt, call out another dribble move ("Spin dribble!"). Keep them dribbling back and forth as many times as you wish until they have practiced all the moves.

15. Cone Dribble

Set up cones in a line from one basket to the next, with 6 to 8 feet between each cone. The team lines up under one basket, each player with a ball. On your signal, the first player dribbles with her right hand to the first cone. When she gets to it, she crosses the ball to her left hand and dribbles around the cone as close to it as possible, leaving it on her right. She dribbles to the next cone, crosses the ball to her right hand and dribbles around that cone as close to it as possible, leaving it to her left. Each time she comes to a cone, she crosses the ball to her other hand. After dribbling around the last cone, she speed dribbles back down the court and gets in the line again.

When the first dribbler reaches the first cone, the second dribbler begins. The third dribbler begins when the second dribbler reaches the first cone, and so on.

Variation: Shorten the distances between the cones. This forces the dribblers to make more crossovers. Stagger the cones so they're in a zigzag pattern. This forces the players to make sharper crossovers.

Emphasis: Players should keep the ball below their knees when crossing over.

16. Dribble Tag

Kids love this drill. Everyone has a ball to dribble. Designate two players who are "It" (who also have a ball) and put them in the center circle. The other players have 5 seconds to dribble anywhere in the gym, other than in the stands (don't let them dribble where they can get hurt). When you say "Go," everyone starts dribbling, and the two players who are "It" dribble after the other players, trying to tag

each player with their hand. When someone is tagged or loses the ball, and thus stops dribbling, she's out. She goes to the center circle and waits, dribbling until all the players are out. Pick two new players to be "It" players and run the drill again.

Your players will quickly learn to double-team the better dribblers in order to tag them. As the season progresses, make sure every player has a chance to be "It."

17. Relay Dribble

Set up two lines of players behind the baseline. The first player in each line has a ball. At your signal, each player speed dribbles to the far basket, makes a layup, rebounds her shot, dribbles back down the court, makes a layup at the near basket, rebounds her shot, and hands the ball to the next player in her line. The drill continues until every player in each line has finished. When a player misses a layup, she shoots at the basket until she makes a shot. This is a fun drill that works on speed dribbling and making layups under pressure.

18. Zigzag Dribbling

Divide the players into pairs, each pair with a ball. The pairs form a line along the baseline, with the first pair at one corner. Each pair has an offensive player and a defender. The offensive player's goal is to dribble the length of the court in a zigzag pattern as fast as she can. The defender's goal is to make it hard for her partner to reach the other end by turning her—forcing her to change directions with a crossover dribble. The defender uses a step-slide motion and she pokes at the ball with her palm up (to avoid fouling) to pressure the dribbler.

The drill starts with the first player dribbling with her left hand to the near elbow. After three dribbles, she crosses the ball to her right hand and dribbles three times to the midcourt corner. There, she crosses back to her left and heads to the near elbow at the far basket. When she crosses over again, she heads for the corner. The players sprint to the other end of the baseline and switch roles. The dribbler becomes the defender, and the defender becomes the dribbler.

They run the same drill down the other half of the court, making the same zigzag pattern.

Run the drill for 3 minutes or until your players are tired. This drill improves conditioning, the ability to handle the ball under pressure, and on-ball defense.

Emphasis: The dribbler should keep her body between the defender and the ball and should keep her head and nondribbling arm up. The defender should play with maximum intensity in order to challenge the ball handler.

19. Two-Ball Dribbling

Two-ball drills are difficult for young players, but they will improve anyone's dribbling.

Each player is in a line at midcourt with two balls. The first player dribbles slowly to the baseline, dribbling one ball with each hand and

timing the dribbles so the balls bounce at the same time. When the player reaches the baseline, she turns around and dribbles to the end of the line of players at midcourt. When the first player reaches the free throw line, the second player begins.

Next, players dribble to the baseline and back to midcourt in a zigzag pattern, changing direction after three dribbles each way.

Then, the players dribble straight to the baseline, this time alternating dribbles—timing their dribbles so each ball hits the floor when the other ball is at its highest point.

Last, they dribble to the baseline and back, using alternating dribbles and following a zigzag pattern.

Emphasis: Players should stay low, dribbling the balls no higher than their knees. Tell players to go slowly. Speed isn't important—control is.

Passing Drills

20. Pairs Passing

Set up pairs of players around the court, each pair with a ball. The partners stand 12 feet apart and begin with two-handed chest passes. They pass for 30 seconds and then switch to bounce passes. After 30 seconds, they make right-handed push passes. After another 30 seconds, they make left-handed push passes and then outlet passes, baseball passes, and curl passes.

Emphasis: Players should give their partner a target. They should make a two-foot jump stop to catch the ball and keep their passes sharp and accurate.

21. Monkey-in-the-Middle

This is the same game we all played in elementary school. Set up a line of three players with a passer at each end and a "monkey" in the middle. The distance between the passers is 12 feet. The passer must hold the ball until the monkey comes over to guard her. The passer works on ball fakes, pivoting, and ripping the ball for 3 seconds before passing. Change the monkey after 30 seconds.

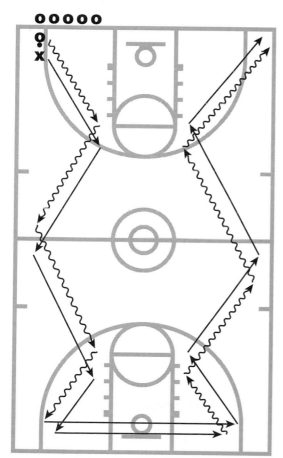

Zigzag Dribbling.

22. Full-Court Passing

Set up six players as passers in stationary positions: four at the free throw lines extended and two at the center circle. The rest of the team is in a line near the basket. Each of the first four players in line has a ball. The idea is for the players in line to go up one side of the court and back down the other by passing to the stationary players, not by dribbling. The only time the ball hits the floor is before shooting a layup. As the first player passes and receives passes, she keeps running up the court. When she reaches the far basket, she shoots a layup, gets the rebound, and starts back the other way. As soon as the first player reaches midcourt, the second player passes to the right-side sideline player, and so on.

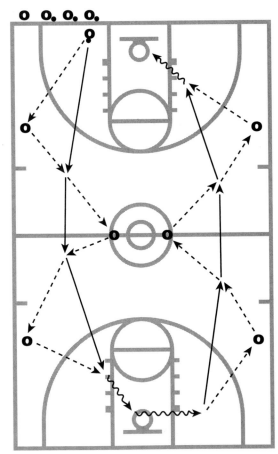

Full-Court Passing.

23. Machine Gun Passing

Line up six passers in a half-circle, each with a ball. A middle passer is positioned at the center of the half-circle, 6 to 8 feet from each perimeter passer. The drill starts with a passer on one end passing to the middle player, who passes back. The second player then passes to the middle player, who passes back, and so on. The goal is for the passers to make rapid-fire, hard passes. Continue the rapid passes for 30 seconds and then replace the middle player. This drill is good for hand-eye coordination.

24. Triangle and Trap

This drill practices passing out of a trap. Set up three players in a triangle, 12 feet apart from each other, one with a ball. Have two trappers in the middle of the triangle. The trappers trap the player with the ball, who can't dribble and can't pass until she's trapped. The passer works on passing around the trap, over the trap, and splitting the trap. After she passes, the trappers trap the new player with the ball. Run this drill for 1 minute and then rotate the players so everyone can practice this important skill.

25. Four-in-a-Line Passing

This drill works on protecting the ball, passing under pressure, ball fakes, curl passes, and on-ball defense. Four players stand in a line with 10 feet between them. The two middle players are defenders. A player at one end has a ball, and the drill begins when the player nearest her comes to guard her. The player with the ball must pivot for 3 seconds (she counts them out loud) before she dribbles by the defender (who lets her go by). When she comes to the next defender, she comes to a jump stop and pivots for another 3 seconds (again counting out loud). She uses a curl pass to pass around the defender to the fourth player in the line. Curl passes are the only passes allowed. After this sequence, the original passer becomes one of the defenders and goes to guard the player she just passed to. The drill continues until everyone has had a turn in each position.

Emphasis: Encourage players to rip the ball through with their elbows out and to use ball fakes to set up the pass.

26. Drive and Dish

This 2-on-1 drill works on dribble penetration and help defense. Set up a line of post players on the baseline and a line of guards at the top of the circle. The first post steps to the block area as the offensive player, and the second post steps out as her defender. The first guard has a ball and drives to the basket (the assumption is she's beaten her defender). As she enters the lane, the post defender comes out to prevent the easy basket. If she's in position to stop the drive, the guard makes a bounce pass to the offensive post, who steps out from the baseline to create a good passing angle. The post should be open for a layup or short jump shot. If she misses the shot or doesn't take it, the players play 2-on-1 until a score or the defender gets the ball. The guard and the offensive post rotate back to their lines. The defensive post is now the offensive post, and the drill starts again.

Variation: Add a perimeter defender. She lets the guard drive by but recovers to guard her man. The players play 2-on-2 until a score or the defense gets the ball.

27. Three-Man Weave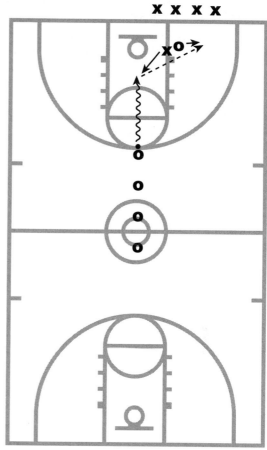

Set up three lines of players on the baseline— one under the basket, the other two at the short corners. The first player in the middle line has a ball. The object is to pass the ball up the court as quickly as possible. At the signal, the player with the ball passes to the player on the right and cuts behind her. The player with the ball passes to the player on the left and cuts behind her. The third player passes to the first player and cuts behind her. As they head up the court, they make a weave pattern.

When the ball is passed to a player near the basket, she shoots a layup. The closer of the two other players takes the ball out of the basket and starts the weave back the other way. When one of the players makes a layup at the original baseline, the next player in

Drive and Dish.

the middle line catches the ball as it drops through the basket, and three new players start up the court. The goal is for the ball to never hit the floor, other than one dribble before the layup. (See left diagram page 194.)

Moving without the Ball Drills

28. V-Cut

The players form two lines at the wings with two passers at the top of the circle. The first player in each line has a ball.

The drill begins when each wing passes to the passer on her side of the court. She cuts to the block, makes a swim move and V-cut, and

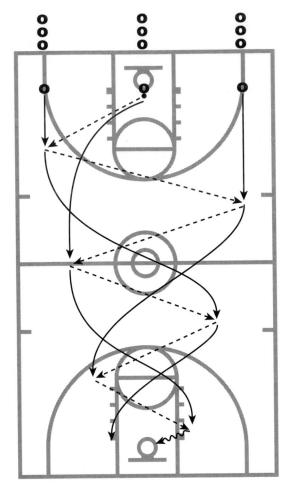

Three-Man Weave.

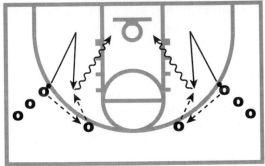

V-Cut.

29. Backdoor Cut

Have two lines of players, one in each short corner, and two passers at the 3-point arc. Each passer has a ball. The drill starts when the first player in each line cuts toward the perimeter. After a few steps, the player plants her outside foot and makes a backdoor cut to the basket. The passer times her pass so the cutter can take one dribble and shoot a layup. The cutter retrieves her rebound, passes back to the passer, and goes to the end of the opposite line. As the cutter retrieves her rebound, the second player in line starts her backdoor cut.

30. Give-and-Go

Have two lines of players, one at each wing, and two passers at the top of the circle. The first player in each line has a ball. She passes to the passer (the *give*) and immediately cuts to the basket (the *go*) for the return pass and the layup.

cuts back to the perimeter. The passer leads her with the ball so the player has to keep coming to catch it. When she catches it, she squares up and gets in the triple threat position. Then she dribbles to the basket for a layup and gets her own rebound. After passing to the next player in line, she goes to the end of the other line.

After each player has gone through each line twice, replace the passers so they can do the drill.

Variation: After your players have the footwork and timing down, add a defender (see Wing Denial, Drill 54).

Emphasis: Remind players to make a V-cut, not an I-cut. They should hold out their lead hand as a target.

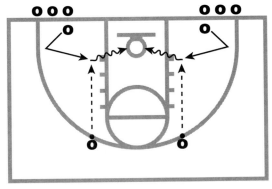

Backdoor Cut.

Variation: Set up two passers, one at each wing, and a line of players at the top of the circle. The first two players in line have a ball. The first player passes to the right wing and cuts to the basket, with her lead hand extended. After she catches the ball, she shoots a layup. As she shoots, the second player in line passes to the left wing and repeats the give-and-go. As a change of pace, the cutters pull up for a short jump shot.

Emphasis: The player should explode to the basket. She shouldn't go at half-speed, waiting for the passer to throw the ball. It's up to the passer to time the pass properly.

31. Screen Away

Have three lines of players, one at each wing and one at the top of the circle. The first two players in the top line each have a ball. The first player passes to the right wing and screens for the left wing, who cuts off the

screener's shoulder into the lane to receive the pass from the right wing. She drives for a layup, retrieves the rebound, and passes to the next player in the top line. Meanwhile, as she shoots her layup, the next group of three players begins the sequence with the player at the top of the circle passing to the player on the right wing.

After each sequence, the players change lines. Once every player has done the drill twice from each position, the player at the top passes to the left wing and screens for the right wing.

Variation: Once the players are comfortable doing this drill, add three defenders. See the Three-Man Shell (Drill 59).

Emphasis: Remind players to wait for the screen, wait for the screen, and wait for the screen.

32. Reading the Screen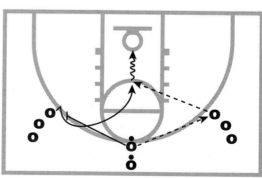

Set up three lines of players, one at each wing and one at the top of the circle. The first player in the top line passes to the right (or left) wing and screens for the opposite wing. Have cutters make different cuts—curl cuts, fade cuts, and back cuts; screeners should react accordingly. For example, on a curl cut, the screener rolls high, and on a fade cut, the screener rolls low. When the cutters and screeners get the footwork down, add defenders so your cutters learn how to read screens. The wing player who receives the ball should sometimes pass to the cutter and sometimes to the screener.

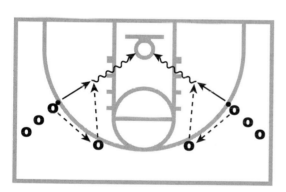

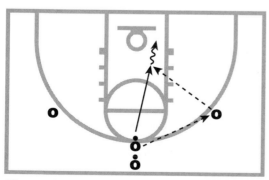

Give-and-Go. Cutting from the wing (top). Cutting from the top of the circle (bottom).

Screen Away.

Variation: Have another player with a ball, so that after every screen, both the cutter and the screener receive passes and work on shooting.

Emphasis: Remind passers not to pass just to a cutter. Screeners also make great receivers.

Shooting Drills

33. Floor Follow-Through

Each player is on her back on the floor, with a ball in her shooting hand, ready to shoot. The player snaps her wrists, practicing her follow-through and catching the ball when it comes down.

This drill can be done at home. As homework, you might want to assign twenty-five floor shots a night before bedtime.

Emphasis: As the ball rolls off the player's fingertips, she should make sure it has backspin.

34. Chair Follow-Through

Place a chair 3 feet in front of the basket. A player sits in it with her back straight and shoots at the basket. Since she can't use her legs to get the ball to the basket, she has to have a good follow-through with maximum arm extension. This drill helps correct common problems such as "short-arming" the shot and not snapping the wrist enough. As the player shoots, have a second player catch the ball out of the basket and hand it to her, so that the shooter can maintain her position in the chair. Switch players after ten shots. This drill takes little time and is well worth it. My players believe it has improved their shooting.

Variation: If you have multiple baskets in the gym, place chairs at every basket, divide your team into small groups, and have them compete against each other. For example, each team shoots for 2 minutes or until one team makes fifty shots.

35. Warm-Up Shooting

The importance of starting in close to the basket when your players begin to work on shooting cannot be overemphasized. How can a player expect to make 15-footers if she can't make 5-footers?

Each player starts on the right block, focusing on the fundamentals—balance, arm extension, and good follow-through. After she makes five shots, she shoots from in front of the basket. After making five shots from there, she shoots from the left block, continuing until she makes five shots. By starting in close, the player gains confidence in her shooting and warms up for longer shots. After she completes that sequence, she's ready to step out to 8 to 10 feet from the basket and start again.

36. Three-Line Form Shooting

Set up three lines of players, one at each block and one in front of the basket. Each player has a ball. The first player in the right-side line shoots a bank shot and retrieves her rebound. As she does, the first player in the middle line shoots and retrieves her rebound, followed by the first player in the left-side line. After a player retrieves her rebound, she rotates counterclockwise to the next line.

Players get only one shot. If a player misses, she doesn't take another shot until it's her turn again. Once your players get the hang of it, this drill has the players shooting a lot of shots in a short time. As they improve, have them step back to a distance of 8 to 10 feet and keep going.

Emphasis: Players should check their feet before shooting. Are they in the right position? Have the players hold their follow-through long enough to make sure their fingers are correct and their arm is straight.

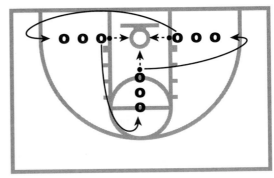

Three-Line Form Shooting.

37. One-Man Stepping into the Shot

This drill works on the proper footwork for stepping into the shot. Have players spread out on the court. Each player has a ball. She *passes it to herself*—tosses it 2 feet in front of her, rotating her hands to create backspin so the ball bounces back to her. As it comes back, she steps into the pass, pivots on her inside foot, and shoots so the ball lands just in front of her.

38. Two-Line Shooting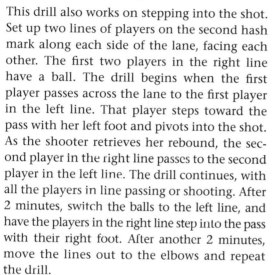

This drill also works on stepping into the shot. Set up two lines of players on the second hash mark along each side of the lane, facing each other. The first two players in the right line have a ball. The drill begins when the first player passes across the lane to the first player in the left line. That player steps toward the pass with her left foot and pivots into the shot. As the shooter retrieves her rebound, the second player in the right line passes to the second player in the left line. The drill continues, with all the players in line passing or shooting. After 2 minutes, switch the balls to the left line, and have the players in the right line step into the pass with their right foot. After another 2 minutes, move the lines out to the elbows and repeat the drill.

Variation: As your players get the footwork down, you can add a lot to this drill, such as a pump fake and one dribble to the right, a pump fake and one dribble to the left, ball fakes, and a one-dribble drive to the hoop.

Emphasis: Players should give the passer a target and should catch the ball in a crouch so they're ready to shoot after they pivot.

39. Shooting off the Pass

Start with two cutter lines in the short corners and two passers above the elbows. The first player in the cutter line makes a V-cut to the perimeter and holds her hand out as a target for the passer. When she catches the ball, she pivots on her inside foot, squares up, and shoots. As she retrieves her rebound (one shot only), the second player in line starts her cut. After shooting, each player goes to the end of the other line.

Variation: The players can make a shot fake, take one dribble, and shoot. They can also make a shot fake and drive. Switch the cutter lines to the wings, then to the top of the circle.

Emphasis: Remind players not to rush. They should always square up into the triple threat position when they catch the ball on the perimeter.

40. Spot Shooting

Divide the players into two teams and set up each team in a line at a block. The first player in each line has a ball. On your signal, she shoots, retrieves her rebound (whether made or missed), passes to the next player in her line, and goes to the back of her line. Each team keeps track of their made shots, shouting the number when another shot scores ("Twelve!"). The first line to reach twenty-five baskets wins.

Variation: Each team shoots five shots from six spots on the perimeter of the lane: the right block, midway up the lane line, the elbow, the other elbow, the other midway point, and the left block. The first team to "go around the world" wins.

Emphasis: Players should focus on shooting with good form and not rush because they're in a hurry to score. They'll score more points when they shoot with good form.

41. Game Shots

Emphasize practicing *game shots*—shots that players will take in games. Every player has spots on the floor where she's most comfortable shooting. I define "good" game shots as being shots that an unguarded player will make at least 60 percent of the time. Lower this figure to match your players' skills.

Have your players shoot game shots from various spots on the floor, not moving from one spot to the next until they've made five at the first spot. After they've finished, have them repeat the sequence, this time with a pump fake and dribble.

42. Knockout

One of the most fun shooting drills is called "Knockout" or "Gotcha." You can do this with as few as two players, but the more shooters you have, the more fun it is. The players form a line at the free throw line. The first two players in line each have a ball. The first player shoots a free throw and follows her shot. If she makes it, she retrieves the ball and passes it to the next person in line without a ball. If she misses, she gets her own rebound and tries to score from wherever she gets the rebound before the second player scores. The second player can shoot as soon as the first player leaves the free throw line. If the second player scores before the first player, the first player is out and leaves the game. The drill continues until only one player remains.

43. Beat the Star

This drill has two players and a ball. One player is the shooter, and the other is the rebounder. The shooter picks an imaginary player to shoot against (such as Michael Jordan or Diana Taurasi). The shooter takes game shots, moving to a new spot after each shot. Every made shot counts as 1 point for the player, and every miss counts as 1 point for the star player. The player continues shooting until either she or the star player reaches 10 points. The shooter and the rebounder trade places and repeat the drill.

44. One Ball, Two Players

The drill begins with one player under the basket with a ball and another player somewhere on the perimeter. The first player passes to the shooter, who catches the ball and shoots. As she does, the passer runs to a spot on the floor where she wants to receive the ball. The shooter rebounds her shot (whether made or missed), passes to the new shooter, and runs out to another spot. Pairs of players pass and shoot simultaneously. Run this drill for 2 minutes or until one set of players makes twenty-five shots.

This drill is a good conditioner and teaches players to follow their shots. You can award extra points if a shooter catches the shot (whether made or missed) before it hits the floor. I have my players call their partner's name as they wait for the pass. This reinforces the habit of calling for the ball in games when they're open.

Variation: Have the passer run at the shooter with a hand up to contest the shot, so the shooter will get used to defensive pressure. Add moves with the shot, such as one or two dribbles, or have the shooters drive to the basket for a layup.

45. Two Balls, Three Players

This is an excellent drill that my teams use often. It works on game shots, conditioning, following shots, rebounding, and passing. Set up three players at various shooting spots on the floor. Two players have balls, and one player begins the drill by shooting. She follows her shot, rebounds, passes to the player without a ball, and runs to a new spot. Meanwhile, the second player shoots and follows the same sequence, resulting in an active nonstop drill. The players keep track of the made shots. Each player who scores shouts the new number of made shots. Run this drill for 2 minutes or until one trio scores 25 points.

Variation: As with One Ball, Two Players, you can add moves with the ball or drives, or you can designate a certain number of shots from certain spots. As your players become familiar with the drill, adjust it to best meet the needs of your team.

46. Two-Line Layups

This is the standard half-court drill many teams use to warm up. Set up two lines of players above the 3-point arc at a 45-degree angle to the basket. The first three players in the right line each have a ball. As the first player dribbles to the basket to shoot a right-handed layup, the first person in the other line comes in to rebound the shot (whether made or missed). After the shot, the dribbler runs to the rebound line. The rebounder dribbles to the corner, passes to an open player in the dribbler line, and runs to the back of the line. After each player shoots several layups, switch the balls to the other line. The dribblers now shoot left-handed layups.

Variation: Add a pass. The player in the right line dribbles in, comes to a jump stop at the edge of the lane, and makes a bounce pass to the other player, who shoots a left-handed layup. Add a jump shot. Instead of shooting layups, the players pull up for an 8- to 10-foot shot.

47. Three-Line Layups

This is a more complicated layup drill that uses three lines: two as in Two-Line Layups plus a third line at the center circle. Each player in the middle line has a ball. To start the drill, all three players cut for the baseline. Assume the left-side player is 2, the middle player is 1, and the right-side player is 3. When 2 and 3 reach the free throw line extended, they cut on a 45-degree angle to the basket. Player 1 dribbles to the free throw line and passes to 3, who shoots a layup. As 2 rebounds the shot (whether made or missed), 1 cuts to the right short corner. After shooting, 3 cuts to the left short corner (part 1).

Next, 2 passes to 1, who shoots a layup and then goes to the left short corner. Player 3 rebounds the made or missed shot (part 2).

After the rebound, 3 passes to 2, who shoots a layup. After 1 rebounds, the players quickly move off the court and run to the end of a different line (part 3). This drill is an excellent pregame warm-up because each player shoots a layup, rebounds, and passes to a cutter.

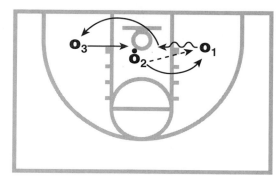

Three-Line Layups, part 2.

48. X Layups

This is a two-player drill. One player starts at the right elbow with a ball while her teammate stands off the court. At your signal, the player with the ball drives to the basket, taking only one dribble with her right hand, and shoots a right-handed layup. She gets the rebound (whether made or missed), dribbles twice to the left elbow with her right hand, stops, turns to the outside (away from the right elbow), takes one dribble to the basket with her left hand, and shoots a left-handed layup. She rebounds the shot (whether made or missed), and dribbles twice with her left hand out to where she began. She continues this sequence for 1 minute as her teammate counts the made baskets. Then the players switch roles, and the other player shoots layups for 1 minute.

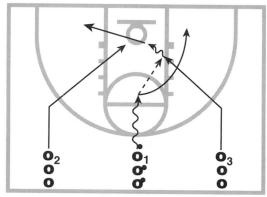

Three-Line Layups, part 1.

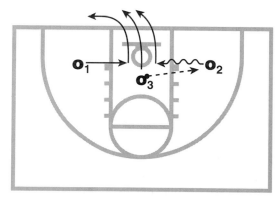

Three-Line Layups, part 3.

This drill is excellent for working on proper footwork in driving and making layups with both hands. The sequence takes some practice to learn. The key to remembering which hand to dribble with is remembering that the ball should stay away from the center of the lane. The number of dribbles is always two out and one in.

49. Mikan

This two-player drill is named after George Mikan, the NBA center who made it popular. The player with the ball starts at the right block while her teammate stands off the court. At the signal, she makes a right-handed layup. She catches the ball as it drops through the net (or misses), steps with her right foot toward the left wing, and shoots a left-handed layup. She catches the ball, steps with her left foot toward the right wing, and makes a right-handed layup. She alternates layups for 1 minute as her teammate keeps track of the made shots. Then the players switch roles, and the other player shoots layups for 1 minute.

The goal is to shoot continuous layups as fast as possible, never letting the ball hit the floor.

50. Foul Shots

Your team should practice foul shots at every practice. The more baskets you have, the better, but even if you have only two baskets, don't ignore this crucial part of the game. Many games are won or lost at the free throw line.

The simplest drill is to divide your players into pairs at the baskets and have each player shoot ten free throws, while the rebounder keeps track of the made shots. We record our players' shooting at every practice so we can chart their progress during the season.

51. Three-Player Foul Shots

This is a good drill when you have enough baskets to divide your players into three-person teams. Each team designates a shooter, a rebounder, and a runner. As the shooter and rebounder stay at the basket, the runner runs a lap. When she finishes, she goes to the free throw line and replaces the shooter, who becomes the new rebounder. The previous rebounder becomes the new runner. As the players tire, they'll learn how to make foul shots in game conditions. Stop the drill after a certain number of made shots or after a certain length of time.

Defensive Drills

52. Defensive Slides

Stand in front of the basket with three lines of players facing you, the first line along the free throw line extended. There should be 3 to 4 feet between players. Have the players get into a defensive on-ball stance. When you point to either sideline, the players step-slide in that direction until you point in the other direction. When you point behind you, they make an advance step, and when you point behind them, they make a retreat step. Do this for 30 seconds at a time, changing signals in a random pattern. After a 15-second pause, go for another 30 seconds. As the season progresses, extend the time to what the players can handle.

53. Slide the Court

Line up your players at one corner of the court. The first player faces the near lane area. When the drill starts, she step-slides to the near elbow, makes a swing step so she now faces the near sideline, and step-slides to the midcourt corner. When she arrives there, she sprints to the other sideline. Then, facing that sideline, she step-slides to the other elbow, makes a swing step, and continues to the corner. She goes to the back of the line. When the first player reaches the near elbow, the second player begins the drill. When the second player reaches the near elbow, the third player begins, and so on.

Variation: In the full-court version of this drill, the players follow the same path they used when doing Zigzag Dribbling (Drill 18).

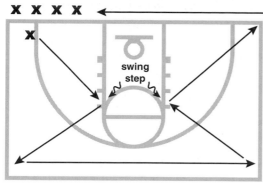

Slide the Court.

54. Wing Denial

Set up two lines at each wing and two passers above the 3-point line at the top of the circle. Put eight or more balls next to the passers and designate several *shaggers* (players who collect balls that are caught or batted away). The first player in each line is the defender, and the second player is the cutter. As the cutter heads toward the block, the defender step-slides in a denial stance, looking at the ball over her shoulder. The cutter makes a swim move, V-cuts, and cuts to the perimeter. Whether or not the cutter is open, the passer throws the pass. If the cutter is open, she catches the ball, passes it to a shagger, and cuts again. If the defender is in position, she deflects the ball with her outstretched hand. The cutter and defender go back and forth several times, and the passer passes every time the cutter comes out for the ball.

Variations: Add a 1-on-1 element. When the cutter catches the ball, she squares up and drives on the defender. As your players get better at this drill, limit the number of dribbles (two for high school players) they can take when driving to the basket.

Add cutting through the lane. After three V-cuts, the cutter makes a banana cut under the basket and cuts to the other wing. Again, the passer passes whether the cutter is open or not. After three V-cuts on this side, the drill ends with the cutter making one more banana cut back to the first side.

Emphasis: The defender should use her hand nearest the ball to deflect the ball. Too often, players try to steal the ball using both hands. It takes an extra split second to turn their bodies, and they're often too late. Their momentum takes them beyond the cutter, who is now open for a drive.

55. 1-on-1 Half-Court Drive

Set up one line of players at midcourt with a ball. The first player is the defender, and the second player is the offensive player. The offensive player must check the ball. She then tries to drive to the basket. The defender works on cutting her off with step-slides and tries to disrupt what she wants to do. When the offensive player shoots, the defender blocks her out. They play until the offensive player scores or the defender gets the ball. The offensive player then goes to the end of the line. The defender stays on defense until she makes three defensive stops. If the defender doesn't block out on a shot but still gets the rebound, don't consider it a stop. This emphasizes blocking out. After she's made the third stop, the current offensive player becomes the new defender.

56. Dribble Drive

This drill works on on-ball defense as well as closing out. Set up a line of players under the basket and put an offensive player at the free throw line. The first player in line rolls a ball to the offensive player and closes out on the player. The offensive player can't shoot. She must drive to the basket, using no more than two dribbles (three dribbles for younger players). The defender contests the drive and the shot. They play 1-on-1 until the offensive player scores or the defender gets the ball. If the offensive player scores, she plays against the next defender. If the defender makes a stop, she becomes the offensive player.

Emphasis: Defenders need to close out low, using choppy steps. They shouldn't leave their feet for shot fakes.

57. 2-on-2 Defense

Have four players play 2-on-2 at each basket, guarding each other man-to-man. They can either be guards against guards, posts against posts, or a guard and a post against a guard and a post. The offensive team can do what it wants (no set plays). When a team scores, the other team takes the ball out at the top of the circle. Set a time limit or a score limit. When the limit is reached, rotate the teams so every team plays against every other team.

Variation: Run the drill 3-on-3 or 4-on-4 .

Emphasis: Tell your players not to lose sight of the ball and to be ready to help out the other defensive player.

Shell Drills

58. Two-Man Shell

Start with the Two-Man Shell. Set up two offensive players, one with the ball at the top of the circle and one at the right wing, each guarded by a defender. The defender guarding the player with the ball is in the on-ball position and stance. The wing defender is in the denial position and stance. The player with the ball passes to the wing. When the ball is in the air, the passer's defender switches to the denial stance, and the receiver's defender switches to the on-ball stance. Have them pass back and forth, the defenders jumping to the ball and switching positions. Each time the defenders jump to a new position, they should shout the name of their new position: "Ball, ball, ball!" or "Deny, deny, deny!"

Variation: Put one offensive player at the wing and one at the high post. Move them again so one is at the wing and the other is at the low post. This practices post defense.

Emphasis: Defenders should jump to the ball on the pass.

59. Three-Man Shell

For the next level, set up players as in the Two-Man Shell and add a third offensive player and a third defender on the left wing. At the start of the drill, the defender guarding the player with the ball should be in the on-ball stance, and the other two defenders should be in denial stances.

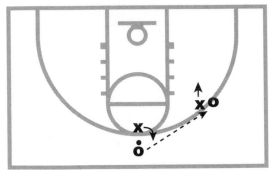

Pass to the wing in the Two-Man Shell.

The drill begins when the player with the ball passes to the right wing. The right wing's defender switches to the on-ball stance, the passer's defender switches to the denial stance, and the left wing's defender switches from the denial stance to the help-side stance (her man is two passes away). Since the ball is above the free throw line extended, the help-side defender has a foot in the lane.

Have the right wing make a skip pass to the left wing. Her defender should switch to a help-side stance, and the defender at the top should go from a denial stance on one side of the offensive player to a denial stance on the other side. The right wing's defender should switch from the on-ball stance to a help-side position.

Each time a player makes a pass, the receiver should hold the ball until you're satisfied the defenders are in the right positions. As the defenders get better at the drill, have the passers pass after a count of two. As your defenders

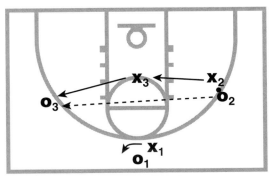

A. Skip pass in the Three-Man Shell.

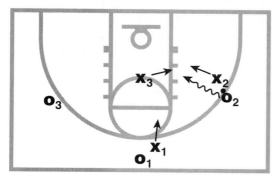

B. Helping on the drive in the Three-Man Shell.

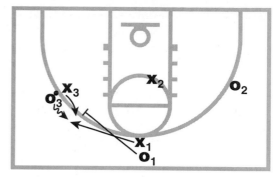

D. Defending the ball screen in the Three-Man Shell.

improve, have the passers throw the ball after a count of one.

The next step in the progression is to add *help defense*. As the players execute the drill, whenever you call "Drive," the player with the ball immediately drives by her defender, who makes no attempt to stay with her. The other defenders practice dropping into the lane to stop the drive.

Next, work on bumping the cutter. Every time you call an offensive player's name, she cuts to the ball. Her defender should bump her (without fouling) so she won't be open for a pass.

Last, work on defending screens. Call for ball screens and player screens to make sure the defenders know what to do.

Variation: Move one of the offensive wings to the low post. Have one player on the wing, one player in the high post, and one in the low post.

60. Four-Man Shell

Once your players become skilled at the two- and three-player drills, add another offensive player and another defender. Set up two offensive players on the 3-point arc at the elbow areas and two offensive players on the wings. Follow the same progression as in the Three-Man Shell.

Variation: Move one of the wing players to the low post. Have one player at the point, one at the wing, and two at each block.

61. Five-Man Shell

For the Five-Man Shell, add another post player on the opposite block and a fifth defender. Go through the same progression as in the Three-Man Shell. Once the players get good at this, vary the five-man setup to mirror the offensive setups your opponents might use: 3-out, 2-in; 4-out, 1-in; 4-high, 4-low; and so on. At this point you're simulating game conditions.

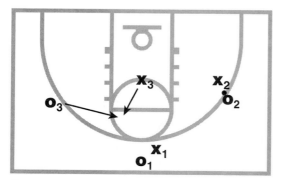

C. Bumping the cutter in the Three-Man Shell.

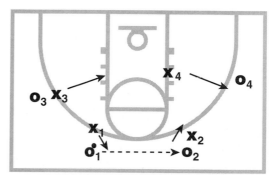

Four-Man Shell.

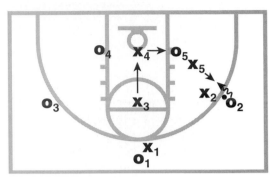

Defending the wing drive in the Five-Man Shell.

Rebounding Drills

62. Touch the Ball

Put a ball in the middle of the center circle area. Have four players stand in the circle, facing out, equidistant from each other. Have four other players stand outside the circle area, each directly across the line from a player inside the line. At your signal, the players inside the circle block out the outside players, while the outside players try to get around them to touch the ball. The goal is for the players blocking out to keep their opponents away from the ball for 3 seconds. Once they do that, the drill is over, and the next group of players repeats the drill. Make sure you match up players of similar height.

When you do this drill with taller players, have only two pairs go at one time to avoid the possibility of players colliding as they go for the ball.

63. Line Rebounding

Set up pairs of players on the free throw line extended. The players closest to the basket are defenders and face the other players, who are offensive players but don't have a ball. On your signal, the defenders pivot and block out their man. The offensive players try to get around the defenders.

Emphasis: Each defender should stay low, make contact, and use choppy steps to keep the player she's guarding on her back.

64. 3-on-3 Rebounding

This drill works on defensive positioning and rebounding. Set up three offensive players, two outside the blocks and one 6 feet in front of the basket. Assign three defenders to them. As you or an assistant dribbles the ball, the defenders adjust their positions (the offensive players don't move). Then shoot the ball. The defenders block out as the offensive players try to get around them. If an offensive player gets the rebound, she puts it back up. Play continues until there's a score or the defense gets the ball. Make this competitive. Every defensive rebound counts as 1 point, and every offensive rebound counts as 2 points. After running the drill five times, switch the offense and the defense.

65. 3-on-4 Rebounding

Put two offensive players above the elbows, two on the wings, and three defenders in the lane. You or an assistant has the ball and dribbles around for a bit. As you dribble, the defenders adjust their positions. Shoot at any time. The offensive players go after the ball, and the defenders try to block them out. The defenders must communicate and block out the players most likely to get an offensive rebound. Keep the same groups in the drill until the defenders snag three rebounds in a row. This drill teaches communication, good block-out angles, and anticipating where the rebound will go.

Variation: Run the same drill with four defenders and five offensive players.

Emphasis: The defender's first step after a shot goes up should be toward an offensive player, not toward the basket. She should make contact and hit someone with her body.

66. Warrior

This isn't a drill for young players or meek players. Pick three players of comparable height. You or an assistant has the ball. When you shoot, each player fights for the rebound, going against the other two players. If the rebounder can't get open for a putback shot, she has the option of passing to you and posting up. You pass back to anyone who passes to you. Award 1 point for each rebound and 1 point for each made shot. The first player to score 5 points gets to sit down, and a new rebounder comes in. The remaining two players can carry over their points. If you don't keep things under control, this drill can get rough. Deduct 1 point for every foul.

Fast-Break Drills

67. Pressure Layups

The first skill to teach for fast-break basketball is making breakaway (1-on-0) full-court layups under pressure. Set up two lines of players behind the baseline, a dribbler line (with balls) at the right lane line extended and a defender line at the left lane line extended. Pair up dribblers and defenders by height. On your signal, the first dribbler speed dribbles in a straight line to the other basket and makes a right-handed layup. The first defender sprints up the court to try to prevent the layup. (Since the defender will be able to run faster than the offensive player can dribble, the defender can't begin to sprint until the dribbler has taken one full dribble.) If the dribbler misses the layup, the players keep playing 1-on-1 until a score or the defender gets the ball. Then they move to one side of the basket, out of the way, and sprint back down the court, passing to each other all the way. They then go to the end of the opposite line.

When the first pair reaches the far basket, the next two players begin. After every player has been a dribbler and a defender, switch the ball line to the left line so players can work on making left-handed layups under pressure.

Emphasis: Dribblers should make as few dribbles as possible. Defenders should not bump and foul dribblers as they race up the court.

68. Outlet Layups

Set up two lines of players, a rebound line on the baseline to the right of the basket and an outlet line along the right sideline near midcourt. The first four players on the rebound line have a ball. The first player throws the ball against the left side of the backboard to create a rebound. She jumps for the ball, pivots away from the basket, and throws a sharp outlet pass to the first player in the outlet line, who is shouting "Outlet! Outlet!" When that player catches the ball, she speed dribbles in a straight line to the top of the opposite circle. After the rebounder makes the pass, she runs the right lane, which was vacated by the outlet player. This reinforces the concept of filling open lanes. The rebounder sprints to the free throw line extended and cuts to the basket.

When the dribbler reaches the top of the circle, she comes to a jump stop and passes to the cutter with a right-handed bounce pass. After the cutter makes a layup, she rebounds the ball and passes it to the dribbler, who has sprinted to a new outlet position on the left side of the court (as viewed from the original baseline). They then run the drill going the other way. When they finish, each player goes to the end of the other line. (See left diagram page 206.)

As the first pair of players crosses midcourt, the second pair begins the drill. There should be four pairs of players running the drill at the same time. The balls should never hit the floor other than on the bounce pass. This drill is tiring, so after 3 minutes or so, change the lines so the players are on the left half of the court, as viewed from the baseline. Now the players work on shooting left-handed layups at each basket.

This drill not only works on outlet passing, rebounding, running the lanes, and full-speed layups using both hands, but it's also an excellent conditioner.

69. 2-on-1 Fast Break

This is a half-court drill, so split your team into two groups and have an assistant coach run the drill on the other half of the court while you run it on your half.

Set up two lines of players at midcourt, a ball line on the left and a cutter line on the right, each halfway between the center circle and the sideline. The first three players in the ball line have a ball. Put a defender at the free

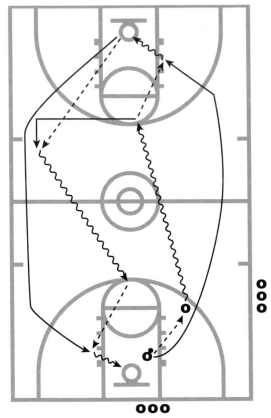

Outlet Layups.

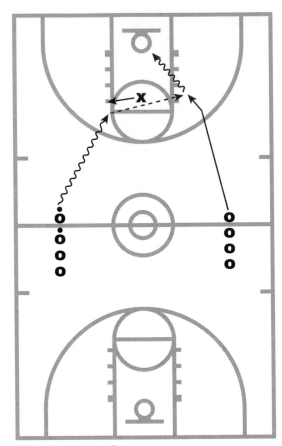

2-on-1 Fast Break.

throw line. The first player in the ball line dribbles hard toward the basket as the first player in the cutter line runs the right lane. When the defender comes over to guard the dribbler, the dribbler comes to a jump stop and passes to the cutter, using her right hand to make a bounce pass. The cutter should have an easy layup. If the cutter misses the layup, the group plays 2-on-1 until the offense scores, the defender gets the ball, or the ball goes out-of-bounds. After they're finished, the defender runs out to defend the next pair, and the dribbler and the cutter switch lines.

In a 2-on-1 fast break, the dribbler should dribble at the nearest elbow. This creates good offensive spacing. If the dribbler goes to the middle of the free throw line, the defender will be closer to the cutter and more able to defend both players. When the dribbler heads to the elbow away from the cutter, the defender has to choose whether to guard the dribbler or the cutter. A defender's first priority is always to stop the ball. If she cheats toward the cutter in anticipation of a pass, the dribbler should drive to the basket.

Once the defender has defended against every offensive pair, she joins one of the lines, and another defender replaces her. After every player has played defense, switch the balls to the other line. Now the dribblers will pass with their left hand, and the cutters will make left-handed layups.

70. 3-on-2 Fast Break

Set up three lines of players at midcourt, a ball line in the middle and two cutter lines next to the sidelines. Put one defender at the free throw line and another defender two steps in front of the basket. The first player in the ball line dribbles hard to the basket. The dribbler should head to the middle of the lane on a 3-on-2 break, as opposed to heading to the elbow on a 2-on-1 break. As the dribbler takes off, the first player in each cutter line runs her lane, heading straight at the baseline. The players cut to the basket when they reach the free throw line extended. The front defender stops the ball so the dribbler can't penetrate into the lane. This forces her to come to a jump stop and pass to one of the cutters (part 1).

After she passes, she *follows the pass* by going to the elbow nearest the player to whom she passed. The back defender waits until a pass is made. When the ball is in the air, she *closes out* on the receiver—sprints to the receiver to guard her. As she does this, the front defender drops down to the basket to prevent a pass from the receiver to the opposite cutter for an easy layup. The cutter who received the ball has several options (part 2):

- pass to the opposite cutter, if she's open
- drive, if the defender closing out isn't in a good on-ball position
- shoot, if the other options aren't available and she's open
- pass back to the dribbler at the elbow

If the cutter passes back to the dribbler, the dribbler can drive, shoot, or pass to the other cutter. At this point it's important to take a shot, because the rest of the defense will be back.

After each pair of defenders has defended against every offensive trio, replace them with new defenders. Run the drill until everyone has played defense.

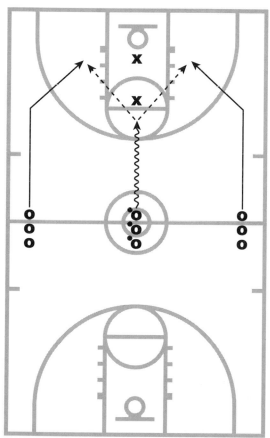

3-on-2 Fast Break, part 1.

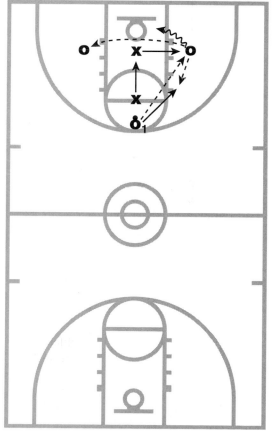

3-on-2 Fast Break, part 2.

71. 3-on-2, 2-on-1

This drill features continuous 3-on-2 and 2-on-1 fast breaks, working on offensive and defensive transition. Don't run this drill until your players are familiar with the 2-on-1 Fast Break (Drill 69) and the 3-on-2 Fast Break (Drill 70).

Set up three lines of players along the baseline and two defenders at the far basket, one in front of the basket and the other at the free throw line. The first three players in the lines head up the court on a 3-on-2 fast break. They're limited to one shot. After the shot, no matter if it's made or missed, the shooter sprints back down the court to defend against the two defenders, who now become offensive players. The offensive players who didn't shoot stay at that basket and become defenders. After one shot at the 2-on-1, the next player in the middle line grabs the made or missed shot and starts another 3-on-2 break.

72. 3-on-3-on-3

Split your players into teams of three. Assuming you have four teams, pick two to start play. The other two teams will each be under a basket with a ball, ready to come into the game. The teams play full-court man-to-man defense. When a team scores, it leaves the court and is replaced by the team under the basket where the score occurred. The new team inbounds the ball. When a team is scored on, it stays on defense. This is a full-throttle, tiring drill that works on transition and all other phases of the game.

Variation: Add a limited-dribble rule, so that the players are limited to, for example, one

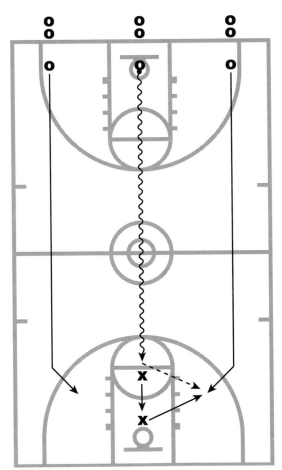

3-on-2 action.

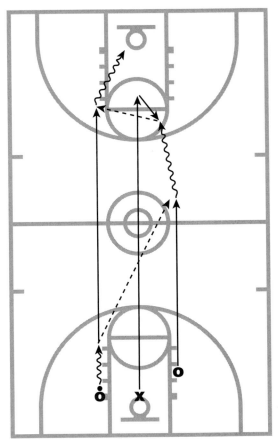

2-on-1 action.

dribble. This forces the player with the ball to be patient, to see the court, and to make better passes. It also forces her teammates to work harder to get open.

73. 3-on-3 Recovery Transition

Set up three lines of players on the baseline: one in the middle and one in each short corner. The first player in each line steps out to the free throw line extended. These players are now the defensive team, going against the next three players in each line, who are the offensive team. The three defenders face the baseline. To start the drill, pass a ball to an offensive player. She and her teammates advance the ball up the court, following sound fast-break principles. The two outside defenders sprint back to guard the basket, but the defender across from the player with the ball must first run to the baseline and touch the floor before she can get back on defense. This allows the offense a few seconds to run a 3-on-2 fast break. If they waste time and don't get a shot off, they have to play 3-on-3. After one shot, the teams switch roles: the defenders go on offense, and the offensive players become defenders. The offense now runs a fast break back down the court. After one shot, play stops. The original offensive players are now defenders and a new trio of offensive players steps up.

74. 4-on-4 Recovery Transition

This drill works like 3-on-3 Recovery Transition but adds another line of players on the baseline. The fast break is now a secondary break (4-on-3), which is suited only to advanced players.

75. Change

This drill is excellent for improving your team's ability to play transition basketball. Start with your players scrimmaging 5-on-5. Whenever

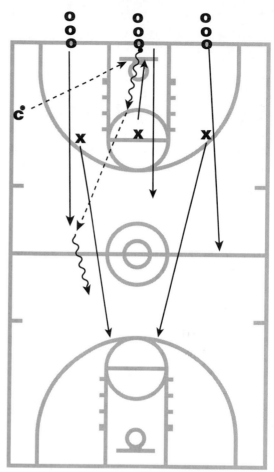

3-on-3 Recovery Transition.

you shout, "Change!" the player who has the ball passes it to you (or an assistant) and you pass it to a player who was just on defense. The players who were on offense must communicate so they can prevent an easy fast-break basket, and the players who were on defense must communicate and run the proper lanes to see if they can create a numbers advantage. This drill is excellent for conditioning.

APPENDIX

Sample Tryout Evaluation Sheet

NAME _____ Grade_____ Position_____

Physical:
Height_____ Sprint speed (up and back)_____ Dribble speed (up and back) _____
Push-ups_____ Vertical jump_____

Conditioning: *_____

Mental: *
Hustle_____ Aggressiveness_____
Toughness_____ Attitude_____

Ballhandling: *
Strong-hand dribble_____ Weak-hand dribble _____ Eyes up_____ Crossover_____
Hesitation_____ Between the legs_____ Spin dribble_____

Passing: *
Weave drill _____ Outlet drill _____ Scrimmages_____

Shooting:
RH layups_____ LH layups_____ Mikan_____ Shooting form_____ Jump shots off the catch_____
Jump shots off the fake and dribble_____ Free throws_____ _____ _____
Post shots_____ 3-point shots_____

Offense: *
1-on-1_____ Getting open_____ Shot selection_____ Court savvy_____

Rebounding: *
Three-man drill_____ 1-on-1_____ Scrimmages_____

Defense: *
Zigzag_____ 1-on-1_____ Dribble drive_____ Scrimmages_____ Stance_____
Positioning_____ Help_____ Intensity_____ Communication_____

* Rate from 1 to 5

Scores (totals):

Physical_____ Mental_____ Ballhandling_____ Passing_____
Shooting_____ Offense_____ Rebounding_____ Defense_____

TOTAL SCORE _____ Player made team_____ yes _____ no

Evaluator_____ Date_____

Sample End-of-Tryouts Letter

Dear_____,

Thank you for trying out for the Varsity basketball team. We're sorry to tell you we can't give you a spot on the team. We wish we could make room for everyone who tried out, but we have room for only twelve players.

It was a difficult decision for us, because you gave it your best in tryouts. Your efforts were noticed and appreciated. In the end, it came down to the fact that other players are more experienced than you. Here's how we evaluated your skills:

Dribbling: Average; you need to work on dribbling with your left hand.

Passing: Good; you made a number of good passes in the scrimmages.

Shooting: Average; your follow-through is inconsistent.

Defense: Good; you move your feet well and are aggressive.

Rebounding: Fair; when you grow taller, you'll be a better rebounder!

Attitude: Very good; we really liked your enthusiasm . . . keep it up!

We hope you won't let your disappointment stop you from playing basketball. It's a great sport, but it takes time to learn how to play. If you're patient and work hard, you can become a good player.

Sincerely,

The Coach

Sample Player-Parent Handout

To: JV Basketball Players (and your parents)
From: The Coach

I can't tell you how excited I am to begin the season! I'm looking forward to coaching you and having a productive, fun-filled season.

These are our team rules and expectations:

1. **Equipment.** Wear shorts, a clean T-shirt, and basketball shoes to practice. Bring a water bottle as well as any medical equipment you need, like an inhaler or an ankle or knee brace. Don't bring a ball.

2. **Punctuality.** Be on time to practices and games. We have little gym time available, so it's important to take advantage of every minute.

3. **Absences.** When you play a team sport, you're committing to attend every practice and game. When you're absent, you miss a chance to improve and help the team. If you miss the practice before a game, you can't play in that game. If you miss practice or a game for an "unexcused reason" (like choosing to play another sport), it will hurt your playing time in the next game.

4. **Effort.** Do your best every time you walk on the court. Your teammates and coaches are counting on you.

5. **Enthusiasm.** Bring a positive attitude to every practice and game, regardless of whether the team is winning or losing games. We expect players and parents to provide unconditional enthusiasm throughout the season.

6. **Respect, dignity, and tolerance.** Treat your teammates and coaches like you want them to treat you—with respect, dignity, and tolerance.

7. **Team player.** The team comes ahead of any person on the team. Do your best to help your teammates play better.

8. **Sportsmanship.** We expect you to display good sportsmanship at all times. We'll talk about what that means during the season.

9. **Playing time.** Playing time isn't automatic. You have to earn the right to play in games. If you work hard in practice and have a positive attitude, you'll play in every game. If you don't, you won't.

10. **Successful season.** Sure, we'll try to win as many games as possible, but the key goals are to improve, to work as hard as we can, and to have fun. I have no doubt we'll achieve those goals!

If any of you have any questions or concerns, please call me at 111-1111 or e-mail me at imyourcoach@ bball.hoops.

Did I mention how excited I am about the season?

Sample Master Practice Plan

FUNDAMENTAL SKILLS:

Offense

Jump stop

Triple threat

Pivoting: front pivot, rear pivot, ripping the ball

Dribbling: strong hand, weak hand, front crossover, pull-back crossover, hesitation, control dribble, speed dribble

Attacking defender with dribble

Moves without ball: V-cut, backdoor cut, basket cut

Moves with ball: catch and drive, catch and shoot, catch fake dribble and shoot, drive and shoot, drive and dish

Posting up

Passing: bounce, chest, push, curl, overhead, baseball, fakes

Catching

Catch and pivot on inside foot

Screening: cross screens, down screens, up screens, back screens

Using screens: popout cut, curl cut, backdoor cut

Sealing the defender for lobs

Give-and-go

Pick-and-roll

Drawing fouls

Beating traps

Defense

Talking on defense

Defensive stance

Defensive slide

On-ball defense

Denial defense

Help-side defense

Post defense: denial, fronting

Doubling down

Bumping cutters

Defending backdoor

Defending screens

Sprinting back on defense

Trapping

Guarding inbounder

Taking charges

Recovering when beaten

Closing out

Fouling intentionally

Shooting

Free throws

Layups

Power layups

3-pointers

Shooting off the pass, dribble, and screens

Dribble drive

Post shooting: posting up, drop step, turnaround, jump hook

Rebounding

Positioning

Blocking out

Grabbing ball

Pivoting

Outlet passing

TEAM SKILLS:

Offense

Give-and-Go Offense

Screen-Away Offense

UCLA-Cut Offense

1-4 Low Play

Box Play

One-Guard Offense

Two-Guard Offense

2-on-1 fast break

3-on-2 fast break

Transition offense

Sideline Screen Play

Box Man Play

Stack Man Play

Box Zone Play

Stack Zone Play

V Press Break

Zoom Play

Double Screen Play

Defense

Pressure Man-to-Man

1-3-1 Zone

2-3 Zone

Full-Court Man-to-Man (and Rover variation)

Sample Daily Practice Plan

Time	Minutes	Activity	Emphasis
2:00	8	Warm-ups: Full-court layups Three-Man Weave (Drill 27)	No dribbling allowed
	2	Stretching	
2:10	10	Ball handling: Stationary dribbling Zigzag Dribbling (Drill 18)	Keep head up and nondribbling arm out
2:20	8	Passing: Pairs Four-in-a-Line Passing (Drill 25)	Curl passes only
2:28	2	Water break	
2:30	5	Form shooting	
	5	Triangle shooting	Hold and check follow-through
2:40	10	Pairs—Game Shots (Drill 41)	
2:50	8	Layups: Three-Line Layups (Drill 47) X Layups (Drill 48)	
2:58	2	Water break	
3:00	8	Three-Man Shell Drill (Drill 59)	Help-side defense
3:08	8	2-on-2 Defense (Drill 57)	Blocking out
3:16	12	3-on-3-on-3 (Drill 72)	
3:28	2	Water break	
3:30	10	Two-Guard Offense	Ball reversal
3:40	15	5-on-5 full court	
3:55	5	Wrap-up talk	Saturday's game

Sample Stat Sheet

Opponent:_____ Where:_____ Date:_____

Score: 1st QTR_____ 2nd QTR_____ 3rd QTR_____ 4th QTR_____

Fouls	Player	Off Rebs	Def Rebs	Assists	Steals	Turnovers	Blocks
123 45		1 2 3 4 5 6 / 7 8 9 10 11 / 12 13 14 15	1 2 3 4 5 6 / 7 8 9 10 11 / 12 13 14 15	1 2 3 4 5 / 6 7 8 9 10 / 11 12 13	1 2 3 4 / 5 6 7 8 / 9 10 11	1 2 3 4 5 / 6 7 8 9 10 / 11 12 13	1 2 3 / 4 5 6
123 45		1 2 3 4 5 6 / 7 8 9 10 11 / 12 13 14 15	1 2 3 4 5 6 / 7 8 9 10 11 / 12 13 14 15	1 2 3 4 5 / 6 7 8 9 10 / 11 12 13	1 2 3 4 / 5 6 7 8 / 9 10 11	1 2 3 4 5 / 6 7 8 9 10 / 11 12 13	1 2 3 / 4 5 6
123 45		1 2 3 4 5 6 / 7 8 9 10 11 / 12 13 14 15	1 2 3 4 5 6 / 7 8 9 10 11 / 12 13 14 15	1 2 3 4 5 / 6 7 8 9 10 / 11 12 13	1 2 3 4 / 5 6 7 8 / 9 10 11	1 2 3 4 5 / 6 7 8 9 10 / 11 12 13	1 2 3 / 4 5 6
123 45		1 2 3 4 5 6 / 7 8 9 10 11 / 12 13 14 15	1 2 3 4 5 6 / 7 8 9 10 11 / 12 13 14 15	1 2 3 4 5 / 6 7 8 9 10 / 11 12 13	1 2 3 4 / 5 6 7 8 / 9 10 11	1 2 3 4 5 / 6 7 8 9 10 / 11 12 13	1 2 3 / 4 5 6
123 45		1 2 3 4 5 6 / 7 8 9 10 11 / 12 13 14 15	1 2 3 4 5 6 / 7 8 9 10 11 / 12 13 14 15	1 2 3 4 5 / 6 7 8 9 10 / 11 12 13	1 2 3 4 / 5 6 7 8 / 9 10 11	1 2 3 4 5 / 6 7 8 9 10 / 11 12 13	1 2 3 / 4 5 6
123 45		1 2 3 4 5 6 / 7 8 9 10 11 / 12 13 14 15	1 2 3 4 5 6 / 7 8 9 10 11 / 12 13 14 15	1 2 3 4 5 / 6 7 8 9 10 / 11 12 13	1 2 3 4 / 5 6 7 8 / 9 10 11	1 2 3 4 5 / 6 7 8 9 10 / 11 12 13	1 2 3 / 4 5 6
123 45		1 2 3 4 5 6 / 7 8 9 10 11 / 12 13 14 15	1 2 3 4 5 6 / 7 8 9 10 11 / 12 13 14 15	1 2 3 4 5 / 6 7 8 9 10 / 11 12 13	1 2 3 4 / 5 6 7 8 / 9 10 11	1 2 3 4 5 / 6 7 8 9 10 / 11 12 13	1 2 3 / 4 5 6
123 45		1 2 3 4 5 6 / 7 8 9 10 11 / 12 13 14 15	1 2 3 4 5 6 / 7 8 9 10 11 / 12 13 14 15	1 2 3 4 5 / 6 7 8 9 10 / 11 12 13	1 2 3 4 / 5 6 7 8 / 9 10 11	1 2 3 4 5 / 6 7 8 9 10 / 11 12 13	1 2 3 / 4 5 6
123 45		1 2 3 4 5 6 / 7 8 9 10 11 / 12 13 14 15	1 2 3 4 5 6 / 7 8 9 10 11 / 12 13 14 15	1 2 3 4 5 / 6 7 8 9 10 / 11 12 13	1 2 3 4 / 5 6 7 8 / 9 10 11	1 2 3 4 5 / 6 7 8 9 10 / 11 12 13	1 2 3 / 4 5 6
23 5		1 2 3 4 5 6 / 7 8 9 10 11 / 12 13 14 15	1 2 3 4 5 6 / 7 8 9 10 11 / 12 13 14 15	1 2 3 4 5 / 6 7 8 9 10 / 11 12 13	1 2 3 4 / 5 6 7 8 / 9 10 11	1 2 3 4 5 / 6 7 8 9 10 / 11 12 13	1 2 3 / 4 5 6
23 5		1 2 3 4 5 6 / 7 8 9 10 11 / 12 13 14 15	1 2 3 4 5 6 / 7 8 9 10 11 / 12 13 14 15	1 2 3 4 5 / 6 7 8 9 10 / 11 12 13	1 2 3 4 / 5 6 7 8 / 9 10 11	1 2 3 4 5 / 6 7 8 9 10 / 11 12 13	1 2 3 / 4 5 6
23 5		1 2 3 4 5 6 / 7 8 9 10 11 / 12 13 14 15	1 2 3 4 5 6 / 7 8 9 10 11 / 12 13 14 15	1 2 3 4 5 / 6 7 8 9 10 / 11 12 13	1 2 3 4 / 5 6 7 8 / 9 10 11	1 2 3 4 5 / 6 7 8 9 10 / 11 12 13	1 2 3 / 4 5 6
23 5		1 2 3 4 5 6 / 7 8 9 10 11 / 12 13 14 15	1 2 3 4 5 6 / 7 8 9 10 11 / 12 13 14 15	1 2 3 4 5 / 6 7 8 9 10 / 11 12 13	1 2 3 4 / 5 6 7 8 / 9 10 11	1 2 3 4 5 / 6 7 8 9 10 / 11 12 13	1 2 3 / 4 5 6

TOTALS

Sample Game Sheet

Opponent:_____ Where:_____ Date:_____ Score:_____

===
Pre Game

Starters: Goals: Results:

1   1

2   2

3   3

4   4

5   5

Absent:_____ Sick, injured_____

===
Post Game Review

Them

Strengths:

Weaknesses:

Offensive tendencies:

Defensive tendencies:

Best players:

===
Us

What we did well:

What we did poorly:

Sample Scorebook Sheet

HOME ELKHORN   **COACH** G. KRUGER

CIRCLE FIRST POSSESSION   HOME / VIS

FINAL 89

SCORE BY QUARTERS

	1st qtr.	2nd qtr.	3rd qtr.	4th qtr.	O.T.
	17	18/35	26/61	22/83	6/89

SUMMARY

QTRS.	PLAYER	NO.	1ST QTR.	2ND QTR.	FOULS	3RD QTR.	4TH QTR.	OVT.	FG FGA	3 PT. FGA	FT FTA	REB	AST	F	TP
S	L. SPILMAN	14		2	P1 P2 P3 P4	2			2/4	0/1	2/2	3	5	1	6
S	J. KRUGER	20	2	33	P1 P2 P3 P4	22220	2 3		6/9	3/5	1/2	7	3	2	22
S	D. ALDINGER	22			P1 P2 P3 P4	0	2		1/4		0/1	1	1	1	2
S	M. TRADER	30			P1 P2 P3 P4		3		0/2	1/2	2/2	3	3	2	5
S	C. SELTZ	32			P1 P2 P3 P4		200		1/2		2/4	3	3	3	4
S	T. THOMSEN	40		2	P1 P2 P3 P4	222			4/6	1/2	2/3	9	2	3	10
S	D. OHM	44	22222	2	P1 P2 P3 P4	2	0		7/16	0/1	1/2	11	2	2	15
S	S. FELLER	42	2		P1 P2 P3 P4	22	0		3/8		0/1	4	3		6
S	M. LINDQUIST	50	200		P1 P2 P3 P4		00		2/4		0/4	5	3	4	4
S	J. WESOLOWSKI	52			P1 P2 P3 P4	00	200		1/4		2/4	1	1	2	4
S	B. MCARDLE	12		22	P1 P2 P3 P4		2		3/6	0/2	3/3	2	1	3	9
S	M. KRUGER	00			P1 P2 P3 P4				1/1			2			2
	TOTALS								31/66	4/11	15/23	46	24	23	89

SCORER H. HUSTON - S. SKAUG   **TURNOVERS** 11   **FG%** 45.5   **FT%** 53.6

Sample Scouting Sheet

Player evaluation

Starters:

	Position	Ball-handling	Shooting	Driving	Comments
#___					
#___					
#___					
#___					
#___					

Key subs:

#___ _____

#___ _____

#___ _____

Team evaluation

Pace they like to play_____

Who inbounds the ball_____

When do they press_____

Team speed_____

Team aggressiveness_____

Team intensity_____

Sample Scouting Sheet (continued)

1st Half

Half-court defense:_____

Full-court defense:_____

Strongest defenders:_____

Weakest defenders:_____

Half-court offense:_____

Press offense:_____

Scorers:_____

Shooters:_____

2nd Half

Half-court defense:_____

Full-court defense:_____

Strongest defenders:_____

Weakest defenders:_____

Half-court offense:_____

Press offense:_____

Scorers:_____

Shooters:_____

Sample Scouting Sheet (continued)

Inbounds plays, sidelines plays, etc.

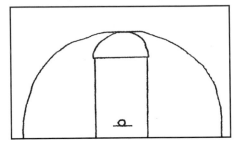
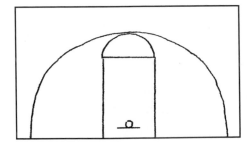

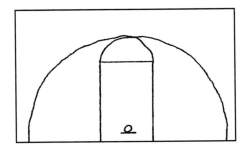
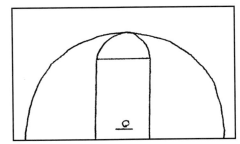

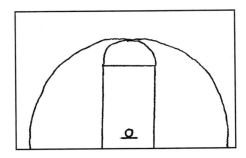
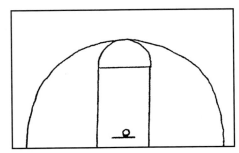

Referee Signals
Official NFHS Basketball Signals

GLOSSARY

Advance step: A step in which the defender's lead foot steps toward her man, and her back foot slides forward.

Air ball: A shot that hits only air—it misses the rim and the backboard.

Air pass: A pass that goes straight through the air to the receiver.

And one: The *free throw* awarded to a shooter who is fouled as she scores.

Assist: A pass thrown to a player who immediately scores.

Backcourt: The half of the court a team is defending. The opposite of the *frontcourt*. Also refers to a team's guards.

Back cut: See *backdoor cut*.

Backdoor cut: An offensive play in which a player on the perimeter steps away from the basket, drawing the defender with her, and suddenly cuts to the basket behind the defender for a pass. The opposite of a *V-cut*.

Back screen: An offensive play in which a player comes from the *low post* to set a *screen* for a player on the perimeter.

Ball fake: A sudden movement by the player with the ball intended to cause the defender to move in one direction, allowing the passer to pass in another direction. Also called "pass fake."

Ball reversal: Passing the ball from one side of the court to the other.

Ball screen: An offensive play in which a player sets a *screen* on the defender guarding the player with the ball.

Ball side: The half of the court (if the court is divided lengthwise) that the ball is on. Also called the "strong side." The opposite of the *help side*.

Banana cut: A wide, curving *cut*, as opposed to a cut that is a straight line.

Bank shot: A shot that hits the backboard before hitting the rim or going through the net.

Baseball pass: A one-handed pass thrown like a baseball.

Baseline: The line that marks the playing boundary at each end of the court. Also called the "end line."

Baseline out-of-bounds play: The play used to return the ball to the court from outside the baseline along the opponent's basket.

Basket cut: A *cut* toward the basket.

Bench: Refers to substitutes sitting on the sideline, as well as to the bench or chairs they sit on.

Blindside screen: A *screen* set directly behind a defender where she can't see it.

Block: (1) A violation in which a defender steps in front of a dribbler but is still moving when they collide. Also called a "blocking foul." (2) To tip or deflect a shooter's shot, altering its flight so the shot misses. (3) The small painted square on the floor next to the basket just outside the lane.

Block out: To make contact with an opposing player to establish rebounding position between the player and the ball. Also called "box out."

Bonus: A team is "in the bonus" when it accumulates seven or more team fouls in a half, giving the other team a *free throw* on each subsequent foul. Also called being "over the limit."

Bounce pass: A pass that bounces once before reaching the receiver.

Box-and-one: A combination defense in which four defenders play *zone* in a box formation, and the fifth defender guards one player *man-to-man*.

Box out: See *block out*.

Box set: A formation in which four players align themselves as the four corners of a box. Often used for *baseline out-of-bounds plays*.

Brick: A bad shot that clanks off the backboard or rim.

Bump the cutter: To step in the way of a cutter who is trying to *cut* to the ball for a pass.

Carrying the ball: A violation that happens when a player dribbling the ball brings her hand underneath the ball and momentarily carries it. Also called "palming."

Center: (1) The position in which a player, usually the tallest player on the team, stays near the basket. (2) The player who plays that position.

Center circle: The painted circle at midcourt used for the opening *jump ball*.

Charge: (1) A violation when a player with the ball runs into a defender who is standing still. Also called a "charging foul." (2) To commit that violation.

Chest pass: An air pass thrown from the passer's chest to a teammate's chest. It can be a one-handed or two-handed pass.

Chin the ball: To hold the ball with both hands under the chin, elbows out, to protect the ball.

Clear-Out Play: A *set play* designed to clear an area of the court of all offensive players without the ball so the player with the ball can play 1-on-1.

Closing out: When a defender sprints to *guard* a player who has just received a pass.

Combination defense: A defense that is part *man-to-man* and part *zone.* Also called a "junk defense."

Continuity offense: A sequence of player and ball movement that repeats until a good shot is created.

Control dribble: A dribble maneuver in which the player keeps her body between the defender's body and the ball.

Court savvy: A term describing a player who makes good decisions on the court—who plays smart basketball.

Court vision: A term describing a player who sees and understands what all the other players on the court are doing. This usually leads to having *court savvy.*

Crossover dribble: A dribble maneuver in which a player dribbles the ball in front of her body so she can change the ball from one hand to the other.

Cross screen: A movement in which a player *cuts* across the lane to *screen* for a teammate.

Curl cut: A *cut* that takes the player around a *screen* toward the basket.

Curl pass: A low, one-handed pass made by stepping around the defender's leg and extending the throwing arm. Also called a "hook pass."

Cut: (1) A sudden running movement to get open for a pass. (2) To make such a move. Also called "flash."

Dead ball: A stoppage of play called by the referee.

Dead-ball foul: A *foul* committed while the clock is stopped and the ball is not in play.

Defensive rebound: A *rebound* made off a missed shot at the basket a team is defending.

Defensive slide: The quick "step-slide" movement a defender makes when closely guarding the dribbler.

Defensive stance: The stance used to play defense—knees bent, feet wide, arms out, etc.

Defensive stop: Gaining possession of the ball before the offensive team scores.

Defensive transition: When the team on offense suddenly gives up possession of the ball and has to convert from offense to defense.

Delay offense: An offense used to take more time with each possession.

Denial defense: A defense in which a defender tries to prevent her man from receiving a pass.

Denial stance: The stance used to play *denial defense*—body low, knees bent, hand and foot in the passing lane.

Deny the ball: To use a *denial stance* to keep the offensive player from receiving a pass.

Diamond-and-one: A *combination defense* in which four defenders play *zone* in a diamond formation and the fifth defender guards a specific offensive player *man-to-man.*

Diamond Press: A *full-court press* with a 1-2-1-1 formation.

Dishing: A slang term for passing the ball to a player open for a shot, usually after *dribble penetration.*

Double down: To drop from the perimeter, leaving your *man* or *zone,* to *double-team* a *low post* player.

Double dribble: A violation in which a player picks up her dribble and starts to dribble again. A common occurrence with young players.

Double low stack: When two offensive players set up at one of the *blocks* to run a play.

Double screen: When two players line up next to each other to set *screens* for the same cutter.

Double-teaming: A defense in which two defenders guard the same offensive player at the same time.

Down screen: A play in which a player comes down from the perimeter or *high post* area to set a *screen* for a player in the *low post* area.

Dribble: (1) To advance the ball by bouncing it on the floor. (2) The bounce of the ball caused by a player pushing the ball downward.

Dribble penetration: When a dribbler is able to *drive* into the *lane;* she "penetrates" the defense.

Drive: To attack the basket by dribbling hard at it.

Drop step: A *low post* move when an offensive player with her back to the basket swings one leg around the defender and uses it as a *pivot foot* to gain inside position.

Dunk: A shot in which the player jumps high and throws the ball down through the basket. Also called a "slam," a "jam," and a "slam-dunk."

Elbow: The corner made by the intersection of the *free throw line* and the *lane* line. Each lane area has two elbows.

End line: See *baseline.*

Face up: See *square up.*

Fade cut: A *cut* that takes the player away from the ball.

Fan the ball: When the defense forces the ball toward the *sideline.*

Fast break: A play in which a team gains possession of the ball (through a defensive rebound, steal, or made shot) and then pushes the ball toward the other basket as fast as possible, hoping to catch the other team off guard and score an easy shot.

Field goal: A 2- or 3-point basket.

Filling the lanes: A *fast break* in which players from the offensive team run up the court in the right *lane*, the middle lane, and the left lane.

Flagrant foul: Excessive physical contact (punching, kicking, etc.).

Flash: See *cut*.

Forward: A position usually played by a tall, athletic player. A "small forward" or a "3" plays on the *wing*, and a *power forward* or a "4" plays in the *high* or *low post* area.

Foul: A violation of the rules.

Foul line: See *free throw line*.

Foul shot: See *free throw*.

Foul trouble: (1) Player foul trouble occurs when a player accumulates three or four fouls and is in danger of fouling out. (2) Team foul trouble occurs when a team accumulates seven or more team fouls in a half and is "in the bonus."

Free throw: An uncontested shot taken from the *free throw line* as a result of a *foul*. Also called a "foul shot." A successful (made) free throw is worth 1 point.

Free throw line: The line a player stands behind to shoot a free throw. Also called the "foul line."

Free throw line extended: An imaginary line extending from the end of the *free throw line* to the *sidelines*.

Front: To guard a player by standing directly in front of her and therefore between her and the ball.

Frontcourt: A team's offensive half of the court. The opposite of the *backcourt*. Also refers to a team's *center* and *forwards*.

Full-court press: A *man-to-man* or *zone* defense in which the players guard the other team in the *frontcourt*. Also called a "press."

Funnel the ball: When the defense forces the ball toward the middle.

Give-and-go: An offensive play in which the player with the ball passes (*gives*) to a teammate and cuts (*goes*) to the basket to receive a return pass. One of the game's basic plays.

Goaltending: A violation in which a defender touches a shot as it nears the basket in a downward flight.

Guard: (1) A position on the perimeter. The *point guard* or "1" brings the ball up the court and begins the offense. The *shooting guard* or "2" is usually the team's best outside shooter. (2) To defend an offensive player closely.

Guide hand: The shooter's nonshooting hand. See also *shooting hand*.

Half-court line: The line at the center of the court parallel to the *sidelines* that divides the court in half. Also called the "midcourt line."

Hand-check: To make hand contact with a dribbler while guarding her.

Hedge: In a *pick-and-roll*, when the screener's defender steps into the path of the dribbler so the dribbler has to hesitate, giving her defender time to get around the screen.

Held ball: A situation in which two players hold the ball in their hands simultaneously, but neither can pull it away from the other. Also called a *jump ball*.

Help and recover: A defensive move in which a defender leaves her assigned player to guard a teammate's assigned player and then goes back to guard her own player.

Help side: The half of the court (if the court is divided lengthwise) that the ball is not on. Also called the "weak side." The opposite of the *ball side*.

Help-side stance: The stance used to *guard* a *help-side* offensive player. See also *pistol stance*.

Hesitation dribble: A dribble maneuver in which the dribbler hesitates, pretending to pick up her dribble, but suddenly continues to the basket. Also called a "stop-and-go dribble."

High post: The area around the *free throw line*.

Home run ball: When an *inbounder* or rebounder throws a long pass over the top of the defense.

Hook pass: See *curl pass*.

Hook shot: A one-hand shot taken with a sweeping, windmill motion.

Hoop: The basket or rim.

Hoops: Slang term for the game of basketball.

Hops: A term used to describe how high a player can jump, as in "Eileen has great hops."

Inbound: To pass the ball to a teammate on the court from out-of-bounds.

Inbounder: The player who inbounds the ball.

Inside-out dribble: An advanced dribbling move, a fake *crossover dribble*.

Intentional foul: A *foul* that occurs when a player makes illegal contact with an opposing player without intending to get the ball.

Isolation play: An offensive play designed to have a specific player attack the basket 1-on-1. Also called "iso play."

Jab-and-cross: A play in which the offensive player makes a *jab step* in one direction and then follows it by driving by the defender in that direction.

Jab step: A short (6 to 8 inches) out-and-back step by an offensive player to see how the defender reacts.

Jam the cutter: When a defender steps in the way of a cutter to prevent her from cutting to the ball.

Jump ball: A procedure used to begin a game. The referee tosses up the ball in the center circle between two opposing players, who jump up and try to tip it to a teammate. Also called the "opening tip."

Jump hook: A variation of the traditional *hook shot* in which the shooter takes the shot with both feet in the air.

Jump shot: A shot in which the shooter faces the basket and releases the ball after jumping into the air.

Jump stop: The action of coming to a complete stop, legs apart and knees bent, when dribbling or running; can be a one-foot or two-foot jump stop.

Jump to the ball: When a defender, after her man passes the ball, changes to a denial position so her man can't cut between her and the ball.

Junk defense: See *combination defense.*

Kick the ball out: When a player near the basket passes the ball to a player on the perimeter.

Lane: The rectangular painted area between the *baseline*, the *lane* lines, and the *free throw line*. Also called the "paint."

Layup: A shot taken next to the basket in which the shooter extends her arm, lifts her same-side knee, and aims the ball at the upper corner of the painted square on the backboard.

Loose-ball foul: A *foul* committed when neither team has possession of the ball.

Low post: The area on one side of the basket around the *block.*

Man: The player a defender is assigned to guard. Also short for *man-to-man defense.*

Man offense: See *man-to-man offense.*

Man-to-man defense: A team defense in which each defender guards a specific player or *man.* Also called "player-to-player defense."

Man-to-man offense: A team offense used against *man-to-man defense.* Also called "man offense."

Midcourt line: See *half-court line.*

Mirror the ball: To follow the movement of the ball with your hands when closely guarding a player who is *pivoting.*

Moving pick: A violation that happens when a screener leans or moves after setting a *screen.*

Net: The cord lacing that hangs down from the rim.

Nonshooting foul: A *foul* committed against a player who is not in the act of shooting.

Nothing but net: An expression that means the shot swished through the basket without touching the rim.

Off-ball screen: A *screen* set on a defender guarding an offensive player who doesn't have the ball. Also called a "player screen."

Offensive rebound: A *rebound* at the basket a team is attacking.

Offensive transition: When the team on defense suddenly gives up possession of the ball and has to convert from defense to offense.

On-ball defense: Defense that occurs when a defender guards the player with the ball.

On-ball screen: A *screen* set on a defender guarding an offensive player who has the ball.

One-and-one: *Free throws* awarded to a team once its opponent has committed seven personal fouls. If the shooter's first free throw is successful, she shoots a second free throw.

One-Guard Offense: A team offense used against zones with two-guard fronts (2-3 and 2-1-2 zones).

Open stance: The stance used to play *help-side* defense—feet apart, body balanced, knees bent, arms out.

Outlet: (1) To pass the ball after a defensive *rebound* to start the *fast break.* (2) The player who stays in the *backcourt* to receive an *outlet pass.*

Outlet pass: An *overhead pass* thrown by a defender that starts the *fast break.*

Overhead pass: A two-handed pass thrown from above the player's head.

Overtime: A 5-minute extra period played when the game is tied at the end of regulation play.

Paint: See *lane.*

Palming: See *carrying the ball.*

Pass fake: See *ball fake.*

Passing lane: An imaginary line from the player with the ball to a teammate. If a defender is in the way, the passing lane is closed.

Personal foul: A penalty assessed on a player who commits an illegal action.

Pick: See *screen.*

Pick-and-roll: A two-person play in which one offensive player sets a screen *(pick)* on the ball handler's defender and cuts *(rolls)* to the basket after the ball handler drives by the screen. Also called a "screen and roll." A common play in college and the pros.

Pistol stance: When a *help-side* defender is guarding her man, she points one hand at her man and one hand at the ball (as if she's holding a pistol).

Pivot: The action when the player with the ball spins on one foot and steps with her other foot to protect the ball from a defender.

Pivot foot: The foot that the offensive player spins on while *pivoting.*

Player-control foul: A nonshooting offensive *foul.*

Player screen: See *off-ball screen.*

Player-to-player defense: See *man-to-man defense.*

Point guard: (1) A position played by a team's primary ball handler, the player who brings the ball up the court and begins the offense. Also called the "1." (2) The player who plays that position.

Popout cut: A *cut* taken around a *screen* straight to the ball.

Post: (1) A player who plays in and around the *lane* area. A *center* or *forward* (a "4" or a "5"). (2) An area of the court, as in the *low post* or the *high post*.

Post moves: Back-to-the-basket scoring moves made by players near the basket.

Post-up: (1) An offensive move in which an offensive player (usually a *forward* or a *center*) positions herself close to the basket with her back toward the basket and the defender behind her so the offensive player can receive a pass. (2) To make that move.

Power forward: A position played by the larger of the *forwards* on the floor, usually a good scorer and rebounder. Also called the "4." (2) The player who plays that position.

Power layup: A two-footed *layup*.

Press: (1) See *full-court press*. (2) To engage in a full-court press.

Press break: A team offense used against a press defense. Also called "press offense."

Press offense: See *press break*.

Pressure man-to-man defense: An aggressive defense where the defenders stay between their man and the ball.

Primary break: A *fast break* that involves only a few players from each team.

Pump fake: See *shot fake*.

Push pass: A one-handed *air pass*.

Quicks: A slang term used to describe how quick a player is, as in "Darnelle has average quicks."

Ready stance: The balanced position from which a player is ready to run, jump, slide, or pivot. Her knees are bent, hands are up and out, back is straight, and head is up.

Rebound: (1) A missed shot that comes off the backboard or rim. (2) To fight for and gain control of a missed shot that comes off the backboard or rim.

Rejection: A blocked shot.

Reserve: See *substitute*.

Retreat step: A step in which the defender's back foot steps toward the baseline, and the lead foot slides in place.

Runner: A shot that the player shoots while running, without taking the time to set up the shot. Also called a "floater."

Running clock: When the clock in a game isn't stopped every time the referee blows the whistle to ensure that the game ends on time and the next game can begin when scheduled. Often used in middle school and AAU games.

Safety: The offensive player at the top of the circle.

Sag: A tactic in which a defender leaves her *man* or *zone* and drops into the *lane* to help protect the basket.

Sagging man-to-man defense: A conservative defense in which the defenders stay between their man and the basket.

Screen: A play in which an offensive player runs over and stands in a stationary position next to a teammate's defender to free up the teammate to dribble or to receive a pass.

Screen away: To pass in one direction and set a *screen* for a teammate in the opposite direction.

Screener: A player who sets a *screen*.

Sealing the defender: After setting a *screen*, the screener does a reverse *pivot* to "seal" the defender—put the defender on her back.

Secondary break: A *fast break* that involves most of the players from each team.

Set play: A sequence of player and ball movement that has an end.

Shagger: A player who, in a drill, collects loose balls and returns them to the passer.

Shell drills: Defensive drills designed to work on all aspects of defense.

Shooter's roll: When a shot doesn't go through the basket cleanly, but bounces around softly before dropping through.

Shooting foul: A violation that happens when a defender fouls the shooter and the shot scores. The shooter is awarded 2 points and a *free throw*.

Shooting guard: (1) A position played by a perimeter player who is usually the team's best outside shooter. Also called the "2." (2) The person playing this position.

Shooting hand: The hand used to shoot the ball. See also *guide hand*.

Shot clock: The clock used to limit the time allowed for a team to attempt a shot. Shot clocks are used in pro and college games, in some high school leagues, but not in middle school and youth leagues.

Shot clock violation: A violation that occurs when the team with the ball doesn't get a shot off during the allotted time. It results in a change of possession.

Shot fake: A movement in which the player with the ball acts as if she's about to shoot. It is designed to trick the defender into straightening up, allowing the player with the ball to dribble past her. Also called a "pump fake."

Sideline: The line at each side of the court that marks the boundary of the playing surface.

Sideline play: A play used by the offensive team to put the ball back in play from the *sideline*.

Sixth man: The first *substitute* who comes off the bench to replace a starter.

Skip pass: An *overhead pass* from one side of the court to the other over the defense.

Slasher: A *wing* player with an ability to drive into the *lane* for easy shots and an ability to slice into the lane for *rebounds*.

Soft hands: A term used to describe a player who has good hand control with the ball—who is a good passer and receiver.

Speed dribble: A dribble maneuver in which the player pushes the ball ahead of her and bounces it at chest height.

Spin dribble: A dribble maneuver in which the player does a reverse *pivot* while bringing the ball around her so it ends up in her other hand.

Splitting the screen: When the screener, seeing her defender *hedging*, gets out of her screening stance and cuts to the basket for a pass.

Splitting the trap: When a trapped player steps in between the defenders to pass the ball.

Square up: To pivot so the shoulders and feet face the basket. Also called "face up."

Staggered screen: When two players not next to each other set simultaneous *screens* for the same cutter.

Steal: (1) To intercept a pass and gain possession of the ball. (2) The name for the action.

Stop-and-go dribble: See *hesitation dribble*.

Stop and pop: An offensive move in which a player comes to a sudden stop, picks up her dribble, and shoots the ball.

Strong side: See *ball side*. The opposite of "weak side."

Substitute: A player who comes in the game to replace another player. Also called a "sub."

Swing step: A defensive step in which the defender does a reverse *pivot* with one foot and stays in her on-ball stance.

Switch: A movement in which two defenders change the offensive player each is guarding.

Technical foul: A violation, such as a player or coach using profanity, that results in the other team getting *free throws* and possession of the ball. Also called a "T," as in "T him up."

10-second call: A violation that occurs when a team is unable to advance the ball over the midcourt line before 10 seconds have elapsed.

3-point arc: A line drawn on the court 19 feet 19 inches from the basket. *Field goals* scored from outside the arc count 3 points. Also called "3-point line."

3-point line: See *3-point arc*.

3-point shot: A shot taken from outside the *3-point arc*.

3 points the old-fashioned way: Scoring 3 points by making a 2-point shot, being fouled in the process, and making the *free throw*.

3-second call: A violation that occurs when an offensive player remains in the lane for 3 or more seconds.

Tip-off: The opening *jump ball* at the *center circle* that begins a game.

Trailer: An offensive player, usually a *center* or a *power forward*, who trails the first wave of players on the *fast break*.

Transition: A movement that occurs when a team changes from offense to defense (*defensive transition*) or from defense to offense (*offensive transition*).

Trap: A defensive move in which two defenders guard the player with the ball by forming a V with their bodies.

Traveling: A violation that occurs when the player with the ball takes too many steps without dribbling. This is a common occurrence with young players.

Triangle-and-two: A combination defense in which three defenders play *zone* in a triangle formation and two defenders guard specific players *man-to-man*.

Triple threat position: The bent-knees stance that allows the player three options: dribble, pass, or shoot.

Turnaround jump shot: A shot by a player in the *low post* in which she catches the ball with her back to the basket, makes a forward *pivot* so she faces the basket, and shoots a *jump shot*.

Turnover: A loss of possession of the ball caused by a *steal*, an offensive *foul*, a *held ball*, or a poor pass.

Two-Guard Offense: A team offense used against zones with one-guard fronts (1-2-2 and 1-3-1).

Two-shot foul: A violation that occurs when a defender fouls the shooter, and the shot misses. The shooter is awarded two *free throws*.

Up-and-under move: An advanced *post move* that starts out like a *turnaround jump shot*, but instead of shooting, the post player "pump fakes," causing the defender to rise out of her defensive stance. The post player steps by the defender and finishes with a layup.

Up screen: An offensive play in which a player comes from the *low post* area to set a *screen* for a player in the *high post* area.

V-cut and swim move: An offensive play in which a player on the perimeter steps toward the basket, drawing the defender with her, and suddenly *cuts* to the perimeter for a pass. The opposite of a *backdoor cut*.

Weak side: See *help side*.

Wing: (1) The area on the court where the *3-point arc* meets the *free throw line extended*. (2) The offensive player who plays in that area.

Zone defense: A team defense in which players are assigned to guard specific areas of the court.

Zone offense: A team offense used against a *zone defense*.

INDEX

Numbers in **bold** refer to pages with illustrations